The way it was

The family at the Robert Flusche Farm: Mom, Dad, Elsie, Bill and Alvin

ALVIN FUHRMAN

The
WAY
It
WAS

Alvin Fuhrman

ISBN 978-1-961358-14-0 (paperback)
ISBN 978-1-961358-15-7 (digital)

Printed in the United States of America

TABLE OF CONTENTS

DEDICATION X

FOREWORD XII

INTRODUCTION...XVI

Section I.   FAMILY

Chapter 1   Robert Flusche Farm 3

Chapter 2   Leo Mosser Farm 5

Chapter 3   Milking Cows.. 8

Chapter 4   Picking Corn.. 12

Chapter 5   Raising Cotton... 14

Chapter 6   Phillip Berend Farm—
             Then a Whole New World for Us 17

Chapter 7   Lessons Learned (Usually the Hard Way)........................ 19

Chapter 8   Butchering Hogs, Raising Chickens and Seeing the Light 21

Chapter 9   World War II Memories 23

Chapter 10   Life in Lindsay 25

Chapter 11   The Yosten Farm 27

Chapter 12   My Inventions 33

Chapter 13   Courting in the '40s 35

Chapter 14   Meeting Gracie.. 37

Chapter 15   The 1942 Ice Storm and the Telephone Company 43

Chapter 16   The Fisherman 45

Chapter 17   A tale of two sons (Kent) 55

Chapter 18   A tale of two sons (Gene)... 60

Chapter 19   Ellen Grace Friske Fuhrman Tells Her Story 74

Section II.   THE TELEPHONE

Chapter 20   Foreword: My Fascination with the Telephone 87

Chapter 21   The First Telephones around Forestburg........................ 89

Chapter 22   Early Telephones in the Rosston Area............................91

Chapter 23   The Beginning of Muenster Telephone Company............ 94

Chapter 24   Communications Center of Muenster 104

Chapter 25   The Mark Sense Ticket...108

Chapter 26   The First Computer Billing 110

Chapter 27   Construction Trucks 117

Chapter 28   The Myra System..121

Chapter 29   Services Returned to Rosston in 1957 123

Chapter 30   Perils of the Telephone Man 128

Chapter 31   Repeat Coils and Phantom Lines....................................132

Chapter 32   All about Poles 135

Chapter 33   The Three-Position Switchboard 138

Chapter 34   House Movers 141

Chapter 35   Improvising Became a Way of Life 144

Chapter 36   Financing the Buyout in 1960....................................... 151

Chapter 37   Cutover to Dial Service in 1963 154

Chapter 38   Mobile Telephone Service..157

Chapter 39   Modern Day Service..161

Chapter 40   Truck Centers 169

Chapter 41   The Evolution of Telephone Service..............................172

Chapter 42   Hello, Texas!—History of Telephony in Texas 174

Chapter 43   Fifth Generation of Telephone Service Is Here 178

Chapter 44   My 80th Birthday Party and Another Party of Note 180

Chapter 45   Company Milestones and the Future.............................182

Section III.   THE ARMY

Chapter 46   The Early Days of My Service...187

Chapter 47   Germany...192

Chapter 48   Where Is My Cu zhild? (More Memories of Germany)...197

Chapter 49   Army Life.. 206

Section IV.   TELEVISION

Chapter 50   The Beginning of CATV..213

Chapter 51   Cablecasting in the 1970s..217
Chapter 52   Distant Learning in the '90s—
              The North Texas Educational Network..........................220
Chapter 53   The First Satellite-receiving Dish...................................223

Section V.   OUR TRAVELS
Chapter 54   We Survived the Great Earthquake...............................231
Chapter 55   Nova Scotia...235
Chapter 56   Our Mediterranean Cruise..246
Chapter 57   Memories from The Grand European River Cruise.......248
Chapter 58   On the Way to Peru..253
Chapter 59   Portugal—Douro River..261
Chapter 60   Our Russian Visit...271
Chapter 61   Communist Cuba...283
Chapter 62   Oklahoma City...297
Chapter 63   Our Trip to Alaska and The Cruise
              (from Gracie's Perspective)...299

**Section VI.   STORIES ABOUT MUENSTER, ABOUT GOD,
              ABOUT OUR FRIENDS AND ABOUT HIS FRIENDS**
Chapter 64   The Muenster Men's Choir (Historically Speaking).......307
Chapter 65   The Choir As I Have Known It......................................311
Chapter 66   Prelude to Germanfest..314
Chapter 67   God Got His Money's Worth..316
Chapter 68   The Medders Hoax...318
Chapter 69   It Was a Great Party...320
Chapter 70   My Army Buddy...323
Chapter 71   The Story of Heritage Park..326
Chapter 72   Germanfest..335
Chapter 73   The Barn Swallows...350

Epilogue   A Tribute To Gene, From His Mother.............................353
Author's Biography...369

DEDICATION

This book is dedicated to my wife of 63 years, Gracie. We have been married almost as long as we have been in the telephone business. Without her dedication we would not be where we are today. Those earlier years we worked long hours at low pay to make ends meet. We have managed the company together. She ran the office, and I dug the rock holes and built the telephone lines and made the telephones work. We each had our area in which we worked. She consulted with me about office affairs, but we never developed a problem. She managed the little things that make a company successful. She saw to it that the office stayed clean and the yards were mowed; she planned the company parties. She could run the office much better than I could have.

This is also dedicated to our son Gene, who wanted to work for everything he received. He was a pleasure to be around. We spent many a pleasant time together fishing. First, we fished in small ponds around Muenster and then move to Texoma and finally took up boat fishing. Gracie and I took him and his friends water skiing until they could ski on their own. We always enjoyed his friends. He was well on the way to taking over the company in 2003 at the age of 39 when he was killed by a drunk driver on his way home from work. His wife of three years was pregnant when he was killed. He wanted a son before he was 40.

He got a son but never had a chance to see him.

FOREWORD

My parents
(My sister Coralee Pulte explains:)

In Cooke County during World War II, the building of Camp Howze and of the Air Base forced the farmers within those areas to seek land elsewhere. One such farmer was the late Henry J. Fuhrman and his wife Elsie Flusche Fuhrman and family. They ended their grim search for a new beginning when they bought the John Yosten farm east of Muenster in November 1942.

Henry J. Fuhrman, born Jan. 28, 1886, was the second oldest child of the 13 children of John and Maria Engert Fuhrman of St. Joseph, Iowa. Henry was 27 when he met 18-year-old Elsie Flusche of Lindsay in 1913 while visiting his uncle and godfather Henry Fuhrmann of Lindsay. His infatuation for the dark-eyed, spirited daughter of Wilhelm and Augusta Flusche endured through an "on" and "off" relationship that culminated in their marriage eight years later on March 29, 1921, in Lindsay. Elsie Flusche was the sixth child of the nine children of Wilhelm Flusche and his second wife, Augusta; she was born Oct. 22, 1894, in Lindsay, Texas.

The history of Henry and Elsie Fuhrman spans from the pre-mechanical age to the world of high tech. Typical of the times, both attended schools through the fourth and fifth grades; then they were considered ready to make a living. Although the topography of Iowa and Texas differed, both of their early lives reflect the work and the simplicity of rural living. Henry told stories of hunting muskrats on the family farm with a harpoon fashioned from a hayfork. Wanting to be in the vanguard of mechanical farming, he went to engineering school in 1905 to learn to operate a steam tractor. Among his diverse duties at Gales General Store in St. Joseph, Iowa, were delivering coffins, picking up new cars in nearby Livermore and teaching the new owners to drive (the women drivers scared him to death). One of his duties as janitor of the parish church where he worked for some four years was to get up at 4 a.m. to heat the church for services—often in the winter it would be 20 to 30 degrees below zero. He broke prairie land at Moose Jaw and Netherdall with oxen on his dad's homestead land in Saskatchewan, Canada. Later, he worked in a lumber mill in British Columbia. One phase of lumbering was the felling of trees that were cut into prescribed lengths by a fiddle saw drawn by two horses. A bachelor until the age of 35, he traveled much in the United States and Canada. One itinerary of travel in 1915 took him through Yellowstone National Park and along the west coast for a fee of $34. But all that changed when he married his "Texas flower."

Elsie Fuhrman wrote of growing up in Lindsay, Texas, in her memoirs, copyrighted in 1986. Because of her remarkable memory, she could share recollections of her bittersweet life in that farming community in the early 1900s. Her stories were of long days in the cotton fields, of hay baling, and of cooking for the thresher crews in cook shacks. She did all the housework for the large Flusche family when she was 14, and in between, often had to catch one of their wild horses and take lunch to the workers in the field. Two events occurred during her youth that date the era. She was thrown from a buggy when the horses bolted, and knocked unconscious as the buggy wheel rolled over her head. She had scarlet fever when she was 11 which is believed to have caused her to be hard of hearing in her teens.

Other contrasts of the times include the reckoning with time and distance, and of life without television. Her brothers Herman and Fritz walked from Lindsay to Muenster (as the crow flies) for music lessons. The lassitudes of summer evenings were eased by games of pump-pump-pull-away for the children, while the older folk visited in the cool of the front porch. The young folks gathered at the town post office and if "nothing else was cooking," they went to the Flusche house, rolled back the carpet, and danced to Herman's music (on the piano). The horse and buggy was the genteel method of transportation; horseback riding was for pleasure or errands. Covering distance could be expedited only by the use of the train that went through Lindsay. The fare to Muenster was 35 cents; the fare to Gainesville was 15 cents. The drudgery of workdays was tempered by lively socials, dances, family celebrations, neighborly visits, and parlor games. It was at one such social affair that Henry met Elsie.

After Henry and Elsie married in 1921, they lived in St. Joseph, Iowa. Their daughter, another Elsie, was born there on Jan. 19, 1922. Because the cold winters aggravated Henry's asthmatic condition, they moved back to Lindsay, Texas, in February 1924. Their son, William (Bill), was born shortly after their arrival on March 10, 1924. Alvin was born on Feb. 3, 1927; the twins Coralee and Rosalee, on Jan. 20, 1930; and Jerry on Dec. 11, 1934. Rosalee and Coralee were the only children of Henry and Elsie who were born in the hospital. They were a bargain package of two for the price of one. At that time as an inducement for mothers to have their babies in the hospital, only $2 per day was charged for the stay in the hospital after birth. With the $25 delivery fee for the doctor and the tab for 10 days in the hospital, the twins cost less than $50. After living in a series of temporary homes, the Fuhrman family settled on what they thought would be their permanent dwelling on the "Berend" place on the north side of the present Gainesville airport.

But Divine Providence intervened.

In 1942 during WWII, the government built Camp Howze and the air base north of Gainesville. The trauma of moving off the farm in the air base is still uppermost in Mrs. Fuhrman's memories. When the government informed the families of the area that their land was being confiscated, they were given two weeks to move off of their farms. The farm crops were ready for harvests; the orchards hung heavy with ripened fruit. They had to leave it all. The previous exodus of farmers from the Camp Howze area caused inflated real estate values in the area. But Henry and Elsie were luckier than most; they were able to live in her mother's home in Lindsay until they decided to buy the Yosten farm in Muenster. Mrs. Fuhrman writes of this period on the farm east of Muenster in her memoirs:

My Mother's memories:

"We lived on this place for twenty-two-years and this is where our children did most of their growing up and their learning. They all married while we lived on this place. Elsie married Gilbert Endres on June 29, 1949, William (Bill) married Kay Eigel on Aug. 11, 1956, in St Louis, Alvin married Ellen Grace Friske on Oct. 20, 1953, in Lindsay, Coralee married Robert J. Pulte of Gainesville on Oct. 18, 1951, Rosalee married

Robert Bayer of Muenster on May 7, 1953, and the last to marry was Jerry who married Carolyn Brinker, Sept. 13, 1958, in San Antonio." With the marriages came "their children's children." Henry and Elsie boast of 22 grandchildren, and nine great-grandchildren.

"In 1964, Henry and Elsie Fuhrman sold their farm to Paul Fetch of Muenster, and built a new home near the church on East Sixth Street. They celebrated their golden wedding anniversary in March 1971, and they marked 60 years of marriage before Henry died April 5, 1976, at the age of 90 of Alzheimer's disease.

"Mrs. Fuhrman will be 94 on her next birthday, Oct. 22, 1988. She has recovered from a fractured hip suffered in 1980, and is able to move about with the aid of a cane. Though her mobility is slowed, she has the rare gift of an expansive, clear memory of experiences throughout her life. She is revered for her longevity, as a unifying influence in her family, and as a remnant of an era and of a people who struck out for a better life in America, and found it in Muenster, Texas."

My Dad and Mom

INTRODUCTION

This is the story of Alvin and Ellen Grace Fuhrman. It is about growing up on the family farms . . . how they lived before the age of electricity and indoor toilets . . . the various ways they made it to school—both graduating from Sacred Heart High School. It recalls their courting days—and the disapproval of Alvin by Gracie's parents.

Alvin tells about starting with the telephone company during ice storm days of the 1940 years. He tells about being drafted into the army and his two year army life, before returning to the phone company and to Gracie. He tells about their marriage and how Gracie became part of the company, and about their attempt to start their family. He tells about the adoption of one son, Kent, and the birth of a second, Gene, who grew up to be a model child who became Chief Operations Officer of the company. He tells about the tragic accident that killed Gene.

Alvin tells about other activities that he has been involved in through the years.

Oh, by the way, I am Alvin.

To Our readers. From: Alvin and Gracie

SECTION I

FAMILY

(My Earliest—and My Favorite—Memories)

Bill had to get the horse hooked up to the two-wheel cart that drove us to school. Then he had to drive us. There was room for three of us on the seat, and the twins sat on a stool with their backs to the horse. Once in a while they would get a bath when the horse "had to go."

PART 1

The family at the Robert Flusche Farm: Mom, Dad, Elsie, Bill and Alvin

Family
(My Earliest—and Some Favorite—Memories)

Bill had to get the horse hooked up to the two-wheel cart that drove us to school. Then he had to drive us. There was room for three of us on the seat, and the twins sat on a stool with their backs to the horse. Once in a while they would get a bath when the horse "had to go."

CHAPTER 1

Robert Flusche Farm

T he hard-rubbered truck tire came to a stop, and my 7-year-old brother William and 10-year-old sister Elsie and I climbed aboard the truck with glee.

My dad hauled cottonseed from the cotton gin in Lindsay, Texas, to the cotton compress in Gainesville. He went right past where we lived on the Robert Flusche farm, and he would stop and we would crawl aboard.

Dad was from Iowa. He came to Texas to visit his uncle and met my mother, who was from Lindsay, Texas. They got married and made a home in Iowa, but because of poor health they were forced to move back to Texas. Dad was doing odd jobs until he could buy a farm.

The rides to Gainesville are among my earliest memories from when I was around 3 or 4 years old (why I remember them I do not know). We lived on Robert Flusche's place on what is now Highway 82 and Moss Creek Road. That was where I was born.

I've been told that Highway 82 was just a gravel road at the time and that it was called Route 5 back when I hitched those rides with Dad. It went through Lindsay and west to Myra over the back roads.

It then continued west on Fisher Road to south of Muenster then north through Muenster on Main Street. It continued to the second four-corners north of Muenster then headed west toward Saint Jo. That was the old Route 5.

Our family in 1973 going to school

The Bill Aggies lived about a mile west of us on Highway 82; the Robinsons lived northwest of us somewhat off the Moss Lake Road. Matt Fuhrmann lived north of us.

We lived there until Dad was able to buy what we called "the Leo Mosser Place."

CHAPTER 2

Leo Mosser Farm

My twin sisters Coralee and Rosalie were born while we lived on this place. They took their first breaths in the Sanitarium hospital in Gainesville, though I can't claim to recall the moment that happened—I was just three years old.

When the twins turned 6 they started school, thus making it five of us attending the Lindsay school. There was Elsie (15), Bill (12), Alvin (me, 9), and "the twins" (just turned 6). Jerry was not around yet. He came along about three years later.

Bill had to get the horse hooked up to the two-wheel cart that drove us to school. Then he had to drive us. There was room for three of us on the seat, and the twins sat on a stool with their backs to the horse. Once in a while they would get a bath when the horse "had to go."

The horse was tied up at a post along the east side of the Lindsay school on the same spot where students now park their cars. Generally, the cart would stay hitched to the horse throughout the school day and until we returned home.

Sometimes, though, the horse was taken to the Leowald place a block away to graze while we were in school.

I do not know where Dad got the cart, but it was built on the front wheels of a car. There was a metal box made from old metal roofing in front of the seat for our feet. The twins had their bench to sit on in this box, always facing south as we headed north.

It was down by the machine shed that Bill chopped into his foot. I do not remember too much about this, per se. But I do recall that he had one toe that never got any bigger after the day it was injured.

I also recall that Dad had a four-cylinder Fordson tractor that he tried to plow with. It did not have a starter or a battery—it had to be cranked.

After the motor was running, it had magnets attached to the flywheel that furnished the power for the spark plugs. Until the flywheel was running you had to hook a battery to the tractor to start it.

There was no air-conditioning then, and in the summertime we would occasionally move our bed outside in the yard to sleep. If we were indoors, we slept in front of a window or door. I do not remember ever having problems with mosquitoes. We could not do this today.

We milked cows, and the milk was run through a cream separator that split the cream from the milk. Dad sold the cream and fed the skim milk to the hogs. (I still have the base of that cream separator in my garden room upstairs in the garage. I made a table by putting a top on the legs.)

Dad kept the cream separator legs, using them to make a flower pot holder for several of our homes. I got it years later when his estate was settled after his death. During bad weather we kids would roller skate upstairs in the hay barn or play in the machine shed east of the windmill. This machine shed was moved during WW II to make room for a highway into Camp Howze.

Talking about the windmill—my twin sisters were five when they decided to crawl up the windmill. Coralee led the way. They were high on the windmill when mother noticed them. She did not want to excite them to the point that they would fall off, so she came up calmly holding a stick behind her and asked them to come down. When they were safely on the ground she gave each a paddling.

There were a lot of pecan trees along the creek east of our home. Each December we would pick up pecans, and our parents would sell them, and Dad used those profits to buy our Christmas presents. I had to crawl up the tree and flail the trees to make the pecans fall to the ground.

There was no refrigeration, so about once a month one of the Mages boys (the Mages were our neighbors) would butcher a steer and have all the cut up servings laid out in the back of his pickup truck and come by for Mom to pick out a roast for Sunday dinner.

In December 1936, Dad came to Lindsay and took me home. I was in the third grade in school and was staying with Grandma Flusche. When we got home all the windows were covered so no light would come in. That was the day that Jerry was born. He was born at home, and the doctor came out to deliver him. Later I would have to rock Jerry in a rocking chair to put him to sleep during the day. There was an age difference, and I do not remember playing with him much. But I remember that while I sat there rocking Jerry, I learned to tell time. On a shelf above the doors was the clock that Mom and Dad received from John and Augusta Bezner for a wedding gift. Once a week this antique wood clock would have to be wound. I still have this clock on a shelf in our computer room.

Alvin's brothers & sisters - 1934

- Back Row:
- Elsie and Bill
- Standing front row:
- Coralee & Rosalee
- Seated
- Alvin and Jerry

CHAPTER 3

Milking Cows

Dad always had cows to milk. As I recall, my first cow milking experience took place at the Leo Mosser home. We would hang a kerosene lantern on a nail in the ceiling in the winter to make it bright enough to milk. We did not have a special barn for milking; we milked the cows in the big barn that is still standing on the Pelzel place on the Moss Lake Road as I write this. We had one-legged stools to sit on while milking. We would give the cows feed to make them want to come into the barn. Milking cows is a never-ending task—no matter how cold or hot it gets, how many weddings, funerals and Christmas parties there are to attend, the cows have to get milked.

No matter how big or little you are, you can milk cows.

In 1936 Dad bought his first tractor. We had all of these dealers hanging around wanting to sell their tractor. There were John Deere, McCormick Deering, Case, Minneapolis Moline, Allis Chambers, Oliver tractors to choose from. Dad finally decided to buy a Model B John Deere with steel wheels with a two-row cultivator and a two-row planter for cotton and corn for $1,800. The tractor would run on kerosene after it got hot. It had a small, one-gallon tank for gas to start it, then we would switch it to kerosene as it got hot. After it ran for a while on kerosene, we would mix some water from the radiator with the kerosene by opening a valve. We had to add water to the radiator when plowing.

The year Dad bought the tractor we were baling prairie hay. I was only 9 years old, but I drove the tractor all day long plowing the field. When it was new it sure did smell good. This field at that time was west of our house. The Seville Bend road now goes through the middle of this field today. As I drove, the rest of the family was baling prairie hay with the horse baler.

West of this field and across the road Dad had a large field of prairie hay that we baled every year. We still had horses. Brother Bill would drive a team of horses to mow the prairie hay. He—and all the farmers in the area—had to watch out for clumps of dried hay because bumblebees would build their nests in them, and they did not like to be disturbed. The bees would sting Bill and cause the horses to bolt. Bill would get them to calm down and get back to mowing.

One time Bill was standing on the tongue of the mower between the horses in front of the mower making adjustments to the harness. Something spooked the horses and he had a runaway. He fell down in front of the mower and it passed over him without injuring him.

There was about 10 acres of pasture land with this prairie field, and many times during the year I would have to herd the cows down the road to this pasture. There was a lot of timber in this pasture. One time I used the leaves of a vine for toilet paper, and I paid the consequences.

That was when I learned a valuable lesson about the dangers of poison ivy.

After the prairie hay was dry, it would be raked into windrows with a sulky rake pulled by a team of horses. The driver would go back and forth with the 20-foot-wide sulky rake and dump the hay into windrows. A bulk rack about 10 feet wide with a horse on each side had 10-foot-long wooden teeth parallel with the ground that would protrude forward and slide under the windrowed hay until it was full—and then it would bring the hay to the hay baler.

We had a horse-drawn hay baler. A horse would go round and round pulling a beam that was attached to a plunger. Dad would pick up the hay and push it down in front of the plunger with the hayfork. As the horse turned, the plunger would move into the baler, compacting hay. Then it would move the hay bale over for the next feed and a large spring would pull it back. The plunger would do this three times whenever the horse made a circle.

Sometimes my job was to sit on a seat on the baler and keep the horse going in the circle. The bolt that held the seat on was too long, so this was not a very comfortable seat.

Dad raised turkeys, and when the hens were laying eggs I would have to follow each hen and find the nest in which they were laying their eggs. They would always lay their eggs in the heavy timber south/east of our farm. Just south of our creek was an area that had never been cleared out. There was heavy overgrown timber with brush, and the turkey hens would go deep into this area to lay their eggs. It was spooky, and after I found where a hen was laying her eggs I would hurry in and pick up the egg and rush back out. I would have to do this every day while she laid eggs.

Dad would take the eggs to the Gobble hatchery in Muenster to be hatched. When they hatched the new turkeys were brought back home, and we raised them for Thanksgiving. Turkeys are the dumbest things on earth. They will actually stand out in a heavy rain and drown. They were not smart enough to get out of the rain. We built a roost for them to sit on at night. They were prime targets for wolves and wild dogs hungry for a meal.

As they got a little older the turkeys would go down to the creek east of our house, and we would have to get them back to the house every evening. There were no 4-wheelers those days, so you had to walk. We had no horses that we could ride—Dad sold his horses when he bought the John Deere tractor. I never did like horses anyway.

Every time we got a heavy rain the creek would flood, and it seemed like the turkeys were always on the other side of the creek. At Thanksgiving they were all sold. I do not remember that we ever ate a turkey—for Thanksgiving or Christmas. We ate plenty of roosters—I know because I always had to catch the rooster and chop off his head. Fried chicken was always so good. It was always my job to carry in the wood from the woodpile. I had to be careful for there would be snakes and scorpions in the woodpile. There was a woodbin in the house that I had to keep full of wood. Mom cooked with wood, and we had a wood stove in the living room of the house that kept us warm in winter. On the side of the wood cook stove was a tank for hot water that we used for taking a bath. On Saturdays Mom would bring in a washtub, and we would all take a bath—in the same water. The twins got to take a bath first. I came later when the water was not clear and not so clean. And cold.

We lived on the Leo Mosser place before there was electricity, so kerosene lamps were used for light. A lamp was mounted on the wall in the kitchen with a reflector behind it. We did our school homework at the kitchen table. There was a wooden bench on the back of the table along the wall on which we sat to eat. It was this bench off which I got pushed, falling hard enough to break my shoulder. I do not remember falling, but today my right arm still is about 1½ inches shorter than the left arm. My dress coats need extra padding to make my shoulders look the same.

Because it was my job to keep the wood bin full, I would have to retrieve it from the wood pile east of the house We had a wooden porch on the south side of the house that was open underneath on both sides. We kids would play under the porch in the summer because it always stayed cool under there.

Now and then, Mom would let us stay with Grandma Flusche Theisan in Lindsay. If it was cold, Grandma Flusche would put a hot iron wrapped in newspapers to put on our cold feet.

BALING HAY – Prairie hay would be mowed down with a horse-drawn mower. Sulky rakes would rake the hay into windrows. The windrows would be picked up with a bulk rake and moved to the baler. On the horse-powered baler the horses would go around and around and cause a plunger to move into the baling chamber, compressing the hay, then pulled back by a big, long spring. Each round of the horses would give two compressions, baling the hay. When the plunger was pulled back hay would be pushed down into the baling chamber with a pitch fork; some workers used their legs.

CHAPTER 4

Picking Corn

I do not remember much about us raising corn until Dad bought the Model B John Deere in 1936. It had a 2-row planter and cultivator attachment that Dad used to plant and cultivate corn.

We handpicked our corn using a grain wagon with backboards. We would pull an ear of corn loose from the corn stalk and throw it into the wagon—hitting the backboard and falling into the wagon. The backboard made it easier to get the ear of corn into the wagon.

The earliest I remember picking corn was when we had a horse-drawn grain wagon pulled by a team of horses. We still lived on the "Leo Mosser place, and Dad had 22 acres rented from Jurassic place. This land bordered us on the south of our place. A road to the creek separated this land from our land. We had the whole 22 acres in corn and it was a rainy fall. We picked this corn by hand and there were scorpions in the ears of corn. I remember bringing a load of corn up to the barn and scorpions would be crawling out of the wagon as we moved. There was even a snake on the wagon one time.

Ear corn is the hardest grain to shovel off of the wagon. You cannot get the shovel under the ears of corn to shovel it and get started. I was always thinking how I could make life easier and decided a corn elevator would make unloading corn so much easier. I built a corn elevator out of parts I found around the place. I used a belt to convey the corn up the elevator. I built a wooden wheel to reduce the speed from an electric motor that I borrowed from the water pump under the windmill. The elevator had a hopper that I placed behind the wagon, and I took the end gate out and let the corn from the wagon fall into the hopper—which would then go up the elevator in the corn bin. This was much easier than shoveling corn. The rest of the load from the wagon was pushed out the back into the hopper.

Later years after we moved to the Brend place we no longer had horses, so the rubber-tired trailer was pulled by the John Deere tractor. Horses did not need a driver to move up as you picked the corn—but the tractor did. My brother Jerry usually was the driver that would drive up as we picked the corn. Sometimes Jerry would go to sleep and to wake him up we would throw an ear of corn at him.

He woke up real fast when an ear of corn hit him on the head.

CHAPTER 5

Raising Cotton

D ad always raised about 15/20 acres of cotton each year. During the hot summertime we had to "chop" the cotton. The planter planted a continuous stream of cottonseed, and when this came up, it had to be thinned out. We had to chop out the excess and leave the plants about 7 to 8 inches apart. When the cotton plant is really small the cultivator could not cover the weeds, and we would have to chop out the weeds. This was during the hottest time of the year. Dad had my twin sisters, Rosalie and Coralee, out in the field the same as us boys. As the cotton got taller, we had to go through again and get the taller weeds, mostly Johnson grass. The cultivators on Dad's John Deere Model "B" tractor would cover up and kill the small grass that came up once the cotton stalk got 8 to 10 inches tall.

Cotton picking time came about the time that school started. In earlier years school would be closed for about two weeks so the farmers could use their children to pick the cotton. The cotton grows in a bowl with four sharp spurs around it. As you pick the cotton your fingers get sore. If it was a rainy season the cotton stake would be very tall and not a whole lot of cotton on it. As you pick the cotton you put it into a cotton sack that you drag along behind you. When you get tired standing and stooping over to pick the cotton you can crawl along on your padded knees. Either way your back soon is killing you, and when you kneel a while your knees are sore. The cotton sack half full of cotton sure makes a very nice bed to use to lie down and take a nap.

When your cotton sack was full you would take it to a rubber-tired wagon that Dad put in the field and weigh it with a cotton scale that was hung on the propped up tongue of the wagon. It would take about 800 pounds of cotton to fill the wagon and make a bale of cotton. Dad would then take the cotton to the cotton gin to be processed into a 500-pound large bale. At the gin it was extracted from the wagon by an ingenious large pipe that had a vacuum that sucked up the cotton into the gin.

The Dieter Brothers' gin in Lindsay was powered by a one-cylinder steam engine. They burned the burrs from the cotton to make the steam to run the gin. They had a steam-powered water pump that provided water for the steam engine. The water was cool coming out of the ground and sure tasted good on those hot days.

The gin would clean the cotton and compress it into a 600-to-700—pound bale. The bale would then be put back on the wagon and taken home and unloaded in the yard. If we got a bale of cotton to an acre we thought we had a good crop.

When all of the cotton was picked and we had about a half dozen bales, and the price of cotton was good. Dad would load the bales on the wagon and take them to the Gainesville Compress.

We chopped and picked the cotton for our neighbors as well. We were paid $1 a day for chopping cotton. We never did see the money; they paid Dad, and he did not give any of the money to us. Of course, he kept us fed, and put clothes on our backs and shoes on our feet.

The same was true of picking cotton. Dad had us picking cotton for all the neighbors around us. Again, we never saw the money. Dad kept it all. However, later when I started dating he gave me the car full of gas and $1 for spending money. At that time $1 is all one needed for a date. We would go to a show that cost us each 25 cents and that left us 5 cents for each of us a coke and 20 cents each for a hamburger. I was still picking cotton after I graduated from high school.

The country having just gone through the depression, my parents were very conservative. They were married in 1928 right in the middle of the depression. After they were married they went back to Iowa to live. Elsie, my older sister, was born in Iowa. Dad developed asthma to the point that he was not sleeping—coughing continuously. They decided to move to Texas, where the climate was much dryer. The land that Dad inherited was located right across the road from Matt Faber old homestead.

Talking about the Faber place, the last time Gracie and I were in Iowa was in 2009, and we drove past the old Faber farm. The house—what's left of it—sits empty; all the other buildings are gone. As I looked around,

I thought about the house that burned, killing the family's five children. They were upstairs and could not get out. The hired hand jumped out of a window. The mother, Anna, my Dad's sister, kept flowers in a flowerbed with the ashes at the place where the house stood, and now the place is abandoned, and the flowerbed is full of weeds.

Mom and Dad's wedding gift from John and Augusta Bezner was a wind-up clock in a wooden case. It sat on a shelf in the living room of the house above the doors to the bedrooms. That was the clock that taught me how to tell time as I was babysitting with my younger brother. As I noted earlier, it now sits on a shelf in our home in our computer room. I took it several times to get it repaired, but it will not keep running.

CHAPTER 6

Phillip Berend Farm—
Then a Whole New World for Us

Our neighbor Phillip Berend died and left his wife with about four small children. At that time, wake service was held in the home, and Phillip's coffin was open in the living room. Dad had to stay up during the night with the body.

Dad was able to purchase the 121-acre Berend place from Mary Berend, Phillip's widow. Dad sold his smaller farm a mile east to Leo Mosser. (This is why we called it the Leo Mosser place.) On the Berend place there was a nice home, a big barn, a two story-double garage, large chicken house and many smaller buildings. Now Dad felt he had a place that he could raise his family and someday retire. Every day Dad had his six children out in the cotton patch chopping that pesky Johnson grass out of his cotton and corn patch. Cotton and Johnson grass do not get along in the same field.

One year we were picking cotton for our neighbor I.A. Zimmerer when Dad picked us up and said we were going to Iowa. Early the next day we left to visit relatives, and Dad was off to sell his land he had inherited.

It was all gravel roads through Kansas. We stopped at a motel along the way. It was on the edge of town with a cornfield behind it. Needless to say, we all slept in one room with two beds. I slept on the foot of Mom and Dad's bed. Bill and the twins slept in the other bed. The next morning, Bill was missing. Dad was afraid that he was lost in the cornfield. We searched all over for him; finally the proprietor looked in the cabin next door. There was Bill sleeping in a bed by himself. Luckily the cabin had been vacant. Bill had sleep-walked during the night and went next door.

When we finally reached Iowa we stayed at the Matt Faber home, my Dad's sister's place. The main crop in Iowa at that time was corn. Dad told us how they gathered corn. It had to be picked by hand. A team of horses would pull a grain wagon that had a high backboard. The corn would be picked and tossed into the wagon. A driver was not necessary while gathering corn. The horses would follow the row of corn. One would tell them to "getta app" to go and "whoa" to stop. The corn was stored in cribs that allowed the crop to dry. Later when all the corn was picked a sheller would come by, and all of the corn would be run through the sheller. The shelled corn was either sold or stored to feed the hogs. The corn cobs were stored in the Faber basement to heat the home at winter.

In Iowa we had plenty of cousins, and they all lived in big houses with basements. The Faber house was heated with a furnace in the basement that burned the corn cobs from the recent harvest. The water that came out of the ground was very hard. Soft water was a real problem. The water from the roof of the house was saved and run into a large storage tank. They used this water for washing.

CHAPTER 7

Lessons Learned (Usually the Hard Way)

Dad sold his land in Iowa and we returned to Texas, where life resumed pretty much where it left off. We milked cows in the big barn. It was convenient to drop hay out of the loft right into the trough in front of the cows so they would come into the barn to be milked. We milked the cows by hand and poured the milk through a large funnel strainer into a 10-gallon can. After each milking, the cans would be moved under the windmill and cooled with fresh, cool water pumped up especially for that purpose. Cats soon learned that they could crawl on the strainer while we were milking and drink the milk. So I insulated the strainer from the 10-gallon can and connected it to our electric fence. When the cat tried to drink they got shocked. Needless to say that stopped them from drinking out of the strainer.

Dad had a machine shop with all kinds of tools, and I started fiddling around with gadgets. I had all kinds of ideas to make life easier so I was always experimenting in Dad's machine shop. It was my job to throw out hay from the loft of the big barn. The second story of the hayloft had a door about 30 feet in the air from which I would throw out hay and then come down and scatter it for the cattle. This was a job I hated, but I had to do twice a day every day, so I fixed a cable from the barn to a tree about 400 feet away.

I had a carriage that rolled on the cable on which I would hang a bale of hay and let it roll down to the tree. I arranged a latch that would release the bale when I pulled on a tag rope. Because the loft was much higher than the tree the hay would roll all the way out to the tree. Then I would come down and scatter the hay. This worked well and saved me a lot of work. One time I dispatched a bale of hay from the loft and went down and pulled the release rope—I stood a moment looking down at the bale of hay when the carriage came off the cable, flew up in the air, came back down and hit me on the head and almost knocked me out. Needless to say, I no longer used the cable.

That was just one lesson I learned in my younger days. One day in the machine shop I also discovered that you do not want to mess around with a shotgun shell. I took all of the power and pellets out of a shell and took a nail and tapped on the round button. I learned that that cap still had a lot of punch. I liked to have lost a few fingers, and it was a while before I could hear again.

Bill liked to piddle in the machine shop, as well. He put a metal fan blade made of tin on a wooden spool in a way that you could wrap a string around the wooden spool and pull on it. The fan would take off and fly into the air. Well, this worked fine for a number of pulls, but one time the sharp metal fan caught on the spool, and while spinning hit Bill in the face. Needless to say, he had to have about 4 or 5 stitches to close the cut. This left a scar on his face.

CHAPTER 8

Butchering Hogs, Raising Chickens and Seeing the Light

When the first cold spell came Dad would butcher a hog. I had to build a fire under the kettle in the yard, and we had a 55-gallon drum with one end cut out of it propped up by a table out in the yard, than we would be ready to get the hog. It was my job to shoot the hog between the eyes—when he dropped Dad would take a butcher knife and cut the hog's throat to make sure he was dead. The blood when he bled was saved to make "Blood Wurst."

The scathing hot water would be poured in the 55-gallon barrel, and we would slide the hog up and down a number of times and then pull it out to see if it was cleaned properly. If not right, the hog would be put back in the hot water and dipped a few times more. Then we would turn the hog around and do the same on the other end. When scalded satisfactory and all hair and outer skin was scraped off the hog was deemed ready to be butchered.

Then the cleaned hog would then be hung upside down by his hind legs on a single tree from the horse wagon hitch and butchered. Because there was no refrigeration the meat had to be cured. We made pork chops from along the backbone to eat before they would spoil, and we cured bacon from the sowbelly and ham bones. Eggs were added to the brains and fried for breakfast.

The head would be put in a kettle of boiling water and cooked till the skin and bones would fall off the bone. This juice would be cooked down and mixed with corn meal to make Pones. The liver, heart and any meat from the head would end up in "Liver Wurst." The legs, including the hoofs, would be cleaned up and cut into pieces and vinegar and spices added to make "pickled pig's feet."

The front and back ham bones would be salt-cured by putting them in a wooden barrel with a salt-water brine to cure. The rest of the hog that did not end up in the pork chops or pork roast and bacon would be ground up into pork sausage. Each family had their own special mix of herbs and spices to season the sausage to their tastes. The intestines' would be scrapped out and cleaned up to make sausage.

Everything else was fried down in a large kettle and packed into jars, and the jars were filled with hot grease to preserve the meat. The only part of the hog not used was the squeals.

As well as we made the best use of hogs, we might have been even better tending to our chickens. It was my duty to keep the chickens from roosting on the wood rafters in the milk barn on the Brend place.

Dry wood does not conduct electric currents so I tacked two wires about 1 inch apart along the top of the 2 x 4 boards in the barn. One wire I had tied to a ground rod and the other was connected to an electric fence. When a chicken roosted on the wires they would get a shock through their feet. That stopped the chickens from sitting on the rafters.

I was about 12 years old, and we were widely using electric fences to keep the cattle where we wanted them. I was charged with putting up the electric fences and keep them working. I do not know if my twin sisters were getting into my dresser drawer, but I didn't want to take any chances. I grounded one metal knob on my dresser and I tied a wire from our electric fence to the other knob. If anyone tried to open my drawer, they would use the two knobs on the drawer to pull the drawer open and they would get a shock. I do not know if anyone ever got shocked.

Speaking of electricity, in 1939 the Cooke County Electric Cooperative built a power line along the road north of us and up to our house, and we finally had electric power. Albert Mosser wired our house for electricity on two circuits. All of the lights in the house were connected on one circuit, and all of the electric outlets were on another circuit. We no longer did school homework by kerosene lamp and listened to a battery-operated radio when our work was finished.

CHAPTER ·9

World War II Memories

C amp Howze was activated in 1941, and all of the farms north of us had already been taken over by the government and made into an infantry-training center. Early in the morning we could hear the rat-a-tat of machine guns and the big boom of the artillery as training took place for soldiers of the 84th, 86th, and 103rd Division of the US Army. At times a platoon of army troops would march along the road on the north side of our farm.

In 1942 the Government took over our farm to build an Air Support Command Base. We were chopping Johnson grass out of our 20-acre cotton patch on August 1. This field was along the road, west of our house. Dad came out to the field where we were working and told us that he received notice from the war department that the U.S. government was taking over our farm to build an Air Support Command Base for the air force. He said we could quit chopping out the Johnson grass. World War II had begun, and the Germans were running over everyone in Europe.

(After the war, this training facility became the Gainesville Airport)

The notice specified that they were only taking our land. The buildings, improvements and fences we could have, but they gave us two weeks to get everything off. The crops were in the fields, but they paid nothing for them. Dad was paid $8,075 for the 121-1/5 acres of land. This included the value of the corn and cotton crop that stood in the field. We could remove improvements located on said land and we had until July 15th to do so, but it was already August 4th before we were notified they were taking the land. We worked feverishly to save what we could. Bulldozers were rooting up our big beautiful trees and peach orchid while we were removing our buildings.

The barn was sold to Matt Mueller, who lived near Muenster. He tore it down with the help of his son-in-law Geo Gehrig. Geo also ran a hardware store in Muenster, and later I spied my missing wristwatch in his store for sale.

I had taken it off to milk cows in the barn and forgot to pick it up before the barn was sold and torn down. Geo gave me the watch after several attempts when I identified it.

We rolled up all of our barbed wire fences, and Ralph Richards, a local oil field operator, used his wrench truck to pull up half of the fence posts.

Our corn crop stood in the field ready to be harvested, but we were not allowed to go in and pick it. At first the gate was open on the north side of the air base and we could go in and get a load of corn. Later the gates were locked, so Dad would have to drop us off on the road by our corn, then drive around to the south side of the air base, and drive into the base through the main gate by himself. (Only one person was allowed to be in the vehicle) We would crawl through the fence and meet him at the corn patch and picked a load of corn. Then Dad would drive back out through the main gate with his load of corn by himself and come around and pick us up again.

Today our land is the north part of the Gainesville Municipal Airport. Recently runways were extended further north across our land to the road north of our old place.

CHAPTER 10

Life in Lindsay

Luckily we were able to move into Mom's old home place the Augusta Flusche home in Lindsay on short notice. Our cattle were herded across the Air Base already under construction for safe keeping at the John Bezner farm on Highway 82. They stayed there until we found a permanent place for them.

Our chicken house, along with the smoke house and wash house, was moved to Lindsay. Our two-story double garage was torn down along with the tool shed and cow barn. We even removed the water pipes in the ground. We dug up both ends, then hooked our John Deere tractor to one end with a heavy log chain and pulled them out of the ground. Sometimes we would have to take a run at it and jerk them out.

The last to go was our home. We had a nice home that sat on a concrete foundation over a concrete basement accessible from the inside as well as the outside. Dad stood on a chair and auctioned it off to the highest bidder. It was purchased by our neighbor Eugene French for $650. Eugene moved it to his place about a mile east and rented apartments to soldiers stationed in Camp Howze during the war. After the war the house was purchased by Ed Pels and moved to 302 N. Pecan St. in Muenster. Today, Jim Fuhrmann lives in the home.

In Lindsay we settled down in my mother's home built around the turn of the century. I liked it, for I had a private bedroom on the second floor. It was during my sophomore year in high school.

Living in Lindsay I did not have anything to do, and I started to get into trouble. I smoked some cigarettes, but I did not like the taste. I wasn't getting along very well at school and was considering quitting. I was running around with another kid. The railroad had a pile of sand and gravel in Lindsay and had a crane for loading railroad cars sitting by the pile. This kid and I got into the crane one day and started the motor. We were going to try to scoop some sand. I pulled the bucket way up and was going to let it drop to the ground—it dropped down, but stopped short of the ground with a jerk. The next day I drove by and they had a mechanic working on the crane.

CHAPTER 11

The Yosten Farm

D ad fortunately found the Yosten place in 1943 in Muenster and soon had me busy working the farm again. We began moving all of our assets to the Muenster Farm. We herded the cows up Highway 82 to our place in Muenster. We moved the chicken house and smoke house from Lindsay on our 4-wheeled, rubber-tired trailer. The fences were in bad shape, and we spent long days rebuilding fences. This was about the third time that Dad rebuilt a farm. Dad built a round roof granary and a machine shed east of the barn. I got disgusted working with Dad on the shed. He had "his way" he was going to build the shed and bushed off any suggestion I made. When we moved to Muenster we were still cutting our grain with a binder, shocking grain and going along with a thresher group to have the grain threshed.

I ran a grain wagon; I used Dad's pickup to haul the grain from the threshing machine to the barn. That year Dorothy and Rita Fuhrman from Chicago visited us and they learned about threshing grain.

Meanwhile, school greatly improved for me. We moved in the middle of my junior year. The nuns took me in and made me feel at home. I was making much better grades in school now. The Junior/ Senior year class was putting on a play named "Simon Smidge from Turnip Ridge," and Sister Grenadine auditioned me for the lead part. I got a lesser part, but I still enjoyed putting on the play.

Harold Luke got the lead part, but I enjoyed being in the play. Our school was in the "Tin University."

Harvest time

When grain harvest time came we hooked the Model B John Deere to the binder and pulled it out of the machine shed. The machine shed had two large sliding doors on each end. The binder was stored on the north end of the machine shed.

The binder had to be made ready to cut grain. We had to install the conveyor belts over the wooden rollers. Conveyor belts carried the grain from the cutter bar to the knotter, where the grain was tied into bundles. We checked the conveyor belts to make sure the rats had not chewed them up. The sickle was taken out and sharpened and missing blades were replaced. The wooden blades in the reel had to be replaced if they got damaged while in storage. Next the machine had to be oiled and greased. Every moving part had a place to oil or a cert to grease.

The binder had transport wheels, one on each side that was used when pulling it to the field. So it would go long-way through gates it was pulled from one end. To get it ready in the field to cut grain the tongue and tractor would be moved around to the sickle side in the front of the binder. A small wheel replaced the tractor. The bull wheel would be lowered and the transport wheels would be removed after hooking the binder to the tractor. The bull wheel powered the binder. A new ball of twine would be threaded through the binder to the knotter, ready to tie bundles.

Cutting grain

Dad sat on the binder and raised and lowered the reel and adjusted the cutting height. He also controlled the carrier that caught the bundles as they were tied and kicked out of the binder and dumped them into windrows. He had to make sure that all was working right and that the bundles were being tied. The bull wheel also powered the sickle that cut the wheat and the reel that made it fall on the conveyor belt. The straw with the grain was gathered and elevated up over the bull wheel and delivered to the knotter. There the straw was tightly packed into bundles and wrapped with twine to hold it together to make it into a bundle, then kicked it out to the bundle carrier.

I drove the tractor pulling the binder. Making the first round opening a field was always the most interesting and dangerous part of the process.

You had to look out for washouts and other hazards when making the first round. After the first round it became routine to continue around and around until you had all the grain cut down, bundled and lined up into windrows.

Shocking grain

Next came the fun of shocking the grain. You cannot leave the bundles of grain lying on the ground too long, especially if it rains. If left too long on the ground when it rains the grain will spout and the straw turns to manure. They are shocked with the grain side up and the stubble side down. One would take two bundles and stack them together with the grain end, making a V. We would stack 8 or 10 bundles around this, making a shock that would not blow over very easily.

All of our grain, wheat and oats were harvested in this manner until our entire grain crop was in shocks.

Threshing grain

While we were on the Leo Mosser place in Lindsay we were part of the Jurassic threshing ring. They owned the threshing machine and the tractor to power it. The tractor was powered by a huge, two-cylinder engine that reminded me of an elephant. Its iron wheels where 8 feet in diameter. The roof over the cab was 12 feet or higher. The radiator was on top of the engine turned 90 degrees driven by a flat belt from the camshaft. Steering was accomplished by a chain attached to the front wheel axle that would pull the wheels in the direction you wanted to go after many turns of the steering wheel. As a kid we would sit on the fender of the huge engine and watch the threshing take place.

All the farmers needing grain to be threshed would have to provide a part of the threshing ring. This included the tractor driver, the threshing machine mechanic, about four bundle wagons with a team of horses, three men in the field pitching bundles, and two-grain haulers to haul off the grain. There was a water boy on horseback that brought cool water to the men working in the field.

The bundle wagons would load up the bundles in the field and haul the bundles to the threshing machine. The men in the field pitched the bundles from the shocks up to the bundle wagon operator, who stacked the bundles so they would not fall off his wagon on the way to the threshing machine. The men pitching bundles always had to be careful—almost every shock by now had a copperhead or rattlesnake under it. After getting to the machine each driver would wait his turn to drive up to the feeder of the threshing machine and feed his load of bundles into it. The bundles would have to be placed in the feeder with the grain forward. A more complete threshing would occur if the bundle went into the machine with grain first, for the bundle would slow down the tractor slightly when the straw went in.

A grain wagon's operator would empty the grain in the grain hopper on the threshing machine in an owner's granary and get back to the machine to begin repeating the process. This was the easiest job on the thresher.

There was a blower on the back of the threshing machine that blew the straw onto a straw pile. If workers threshed several days at one place the straw pile would get quite high.

The thresher crew had to eat, and you were always well fed. Three meals a day were served each day and snacks in the middle of the morning and afternoon. Plenty of hot coffee was always on hand.

There was a large covered wagon that had a large door and steps in the rear to enter it. They called this the cook shack. It had a large wood burning stove on the front facing back on which all meals were prepared. Both sides of the cook shack had doors that dropped down and made seats and a table on which the workers could eat. The table was the full length of the shack and was about waist high to the girls inside. We would eat sitting on benches attached to the outside of the cook shack that folded out during mealtime. The wooden covers of the openings on the sides would be lifted up to provide shade for the men as they ate. This also made it a lot cooler for the cooks inside the cook shack.

When we moved to the Brend place we joined the Zimmerer threshing ring. Both thresher rings operated about the same.

I performed every job on the ring at one time or another. I ran a bundle wagon with somebody else's horses. I always hated hoses. I would have to harness them in the morning, work them during the day, see that they got water during the day, unharness them at night, feed them and water them. I just never did like horses.

Several seasons I pitched bundles to the bundle wagons in the field. This is hard work—the bundles weighed about 20-30 pounds, and you pitched them at the end of a pitchfork over your head to the top of the load. One always had to watch out for snakes and skunks under the shocks. I would pull the shock over and make sure nothing was under it before I started pitching the bundles. Other times I hauled the grain to the granary. By the time I was big enough to haul grain we were using pickups to do the hauling. Of course, in those days there were no portable elevators to unload the pickup, and the grain would always have to be scooped into the granary. There seemed to always be a breeze blowing from inside the granary and you always got the dust back in your face.

In the evening there would be plenty of horse play around among the younger group. That is how I got my nose broken. Bill Hess got in a lucky punch while we were playing around.

Christmas time

Each year at Christmas time all of us children would gather at grandmother's house before Midnight Mass. After grandmother moved to assisted living in 1991 we met at Elsie and Gilbert Endres' home.

Massy Ferguson combine

Around 1940-1941, Dad bought a Massy Ferguson 7-foot combine, and I no longer had to work with a threshing crew. However, I had gone rollerskating right before harvest, fell and severely sprained my wrist. Somehow, I was able to drive the tractor and raise and lower the cutter bar of the combine with one hand.

Arthur Felderhoff's family lived across the pasture west of our place, and Arthur's father died not too long after we moved to Muenster. At that time the neighbors dug the graves, so we were among the neighbors that dug his grave in Sacred Heart Cemetery. The grave had to be dug in Solid rock, so Cooke County Electric Co-op had a crew there that loaded drilled holes in the rock with dynamite and blasted the rock so we could dig his grave.

Muenster Airport

Muenster's airport was a grass strip on the southeast corner of the Ed Schmitz place. On the other (East) side of the fence was the Mages farm. Joe Wilde was looking for a place to keep his airplane and to practice landing and taking off. So he used our pasture. We did that in exchange for some flying lessons. I never was very interested in learning to fly, but my brother Bill was very interested. Joe had only one arm, so he either had it on the stick or on the throttle.

Joe also had a side-by-side Cessna and I rode with him to the Gainesville airport one time. It was on airport road north of Gainesville. When we landed in Gainesville, he had difficulty keeping the plane horizontal and adjusting the speed of the plane with his one arm. He came in too fast, and the fence was rapidly approaching, so he had to turn and go along the fence while he slowed down.

Another time Joe was going to give me some lessons for keeping his plane in our pasture. These lessons were given from the Muenster airport, and that day wind was from the south. This meant I had to take off south, over the power lines along U.S. Highway 82. I was taking off and making a circle and landing. When I came in for the landing I would not stop completely, then "give it the gun" and take off again. Well, Joe would hold back on the control stick and I would have to "hump it" to clear the power lines along Hwy. 82.

CHAPTER 12

My Inventions

Wherever I worked, my mind was always thinking how I could make the job easier. While milking cows I was always studying how to milk cows with machines. When I was chopping cotton or picking cotton I was always trying to make the job easier. If someone had not invented a cotton-picking machine, I would have—I hated that job.

Ear corn elevator

When we gathered corn in a wagon and later in a four-wheel trailer, it was my job to unload the corn in the grainer.

Corn is the hardest thing to scoop, move a distance and deposit. So I built me a grain elevator using the electric motor and belt from the water pump. I made a wooden wheel two feet in diameter to gear down the electric motor to slow down the speed.

Automatic grain elevator

We had oats bins in the barn where we milked the cows. We had a grinder to grind the oats and blow the ground material into a feed bin next to where we milked the cows. We fed the ground oats to the cows when we milked them. The oats bin was about 100 feet from the grinder, and I had to carry the oats by hand from the bin to the grinder.

To make the job easier I took an old auger and augured the grain out of the oats bin to an old threshing machine elevator with the measuring mechanism still intact. After the grain was measured, I dumped it on a conveyer belt and took it to the grinder. This invention took the oats from the grain to the grinder automatically.

Fertilizer spreader

I made a fertilizer spreader that mounted on the back of our Model B John Deere tractor and ran from the power takeoff. It worked so well that I decide to get it patented. I filled out the papers with a patent attorney in Washington. To finish the patenting process, they said I had to put more money into it. I went to J. M. Weinzapfel at the bank, and he was interested in building my invention at Muenster Manufacturing Company, which was making lawnmowers in Muenster at the time. Weinzapfel paid the money needed, and I signed an agreement for them to manufacture it and I would get a commission for each they sold.

Muenster Manufacturing built one for demonstration purposes but never consulted with me in designing the demo. My design was to mount on the back of the tractor on the 3-point hookup. They designed one more like a 20 -foot drill with wheels on each side. Needless to say, it failed.

I then took the backseat out of my car and hauled my model to a manufacturing company in Dallas that made attachments to the Ford tractors. The company's owner was excited about my idea, and we talked about him manufacturing it and agreed that I would get a commission for every one sold. I believe this concept would have been successful. It worked great on the back of our Model B John Deere tractor. When I told him I had signed a contract with Muenster Manufacturing Co., he no longer would touch it.

Later I went back and picked up my demo. Weinzapfel wanted me to pay the money they had in the venture and would not give me a release. I eventually abandoned the idea.

CHAPTER 13

Courting in the '40s

I was a master at dating on a dollar.

I would go to town to Joe Trachea's drug store. There various guys would be hanging out deciding what to do that Saturday night. If we would like to get a date Joe had a telephone hanging on the wall in a back room. You would have to crank the phone to get the operator. You could tell the operator which girl you would like to call, and she would connect you, or she would tell you that the girl has a date already. I had the twin sisters, and the guys were just wanting a date with either one. They did not want to ask one and find out if she had a date already. They could not very well ask her twin sister. To avoid this problem they would ask the operator which girl had a date already, then asked the other.

My first date was with Anna Doris Geray. She asked me; at that time I was too bashful to ask a girl for a date. I took her to the Junior/Senior prom. The prom was in the Schuzten-Hall in downtown Lindsay. One of the songs that the jukebox played was "I Will Keep a Light in my Window Tonight."

Through my dating years I double-dated with Ruben Sturm, William Joseph Miller, Herbie Miller and James Bayer. My first double-dating was with Ruben Strum. Dad would give me the car full of gas and $1. This was enough to date a girl in the evening. It would cost each of us 25 cents to get into a movie show. Then afterward we would go to a restaurant for a bottle of soda and a hamburger. Ruben Strum drove a '38 four-door Chevrolet sedan that had the knee action front wheels worn out. The wheels leaned severely in at the top, making it difficult to drive.

For a while I triple-dated with Bill Miller and Ruben Strum. Bill had Teresa Walter; Ruben was going with Bernice Lutmer. I would go with whoever was available. It was always hard to get Bernice back home if it rained. The road back to her place off of the road would flood easily. They pretty well had settled on the same girls. The only girl Bill ever dated was Teresa. They were classmates. Ruben stayed with Bernice, and that was getting serious, but I was playing the field.

I dated Helen Walterscheid, Gracie Wimmer, Barbara Miller, Imogene Bezner, Betty Jean Fleitman, Rose Becker, and Teresa Rohmer. Helen W. lived way off of the gravel road, and it would get muddy to get her back home. Barbara Miller, I always had to open a gate four times a night to get to her house—twice when I picked her up. Teresa Rohmer, I got soaking wet twice when I brought her home, having to open a gate to get her back home during a rainstorm. Water was gushing a foot high across her gate. Dating in these years was for the fun of it and nothing very serious. A kiss at the door was just a kiss and was part of the formality of dating at the time.

For a while I double-dated with Herbie Miller, and I was going with his sister, Barbara Miller. She was a nice girl, but we both agreed we were not for each other and wished each other good luck.

Also in the summer of the '40s I dug rock holes for the telephone company. We dug holes for a line going west out of Muenster and on the road going west from the third four-corners north of Muenster. We used dynamite to dig the holes. I carved the initials of a girl I was dating in a tree along this road during a break.

CHAPTER 14

Meeting Gracie

My mother's chickens always laid more eggs than we could eat so, we always had eggs to sell. One day I had to take the eggs to the Farmers' Market Association to sell. John Herr worked in the produce department of the store and was buying the eggs. I sat on this table while he was counting and candling my eggs. As he worked, this attractive girl was bringing in eggs to sell, and we exchanged greetings. She seemed to be a bright, intelligent person. I did not ask who she was, but I saw her later in the pickup with her Dad, Martin Friske, so I knew her last name.

At that time the KCs had a Saturday night dance for young people in the upstairs of the KC Hall. There was a bench along the south side of the dance floor on which the girls sat and a bench along the north wall, where the boys sat. If you wanted to dance with a girl you would just go over and ask her to dance. You would do this until you danced with all of the girls. I asked Gracie (I knew her name by then) to dance, and we spent the evening together. I did not take her home, for her Dad had brought her to town and he was playing dominos at his mother's place.

My first automobile

The first new models of cars were coming out after World War II fighting had stopped, and I purchased a new two-door green Plymouth Sedan. James Bayer and I continued to double date together, and James mentioned that he would like to date that Friske girl. It was an unwritten law at the time that you would not try to date the girl that your friend was dating. If I did not move fast I would not be able go with her, so I asked her for a date before James did. This made it difficult for James to go with her. Of course she could go with other boys. When I told James I had a date with Gracie he said, "I wanted to go with her." I was hobbling around with clutches at this time.

Falling in love

I asked Gracie for a date the following Saturday, and I felt a special attraction to her that I did not feel with any other girl. I could tell she felt the same way toward me. I never went with a girl that affected me like she did. She just seemed to melt in my arms. I waited a few days, and I asked her again for a date, but she already had a date. She said that I should call earlier in the future. This was in the days when we had party lines, and everybody heard the all phones ring on the line. I called another girl on her line and made a date. As expected, her mother listened in and told Gracie. She never turned me down again. She was only 15 years old.

We went steady after that, and every time I called her, the others on the line would listen in—since I was the telephone man I added another button on the switchboard for the operators to use when I called her. This fixed it so I could call her without the others on the line hearing it ring.

Drafted into the Army

We started going steady about May or June of 1949—and I was drafted into the U.S. Armed Forces in December 1950. Gracie was still going to school in her senior year, so we could not very well get married. I could not very well tell her, a 16 year old, to stay home and not go anywhere while I was gone. After I left it was difficult for her with the junior/senior prom and other activities at school. She took it on herself not to go with other boys at first, and she asked my younger brother Jerry for her date to her senior prom.

I was in basic training at Fort Hood, Texas, for about six months, and I came home every weekend to be with her. I put a lot of miles on my new car—about 300 miles every weekend. Three other guys—Ewald Fuhrmann, Joe Phillips and Huge Perry from Gainesville—rode with me. The roads were not as good then as now, and we had to go through every town on the way to Killeen, Texas.

In the meantime Gracie's family moved to the Freddie Bezner farm, north of Lindsay.

After six months in basic training I was ordered to go to Germany. I brought my car home, and Bill and Gracie took me to Dallas to catch a train to Fort Hood. I kissed Gracie goodbye, and I would not see her again until December 1952–18 months later. My Army Life will be covered in another Chapter.

The last time I picked her up at her new home north of Lindsay before I went overseas, Harold Nortman was there, obviously thinking I was gone and that he could get a date. When I came up, he pretended that he came for Joan, Gracie's younger sister.

For some unknown reason Gracie's parents did not like me and did not trust me with their daughter. It was their intention to get her married off while I was gone. We could not get married—she was still in school. So Gracie had problems of her own.

Gracie's family problems

After she graduated from school, she got a job with the Kress five-and-dime store in Gainesville and stayed with her grandmother, who lived on North Weaver Street in Gainesville. Her mail still went out to her Dad's farm north of Lindsay. Her mother would open and read her mail. Eventually, it got to the point where Gracie's mom would not give her my letters at all, saying I did not write. Gracie knew better.

She also knew the postal workers in the Gainesville post office, and they would hold her mail and give it to her and not send letters to her out on the route. She caught a city bus to work and home again in the evening. There was a boy that her Grandmother liked that tried to go with Gracie, but she could not stand him. Harold kept calling her and she started dating him again to get to go somewhere. Harold had other ideas; he planned to marry her before I got back. In the meantime, her parents were putting pressure on her to go steady with Harold and break off from me. As the time that I was coming home drew near she wrote me a Dear John letter but waited to see how I would be when I got back.

In December 1952 I was finally discharged, and my ship landed in New York, and a two-engine army airplane few us to Fort Hood to be discharged. I immediately went to the Sears Store in Gainesville where Gracie was working and gave her a big kiss. She neither drew back nor resisted when I kissed her. However, she also did not put any feelings in her response.

She continued to go with Harold until one evening we were both across the river at Johnny Schmitz's club. I was by myself when Gracie came up and said that she was quitting Harold and that would I take her home. As related to me later he had become very aggressive and was all hands. He had apparently become quite desperate to win her—any way he could. She wanted no part of that, and she came to me.

Back to work for the phone company

I went back to work for the telephone company. While I was gone, my brother Bill quit the telephone company and went back to school in Saint Louis, Mo. Herman Younger's brother-in-law, Cotton Jackson, was running the company. He left as soon as I started working—so I had the telephone company to keep going.

Gracie and I continued dating again, but we ran into another problem. Gracie's parents would not allow me to pick her up. James Bayer and I were double dating again, so he would go by and pick up Gracie then get his date, and we would be together for the evening and then James took her back home. This went on for some time when Gracie said she was moving to Gainesville, where she had found a room rented by Marie Geray. After she had been living in Gainesville for some time, I proposed and she accepted. I did not ask her father for her hand, as we did not believe he would give approval.

Soon after we agreed to get married I bought three lots on 624 N. Cedar St. for $600 dollars and got a $6,500 loan from Frank Trubenbach to build the house. I hired Tony Klement and his brother Eugene to build the house, and Henry Henscheid painted some of the rooms so we could move in when we got married. We painted the living room after we were married.

The marriage

We got married on Oct. 20, 1953 about 10 months after I was discharged from the Army. To keep friends from playing tricks on us we hid our car in Gainesville and used a car that Wilde Chevrolet loaned us for the wedding.

We got married in the Lindsay church with Fr. Conrad officiating. James Bayer was to be best man, but he was in the service and could not be there for our wedding, so his brother Randy was our best man. Gracie had her good friend, Joan Geray, as her bridesmaid.

We were not sure her father would give her away, so we had made out that if he did not show up I would come to the back of church and we would walk up together. He showed up and gave her away. When I came out of the sacristy to meet my bride, I hit my head hard on the Visual light that hung on the side of the door. I did not notice it hurting until later in the afternoon.

We got married at 9 in the morning, and our wedding reception was not until 6 in the evening in the basement of the old parish hall. Agnes Lehnertz cooked our meal. The wedding dance was in the old VFW hall on South Main Street. The dance floor had just been enlarged, and we were the first dance after it was made bigger. We danced our first dance to "The Waltz You Saved for Me."

Our honeymoon

After our wedding reception Robert Bayer helped us get away and took us to our car hidden in the garage of Gracie's Sears store boss, Magritte. We spent our first night in an Ardmore Okla., motel. The next night we got as far as Vinita, Okla. Finally, on the third night we got to Saint Louis to visit my brother Bill, who was going to Loyola University. In Saint Louis we had dinner at the home of Grandmother Fuhrman's friends, the Theisens, and we both fell asleep at the dinner table. From there we drove up to Lincoln, Neb., to visit my brother Jerry, who was going to Marquette University.

Then we headed out west across South Dakota, spending the night in Oglala. Oglala was a highlight of our honeymoon. From there we made it to Colorado Springs; we visited the Garden of the Gods; we drove as far up Pikes Peak as we could go until we were stopped by ice and a gate across the road. It was late October, and we were not able to go to the top. We went over to the mining town of Cripple Creek before taking a 32-mile winding mountain road to Canon City, Colorado. It was not a fully developed road and was one-way only with places to pass a car. As we were about half way down it got dark on us—the next day we learned that God must be with us, for the generator of the car was out and we had been driving on the battery. We drove straight home the next day. Later, when we showed pictures of our honeymoon, they were only of motels.

I continued working for the Telephone Company and Gracie went to work again at the Sears mail order store on California Street in Gainesville. Our house was finished except for the living room, and we finished it as we found time from our work. Gracie miscarried three times, and it looked like we may not be able to have a family of our own, so we adopted Kent in 1960, seven years after we married. Three years later, after a trip to Las Vegas, Gracie got pregnant again, and Gene was born in 1963.

I also need to note that shortly before Gracie's mother's death, she apologized for not accepting me as their son-in-law and asked for forgiveness. I told her I had never held any animosity toward her or her husband.

CHAPTER 15

The 1942 Ice Storm and the Telephone Company

I n the 1942 ice storm I worked with a contractor that came in to help rebuild the Cooke County Electric Co-op distribution system. I worked as a Grunt for a climber. We started at the sub-station by the Myra Road on the Geo Bayer farm and Highway 82 rebuilding the south of Muenster line, all the way south of Valley View and then east of I-35 down into the sand country.

At another time in the late 1940s I worked for the electric co-op to build the power line west from Muenster that served the Alphonse Hoeing, Al Fleitman, and Felix Becker farms on west of Muenster.

Telephone company

Cooke County Electric in 1949 was bringing electricity to many new homes, and my brother Bill and I were wiring homes for electricity. We had particularly bad ice storms, and Alphones Hoenig, a director of the local telephone company, came to my brother and me and asked us to rebuild the phone system. The telephone company repair man had left town, and they had no one to rebuild the lines again. All the east and west lines had loaded down with ice and now lay on the ground. Most of the telephone poles had broken off or had fallen over. We had no telephone experience, but we said we would try to rebuild it. We put it back like it was before the ice storm with the poles in their shallow holes. We had everybody back on again.

Then a second storm took it all back down again.

This time we dug the holes four-feet deep and, for the taller poles, five-feet deep. We hit rock about three feet down. We used dynamite to make the holes deeper. We had to drill a small hole in the rock with a crow bar that had the end flattened out. By going up and down in the same place adding a little water we were able to make a hole for dynamite. We had more ice storms, but our poles never did fall over again.

Herman Younger of Fort Worth, Texas, bought controlling interest in the company for $20,000 about this time.

It was in January 1949 when I started working for Muenster Telephone Company. The telephone poles were old and weather beaten and difficult to climb. I was climbing a 25-foot pole in May and fell off. I hit the ground on my feet. On my left leg, the knee was still locked and the impact knocked me out briefly and cracked my leg in the knee since it was locked and did not give.

When I came to, I realized I had severely damaged my left knee, so I unstrapped my climbers and tool belt. I hobbled over to my 1929 Chevrolet truck and headed back to Muenster. I stopped where the telephone line came down within easy reach and I called in to tell them that I had probably broken my leg.

Doctor Myrick was the only doctor in Muenster—a general health doctor—and I felt I would need a bone doctor. Doctor Myrick was in, so I came in to the Myrick clinic and hobbled up the stairs. Doc x-rayed it and said he did not believe it was broken and dismissed me. That night my knee got as big as a watermelon, and I was in severe pain.

The telephone company had no insurance on me, so I paid the hospital bill. Later I was reimbursed for the medical costs.

CHAPTER 16

The Fisherman

Not long ago, I ran across our old fishing equipment in the storeroom of our garage. The rod and reels, gasoline lanterns, the filleting knives—even the old inner tube and water skis—are still there. This reminded me of the times I spent with our boys, Gene and Kent, water skiing and fishing.

Gene loved to fish. When he was about six, we would dig up some worms and go to the pond along Highway 82 halfway between Muenster and Saint Jo. We would usually catch a few perch. Most of the time they were not very big, but he got a big thrill out of catching fish.

Sherwood Shores

As he got older we would go out to Sherwood Shores of Lake Texoma and fish off the shore. We would stop at one of those bait places and pick up a couple dozen minnows for bait. You could look out over the lake and see the fishing boats usually grouped together in different parts of the lake. You would have to assume that they were having better luck fishing than us along the shore.

Nothing tasted better than fresh-filleted Crappie wrapped in foil with an onion, and salt and pepper, cooked in the campfire.

It was in the late 1960s when we camped out all night that the first time. It was across the bayou from Rock Creek along a sandy beach of Lake Texoma. This trip included Kent, Gene and our dog Queenie. I hauled all equipment and supplies in my car, for I did not have a pickup. We pitched a tent, made a campfire, and went fishing to eat. Gene and I fished. Kent was no fisherman, and he sat in the car all the time and listened to the radio. That night we slept in the tent. Queenie took off early in the evening and we did not see her again till early the next morning. An armadillo came stumbling around during the night. Gene did not sleep a wink while the dog was gone but fell asleep soon after Queenie came back.

The next day when we started to come home I found out I had a dead battery in my car. Kent listening to the radio had run the battery down. Turning on the key so the radio played also turned on my two-way radio and killed my battery. We had just installed our Motorola Push Button mobile phone system. Luckily there were some more campers in the area, and they pulled my manual-shift car till it started.

We heard many stories of the Sand Bass fish running on Red River so we would go to Horseshoe Bend in Red River to fish. When the fish were running there were hundreds of people fishing along the river.

For bait we would seine for ghost minnows in a shallow water on a sandbar on the river's edge and get all the bait we would need. I still just had a car, and the ruts were deep getting to the river and my car would drag bottom. The river was heavily infested with poison oak and ivy, and I was very allergic to it. The boys would not get it, but I would break out just being in the area. I found that as soon as I got home from the river I would take a hot bath scrubbing down with a strong soap from hair to toes and put on clean clothes. I would still get a slight rash at times but nothing severe, and it would not last long.

There are a lot of snakes in the area and there would be rattlesnakes swimming across the river. I always gave them plenty of room.

We caught a lot of fish on the river, but it seemed that the best fishing is always on the other side from where you are. The river had accumulated on one side of the riverbed and was only about 50 feet wide. So I loaded up both boys, a bait bucket, rod and reels and started across the river at a narrow point. The water was deeper than I expected and came over my waist. The boys hung on tightly as the water rose. We made it safely and took advantage of the better fishing.

The image of the fishing boats out in Lake Texoma made me feel that our fishing would be so much better on the lake if I could move around, and I started to look at boats.

Boat fishing (the Sea Sprite Boat)

As our boys got older I finally broke down and purchased a Sea Sprite fiberglass boat with a four-cylinder marine inboard engine from North Texas Marine. It was more of a pleasure boat than a fishing boat, but it did both jobs.

North Texas Marine took us to Moss Lake to show us how to operate the boat. I wasn t much of a water person and had never loaded a boat on a trailer, and I had some angst but managed to maneuver the boat and after several tries got it back on the trailer. After that it came easier.

We would go out to Texoma to fish from the boat. We got more fish and had to learn how to filet them. One rule I made from the very beginning: Everyone riding in the boat must have his or her life jacket on at all times.

We spent many weekends at the lake especially when it was new, I would pull the trailer out, and Gracie would bring the boat. Thunderstorms quite often would come through at night and rock our trailer. We would go to the lake as late as the Thanksgiving weekend. Some years it would be cold, and there was some ice on the lake.

One weekend just Gene and I took the travel trailer and boat to Big Mineral resort for a weekend. It was quite a procession to the lake. I pulled the travel trailer with the boat behind the travel trailer.

We had learned before that any time you were on the lake and saw a dark cloud in the distant northwest you needed to head to shore quickly. We were fishing when a dark cloud appeared to signal that a front was coming in. It was still a ways out when, all at once, Gene's and my hair stood straight up. This signaled the possibility of a lightning strike at any time. Needless to say, we got down low in the boat and headed to shore as quickly as we could. When we got to the loading ramp the storm was in full force. Gene was too young to back the pickup and, with the boat trailer down into the water, to load the boat. I had to tie up the boat next to the loading ramp and get the pickup and back the trailer into the water. Then I went about loading the boat.

Because of the storm I could not drive the boat into the trailer. I got down into the water to get the boat around and into the trailer. I was in the lake, water over my waist, trying to maneuver the boat around with the storm brewing—the wind was howling, the waves were hitting the boat, driving it everywhere but on the boat trailer. I finally got the boat on the trailer, and Gene hooked the rope in front and cranked the boat into the trailer. The violent storm rocked our travel trailer that night. The wind was blowing from the side of the trailer that had the vent for our space heater. This caused a terrible harmless odor from the heater to get into the travel trailer. The storm finally subsided, and we got some sleep.

There were always stalled boats on the lake, and we would stop and pull them into their camp. Every summer there would be one or more of those one-man wind skis that had fallen in the water and could not get back up that we would tow back to their camp. We also got pulled to shore a number of times ourselves when a trot line wrapped around the propeller, knocking out the oil seal and letting water get into the drive.

When the lake was high there was no danger of hitting an underwater object, but when it was low, one would have to watch out. Once we were pulling Gene in the middle of Lake Texoma when the boat stopped. Gene got off of his skis and walked to the boat. We were crossing a high ridge under the low water.

Quite a ways from our Camp at Paw Paw Creek in the middle of Lake Texoma is an island. Once or twice a year we would load up the grill with picnic supplies and take a boat ride down the lake, cross under Willis Bridge continuing east until we came to this island. Here we would set up camp and start a fire in the grill. We would spend a leisurely afternoon roosting wieners and marshmallows before heading back to our camp on the north end of the lake.

Gene and I liked to go night fishing under Willis Bridge. After work we would unload our boat at Cedar Bayou at the south end of the bridge and head for one of the big peers holding up the bridge. At our favorite peer we had left a cable around the peers to which we would attach the boat. We had two gas lanterns with a support that pointed them down toward the water. The light would attract bugs that buzzed around and fell into the water. This attracted fish of every kind, and we caught some nice-sized fish. We would fish a couple of hours and head back to shore. The ramp into the water at Cedar Bayou was at the bottom of a steep grade. You had to be very careful when launching or loading a boat from this ramp. There was a streetlight that illuminated the area at night.

Gene was still too young to back the pickup down the ramp in preparation of loading the boat, so I would park the boat alongside the ramp and then go get the pickup and boat trailer and back it down the ramp. Then I would get the boat and drive it on the boat trailer. Gene stood on the boat hitch in front of the boat and attached the rope to an eyebolt then cranked the boat into the trailer until it was all the way in.

One particular night, after fishing until midnight, we loaded the boat like we always did. I drove the boat into the trailer, and Gene hooked the boat and cranked it into the trailer. Then I pulled the boat and trailer out of the water after Gene got in the pickup, and we continued up the steep grade of the parking lot. About halfway up the parking lot the boat suddenly came loose and started out of the trailer and down the hill. I stopped just in time that the front of the boat was still in the trailer. Apparently when Gene cranked the boat into the trailer he cranked it backwards and as the pull on the rope increased as we drove up the hill, the rope came loose and the boat started out of the trailer. We were by ourselves, so I used a bumper jack to start the boat back into the trailer, and eventually I got the boat loaded again.

Travel trailers

Travel trailers were the next item I looked at. I figured if I had a travel trailer with a shower Gracie would enjoy camping more with us. I finally broke down and purchased a medium-sized travel trailer. I still only had a car, so a sturdy trailer hitch had to be installed on the back of my Chevrolet Impala car. We were really living now. It had a space heater, kitchen stove and oven, and a commode with a shower over the top of it. It had a built-in water heater venting out the side and an air conditioner on the roof. There was a place for all four of us to sleep. We removed the kitchen table for Gene to sleep and Kent had to climb a ladder to get to his overhead bunk. We were cozy, but it was a little small.

Later I purchased a two/tone green GMC half-ton pickup to pull the trailer and boat. It only made 12 miles per gallon, and it took a tank of gas to make one round trip to Lake Texoma.

I had one problem on weekends. I belonged to the Men's choir at church, and we always sang at the 8 o'clock Mass every Sunday morning. While the others were sleeping I would come back to Muenster and sing with the choir then drive back out to the lake. We sang three- and four-voice Masses, and it really handicapped the choir if one member was missing.

I purchased a pair of water skis, and Gene and his friends soon learned how to ski. Gene's friends included Troy Wolf, Jamie Moster, Sam Hess and Bob Hamric. They spent almost every weekend with us for many summers. I was always the driver, and Gracie was always with us with her life jacket on, even though she did not really like the water.

On weekends the lake was always busy, and I would have to dodge troutlines, water skis and other boats as I pulled the family around the lake.

They particularly enjoyed being pulled on an inner tube behind the boat. While going fast I could swing them way out—I'd go so fast that they bounced on the waves.

Our small two-wheel travel trailer was a big improvement to camping out at night, but as the boys got bigger it got more crowded. I started looking for a larger trailer.

Larger travel trailer

Eventually, we had an opportunity to trade our small trailer for a 20-foot model. This was our home for at least one summer. We no longer had to take down the kitchen table for Gene to sleep. The shower was no longer over the commode. Kent still had to crawl a ladder to get to his overhead bunk. Gracie and I had a full-size private bedroom.

Astronomy

Gene was interested in the stars, so we gave him an inexpensive telescope for Christmas one year. His interest only grew, so the following year we bought him a much better telescope. The stars are clearest on a cold night, so Gene got some feet and hand warmers to stay warm. Then, using old bicycle parts and surplus electric motors, he built a special chair that, with the push of a button, would rotate and also allow him to comfortably lie while stargazing. We still have this chair and telescope in storage. Our grandson Conner has shown an interest in the stars, as well; whenever he is ready we will let him have Gene's telescope and chair.

Cabin on the lake

I had a chance to trade my 24-foot travel trailer for a mobile home at Paw Paw Creek resort. We could see the advantage of having a permanent home on the lake and not have to drag the travel trailer and boat each time we went to the lake. This gives us a place to keep our boat at the lake and not in the alley behind our house.

It was a relatively new travel trailer, but it needed a great deal of work on it. The underneath portion of the mobile home was open, and you could see that it still had the wheels under it. I put a skirt around it to make it warmer during the winter. The road passing by it was low, so I made a driveway up along the trailer using old telephone poles so that our car was level when parked by the trailer. I worked on this during the summer time, and I was soaking wet with sweat.

The resort was run by Bill Woody. We were amused by Woody's signs that he had stacked up behind a building on his resort. You could see these signs as you drove up. Every time he changed wives he had a new sign made and the old one went behind the building. There were a number of these signs stacked behind of his building.

Our new mobile home had two bedrooms, a bathroom with the shower over the bathtub, a living room and a full size kitchen. It had a forced air heating system but no air-conditioning for the summer time. At that time one could buy air-conditioning systems from Sears and do the installation yourself. I got a system and installed it in the heater closet for cooled air in the summertime.

Each summer we would spend our weekends at the lake. Right after work on Friday we would load up and go out to our cabin on Lake Texoma. At times Gene and I would launch our boat at Cedar Bayou next to Willis Bridge in the evening and go out and do some night fishing under the bridge. We would attach our boat to one of the peers of the bridge. We had our gas lanterns mounted on the side of the boat to shine down into the water.

The light attracted bugs that would fall into the water and attract the minnows. The bugs and minnows swarming around the boat would bring the fish for us to catch. We actually caught a lot of fish in this manner. We would stay until about midnight before returning home.

Even though Gracie was afraid of water she was always with us when the boys were skiing. I mentioned earlier about my life jacket rule. Kent never wanted to put on his life jacket, so he would not always go out to the lake with us. In the earlier years I would be driving the boat.

By the time Gene went into high school we had the mobile home on Lake Texoma and his friends were coming around to water ski and play. They were too young to take the boat on their own, so Gracie and I would take them out to ski. We taught Gene and his friends how to water ski. I would drive the boat watching out for other skiers, trout lines and Gracie watched each of the skiers and let me know when they fell down. Gene learned fast and was a good skier. He could go over the ski jumps without falling, but he enjoyed being pulled on the truck tube. He would sit in it and hang on and I would try to throw him off.

As the years passed and they got older we made Gene in charge of the boat, and they were able to go out on their own and ski.

After that, my chore was to keep the grass mowed around our mobile home and barbecue the chicken so that it would be ready when they came back hungry. Not knowing when they would be back I would brown the chicken over the hot coals, then move the chicken into a large roaster with a grate on the bottom and add some water to steam the chicken. I would then spread the barbecue sauce over the chicken and let it steam until we were ready to eat. The chicken was very good and tender and would just fall off of the bones.

While I was preparing the chicken, Gracie made a big skillet of fried potatoes with onions and heated several cans of pork and beans. The boys would come in from skiing hungry as a bear, and soon there were only chicken bones left. When they left to go home I always reminded them "to come back when they could not stay so long." One time I was not able to be there when they left, and they came back and asked Gracie to tell them "to come back when you cannot stay so long.'

By the time they all graduated from High school Troy Wolf and Jamie Moster were good skiers, but we were never able to keep Sam Hess up on the water skis very long. We always enjoyed having Gene's friends around, and do enjoy them even today. They were all good boys—we kept them off of the streets and out of trouble.

At that time there were many trails in the timbers on Lake Texoma, and we would ride them on our four-wheeler.

One day I came out to our cabin pulling our four-wheeler on a trailer and was met by Bill Woody, operator of the resort. He told me we were no longer allowed to ride our four-wheeler on his resort.

Also, we got new neighbors, and the space between them and us quickly had a wall built right in the middle, not leaving enough room for my boat. When I asked Woody why the change, he said we no longer were allowed to park our boat next to our cabin even though others still had their boats by their cabins. We would have to rent a stall from him in the future. Our relationship with the owner deteriorated rapidly. Gene went on to college, and with a cantankerous resort manager, we had an opportunity to sell the mobile home, so we sold it, shook the dust off of our shoes and went on.

One tradition with Gene's friends continues to this day. Every year after midnight Mass, Gene and his friends would bring a bottle of wine and gather at our place for breakfast. Some of Gene's friends still gather at our place after midnight Mass and bring a bottle of wine.

Before we had the cabin on the lake, rather than hauling the boat back home, we decided to pay for a stall by the lake. I thought it was safe until a storm came along. My boat did not stay completely under the shelter, and the water from the roof poured into my boat and the boat was barely afloat when we found it the next day. The engine was completely under water and I had to have the engine completely overhauled. My boat was in the shop about as much as we used it. The opportunity came along and I traded it for a larger used boat.

A boat can give you a great deal of pleasure—leisure boat riding, water skiing, fishing—but owning a boat gets kind of expensive. When buying a boat you account for the cost of the boat and then you think you have it made. But that is not the way it works. You have to buy a permit to be on the lake—if you will use it on two lakes you have to buy two permits, etc. Then, as with your car, you have to buy insurance in the event someone gets injured in a boat accident. And, as with your car, it is always out of gas—if you buy it on the lake, you get about as much water-in-the-gas as gas, which causes other problems.

Texoma is full of trout lines, and the outboard drive on our boat picked these up and wrapped them around the prop and knocked out the seal. That caused us you to lose our oil and did damage to the outboard drive. It was a never-ending battle to keep the boat running and legal with the yearly permit and insurance renewals, and it is always out of gas. But the pleasure of being out with the family made it all worthwhile.

Island picnic

Occasionally we would load up hot dogs and a portable grill and take the boat out to an island in Lake Texoma, fish and have a roasted hot dog lunch.

Closing the lake property

The boys grew up and graduated from high school and went off to college. Bill Woody, the owner of Paw Paw Creek, got so cranky that we gave up on our lake adventures. We found a buyer for the mobile home, and Larry Eldridge bought the four-wheeler.

I kept the boat a while, and I told Gene he could use it all he wanted, but he had to pay all of the expenses. He used it once or twice with his friends then told me he did not realize how expensive it was to operate the boat. He did not use it anymore, so I sold the boat, as well.

The big truck inner tube, camping equipment, Coleman lights, filet board, fishing rods now lay idle in the upstairs storeroom of our garage. Gene is gone, and only memories are left. Whenever I go upstairs to get something from the storeroom, I always stop for a moment and think about the great times we spent together as a family.

Gene's son Conner is now about the age that Gene was when we started fishing. Hopefully he will be able to spend some time with us, and maybe we can get in some fishing.

After leaving the lake home for about 15 years, recently we drove out to see what our old Paw Paw Creek camping grounds looked like today, and we were really disappointed. We had to drive around washed out areas of the road. Paw Paw Creek Camp no longer existed. There was nothing there. Our old fishing grounds along the lake were fenced off, and we weren't able to have access to them. An era in our lives is now just a memory, and we are glad we have that.

CHAPTER 17

A tale of two sons (Kent)

Once in a while Gracie got sick and I would have to take care of the boys. We ate cannibal sandwiches (ground sirloin steak with onion, salt and pepper, raw on a slice of bread—only I used ground round steak hamburger meat), and I held military-type inspections by their bed each morning before they went off to school. They loved this. Their pockets had to be buttoned, shoes clean. The beds had to be made and the room neat. We made a game of this. If they passed inspection (and they almost always did) I gave them a treat. They even voted me "Best Dad."

Maintaining that distinction was hard, especially with Kent.

Kent Michael Fuhrman

We had been married six years, and Gracie was having trouble. She had miscarried three times, so we applied to Catholic Charities of Dallas to adopt a child. We did not have to wait too long—Kent came into our lives two weeks after he was born in November 1960, and we came down to Saint Paul's Hospital in Dallas and picked him up. We bought a baby bed and a highchair and blankets preparing for a new baby. We picked him up in the same the 1949 Plymouth two-door car that we drove on our honeymoon seven years earlier.

On the way home from Dallas we stopped at my parents' place on the farm east of Muenster and showed my mother her new grandchild. One of our telephone operators was pregnant—it seemed like forever—and I asked her what was taking her so long.

Kent was an outgoing child and wanted to have someone around him at all times. He always wanted someone to play with him, for he liked to play ball or some other sport. I played with him as much as I could. He wanted friends. As he got older it got to the point where he stole a watch and gave it as a gift to Rummy Hess, who was a teacher at the time.

He did not like heights but did crawl around on a peach tree we had in the backyard. One time we heard him hollering, and we looked out and he was hanging upside down with his foot caught in a fork of the tree. While Gene always rode with me to school, Kent always rode his bicycle.

We lived right in town so that both boys could get up early to serve Mass without our help. Both boys were altar boys.

Kent had a terrible overbite of his teeth, and we had Dr. Graham put braces on his teeth to try and correct the problem. Kent would jerk them out as soon as he left the dentist's office. We tried to talk to him and explain why it was important for him to have his teeth fixed. We would put the braces back, and he would jerk them back out. Finally Dr. Graham said there was no need to give him braces because he would not keep them in.

Kent was a very nervous child, and his hands and feet stayed wet with sweat. This caused him to have foot odors. We tried to have him soak his feet in a special solution to keep the odor down, but he would have no part of it. He could never understand that we were trying to help him. He did not pick up his clothes and would not do anything he was told. Gracie and he did not get along at all for they had opposite personalities. Kent would tell a lie, when the truth would have been to his benefit.

He had dyslexia, which made it harder for him to learn. When he was in high school we had Sister Alberta give him special tutoring after hours to help him learn. He would not show up for the lessons. We finally we had to quit.

He did not graduate form Sacred Heart High School with a diploma. He went through the motions of receiving a diploma but it was a blank piece of paper.

After he graduated he moved into a trailer on the south side of Muenster. We helped him furnish it and bought him a large TV set. I came by one day and the TV set was gone. He had hocked it to buy drugs.

After high school I gave him a job with our company. He would ride along with the guys working and sit in the truck, not paying a bit attention to what they were doing and telling them some day he was going to be telling them what to do.

I got Kent a job with our good neighbor, Gene Gieb, working in the oil fields. Gene would come by and pick up Kent and take him to work. This went on for a number of years. One morning Kent told him he was quitting and did not go to work with any more. I found out later that he was not a good hand and the only reason he stayed as long as he did was because of my friendship with Gene Gieb.

We were planning a trip to Germany to visit relations and go to the place where I was stationed when I was in the army in 1951. Kent did not want to go along, so I told him I would buy him a car when we got back. He stayed with my sister, Elsie Endres, and her husband Gilbert and their family.

When we got back I bought him a nice used Tudor Pontiac Sedan. Soon after he received the car he came around the corner on Highway 373 north on the north end of Main Street too fast, lost control and hit a highway sign. There was only minor damage. He never seemed to have money to buy gas, and soon I would find his car about anywhere sitting on the side of the road out of gas. And finally someone dumped several bags of fertilizer in the car. I assumed that Kent owed someone for drugs and did not pay and they fertilized his car.

I was looking for a place that could help him and I read in the Yellow Pages of a home in Fort Worth for troubled boys. I investigated and it seemed like a good institution. So I paid the tuition and enrolled Kent there. They would teach him a trade, and he would be given a job at graduation. After he was there they transferred him to their home in Houston for they needed to balance the number white and black students. We visited him a number of times while he was there. We thought he was doing real well and that he would be graduating very soon.

One day Kent was on our doorstep. He had been expelled from the Boys Home. He was accused of stealing a pair of boots. He said he had approval of the owner to wear the boots. He had caught a ride with Rumpy Hess, who was hauling beer from a brewery in Houston to Muenster for Gilbert Endres, Beer Distributor in Muenster. He had no clothes with him. Later we were able to retrieve his clothes. On another trip Rumpy brought him his clothes.

I got Kent a job with a contractor that was burying a fiber cable for us from Bowie, Texas, to Dallas. I told him then that if he would keep the job for a year I would consider bringing him back into our company. He was working on the section that went through Era, Texas. at the time.

Gracie did not want him in our house, so I paid for him to stay in a motel in Gainesville, and he could ride out with others staying at the motel and working on the project. It was very hot weather, and he got sick and missed a few days' work from drinking cold water while he was hot. He worked a week, got his paycheck and did not show up for work again. The contractor said that he had made him a good hand.

The next communication I received from him came from the Drug and Alcohol Rehabilitation Center in Wichita Falls, Texas. Kent had gotten drunk and was picked up or turned himself into the Center. We did not hear from him for close to 20 years.

Kent resurfaces

About a year and half ago I got word that Kent showed up at the House of Peace, a church in Fort Worth. But he was there a short time. I learned that he had moved to Midlothian, Virginia.

Apparently, Judy Maxie, who has a restaurant in Midlothian,Virginia, sent him the money to take a bus to her state. She took him into her home with her mother, and he worked cooking in her restaurant. Later, she bought him an old pickup and he found other work around town. With the restaurant she has a bar that served beer and alcohol and Kent occasionally would drink a beer. This arrangement worked well for about a year when Kent started drinking more heavily. One day he got drunk and drove back to where he was staying. On the way he hit several other cars before getting home. It did not take long for the police to catch up with him and arrest him for hit and run driving and leaving the scene of an accident. Kent spent some time in jail, and I paid for Gray Gennings, an attorney, to represent him when his trial came up. His driver's license was revoked and he was ordered to pay a fine and report back to the court at given times. Kent neither paid the fines nor reported back to the court as directed. It is now over a year since Kent's accident.

Kent later had a chance to go to a place in Arlington, Va., that helps people like him to get back on their feet, but he could not leave until he received approval from the court in Midlothian. Gray Gennings was helping him to get clearance to leave.

When Kent finally could leave Virginia I sent him bus fare to Fort Worth through Judy. He got back to the House of Peace in Fort Worth and called me. I got his address and drove down to Fort Worth to visit him. I had trouble finding his place, for my GPS in my Taurus would not take his address, but I finally found where he was living. I drove up and waited. There was an old man sitting there, so I thought I would ask him if he knew Kent. When I got close to him he got up and approached me. I asked him if he knew Kent Fuhrman and he said, "I am Kent."

Kent had aged since the last time I had seen him and I did not recognize him. He had a beard and mustache and was gray headed. I put my arm out to give him a hug, but he did not respond, and we shook hands. We exchanged greetings and decided to go down to the corner Jack in the Box to talk.

I gave him some money, which I understand he readily gave to Jack Yarbrough, the operator of House of Peace. We then had the waiter take our picture, and we parted. I was very glad to see him again, and he seemed to be happy where he was—he has been all over the United States working with

H.O.P. for his room and board. He is not getting money for cokes and the like, and I mailed him a debit card that had about $200 on it. He asked me to text him the code, which I did, but I believe he was on the road before he could get money from the card. When he got back from his trip his debit card had only $75 on it.

As I am writing this he is on the road again without money to spend for a coke, so Judy has gotten him a Home Depot reloadable debit card with $200 on it, and I have refunded her the money. He has no way to make himself spending money where he is. I do not mind helping him out.

CHAPTER 18

A tale of two sons (Gene)

Gene Henry Fuhrman

G ene was a remarkable child. He was as inquisitive as a cat. He had to push every button he found to see what it would do. He would go with me to the telephone office and play around while I worked on the equipment. One time he fell off of the rolling ladder in the equipment room to the hard tiled floor. He said he saw stars when he hit the floor. Another time he turned off the main charger in the battery room and the next day the local police came by and told me that the office was dead. The dial equipment ran all night on the batteries, but failed the next day. This was Gene—if he was in my car, or watching television, he turned or pushed every button to see what it would do.

Nov. 25 is the anniversary of our son Gene's death. He was killed by a drunk driver on the north edge of Sanger, Texas. The streets in Muenster around Main Street had been blocked off for the 2003 Christmas parade, which was taking place at the same time as Gene's interment in Sacred Heart Cemetery. The funeral Mass was at the Immaculate Conception Church in Denton, the same church where he married Kaylynn Paterson, three years earlier. He was 39 years old. He always wanted a family before he was 40 years old—he had a family but he did not live to see it before 40.

Gene's birth

It was Good Friday evening, and Gracie and I were keeping an hour of adoration in Sacred Heart Church when Gracie said she was starting to have labor pains and that we had better get to the hospital. She was only in her seventh month. It appeared that Gracie would miscarry this pregnancy, as had happened three times before. Gracie was in labor and the doctor decided to do a cesarean to give the child a better chance to live.

Gene was born on March 27, 1963. Being premature he was just a bag of bones, but he was alive. He was almost three months premature. He weighed 4 pounds and 4 ounces. Shortly after he was born they had him in an incubator, and we could watch him through a window. It amazed us that he would try to hold himself off of a wet diaper. All at once he started to turn blue and the nurse quickly pulled the blinds on the window closed so I could not see what was taking place. It turned out that the incubator started to malfunction and Gene was not getting oxygen. They got the incubator fixed and Gene was all right.

Everything was going well enough that I had gone back to work installing a key system in Endres Motor Company's Ford dealership.

In the meantime Gracie was having a hard time. She was not able to keep liquids or food down. I got a call from Gracie and all she could say was, "Come." When I got to her she was in a terrible condition. Her eyes were sunken—it was obvious that she was going down fast and something had to be done. I asked the doctor what he was going to do, and he said he never had one that did not improve. This is when I ordered him to bring in another doctor for consultation. He brought in a doctor from Denton, and immediately they determined that they must go back into surgery. They found that her intestine had attached itself to the cesarean cut and would not allow food or water to pass. After that, her color came back, and she was able to take food and water was a new person within a day.

It was about two weeks before Gene gained enough weight for us to take him home. He was small enough that I could hold him in the palm of one hand and pass him over the table, and my wedding ring fit on his arm.

As he started walking and got older he would go along with me if he did not have to meet people. He would stand on the seat of my truck. I would put out my arm when I had to put the brakes on and slow down. Only once do I remember that I braked so hard that he fell off of the seat and ended up on the floor of the car under the dash.

When Gene was four, I noticed that Gene was not feeling well. I took him over to our next door neighbor Odessa Morrison (our illness consultant), who said she thought he had scarlet fever. he next day I took him to the Baby Doctor in Sherman, and as I entered the doctor's office I told the receptionist that this baby probably had something very catching. Her reply was, "just take your seat and wait your turn." When Gene's turn came and the doctor diagnosed the illness, they ushered him out the back door. In fact, Gene exposed everyone in the waiting room to scarlet fever. Fortunately none of the other children caught it.

Gene suffered with tonsillitis for several years before he was old enough to have his tonsils removed. When Gene turned five, we had to take him to the doctor 17 times in three months. One day the doctor said, "This is the best I have seen his throat. Let's take his tonsils out tomorrow." Tomorrow was a Saturday.

After that Gene felt so good that we threatened to put them back at times.

When he was five, he had the chickenpox. I could not find a babysitter for him, but he was a pretty responsible little boy. I was only six blocks away, so I left him home by himself and told him I would call him every so often and he should call me if he needed me. I called him, and there was no answer, so I immediately ran home to see if he was okay. I found him playing in his room very contented. I asked, "Why didn't/t you answer the phone?" He said, "I was too busy playing." He did not scratch when the pox itched; he only would press on them. I had told him that scratches would leave scars. He caught chicken pox a week before he was to be in Darlene Lueb's wedding as ring bearer. Fortunately, he was over the disease enough to be in the wedding.

Gene attended kindergarten at Muenster Public School. The morning he started school, as he was eating breakfast he started to cry. Gracie and I asked him why he was crying. He said, "I do not know how to learn." We told him that is why he was going to school—to learn.

We always told our children if they got in trouble in school, they would also get in trouble at home for it. One day while Gene was in kindergarten another boy squeezed his hand hard and Gene hollered, so the teacher seated him in a corner. He did not tell us about it until the third grade because he didn't want to get in trouble at home, also.

Gene liked his day care so well that when he started school, after school he would stop in at the day care on his way to the Telephone office. I called the day care and asked Sylvia to send him on as she had enough to do without him being there. Sylvia said he was a help—he would play with the other children and keep them occupied. He finally outgrew this.

When Gene was in the first grade at Sacred Heart School the time changed in October. Gene, still not knowing how to tell time, was crying at the breakfast table again. This time he said he was late for school. We asked why he thought he was late for school. Gene said, "The sun is way up and the birds are singing." That was how he knew when he should be at school.

We had taught Gene his prayers before he went to school. One day he came home from school and was disgusted. They were learning "The Apostles Creed," he said, and we had not taught him this prayer and "Sharon Voth knew all of her prayers before anyone else. He could not stand that he could not out-do her in prayers.

Gene received his first confession and first communion at Sacred Heart Church. He received his Scapular medal that day and wore it every day of his life. He had it on the evening he was killed. We gave a breakfast for him after Mass. Ray and Toni Lube, his baptismal sponsors, were present.

One year his teacher asked parents to attend a math class. I went up to school along with other parents to see what they were learning. When the teacher asked who wanted to work a math problem on the blackboard several of the students volunteered. Gene just sat there and had his math book open, but when I checked closer I saw that he was reading something else tucked into the book. That evening I asked why he did not pay more attention. He said, "We had those problems last week, and I made 100 on it." I guess he did not feel he had to show off to his Mother.

Gene was a cub scout. Gracie was his Den Mother for several years. He was very conscientious about working for all of his merits.

When Gene graduated from the eighth grade some of his fellow students told me Gene was the smartest student in the class. They did not give any awards for this in the eighth grade. Gene would never brag on himself. So he never said anything about this to us.

Gene served as a Mass Server (altar boy) at Sacred Heart Church. He was always on time for serving. By living in town and only two blocks from church he served 6 a.m. Mass many times. He had to set his alarm and get himself up and ride his bicycle the two blocks to church. The only time I would take him to serve was if it was raining. He also served if a guest priest was in town and said Mass. The last time he served was Christmas Eve Mass the year he graduated from high school.

When Gene was in Sacred Heart High School there were no computers. He and I solicited donations from Sacred Heart Parents until we had enough money to purchase computers. Gene would teach his fellow students about the computer after school and in the evenings. We had a dead beat of a principal at that time, and he did not know how much Gene knew about computers, and he was afraid that Gene would get into some of his programs. The Principal would not let Gene stay at school to teach these students about computers—so one of the Nuns would open the school after the principal would go home and let Gene and these students in to learn the computer. Gene was a very trustworthy child.

When he was in high school Gene did not play football. He always said that he could run fast, and he was pretty sure they would have him receiving the ball. He said you know what they do to the receiver, so he did not want to play football. The other boys were mad because he would not play and told him that he could not play basketball if he did not play football. He came home upset and asked us if this was true. So I took Gene up to school and talked to the basketball coach and said what the other boys were saying. The coach said Gene had the build for a good basketball player and he wanted him to play and said he did not have to play football.

In Gene's freshman year his first basketball coach was not very good with the boys. The next year Coach John LaBressuer came to Sacred Heart. He worked wonders with those players. Gene did not look like the same player—the new coach had worked wonders with him.

As a basketball player, Gene got 90 consecutive tip-offs to his team. As he grew older he liked to take his BB gun and shoot birds out of the trees in our backyard. We had a peach tree in our backyard—the only one of Anna Fleitman's orchard trees left—that Gene liked to play in. He was always crawling in trees. Later we had a larger tree on the side of our covered patio that he always crawled in. When we added on to the house we cut down this tree to make room, and he was very disappointed that this tree was gone.

Gene was a night owl. He liked to stay up late and then never could wake up in the morning. Sometimes when he was supposed to be asleep he would be in bedroom reading with the light of a flashlight.

He liked to push buttons and twist switches. He would go with me to the telephone office and play while I worked. He fell off of the ladder one time and almost knocked himself out—he said he saw stars. Another time he turned off the charger to the office batteries, and the next day our whole office went dead.

Gene was very shy and quiet. When he was 10 he said he did not need the sitter and that he could make lunch. Gracie would have a dish ready to go into the oven when she left for work. He would turn on the oven and have the meal cooked when we got home at noon for lunch. He kept the house clean and never messed it up. He soon was mowing grass and trimming around the house. I kept a garden, and he always liked to work with me in the garden.

More memories of Gene

Gene was always snoopy. When we went to Bill and Kay's he would always crawl under Kay's sofa and look around. We could only see his feet sticking out.

After school when Gene would come to the office, Chris Moster started coming also to play. Chris always got them in trouble. So Gene would hide when Chris came and then come out after Chris left.

Gene was always thinking and doing different things and getting into trouble. He had a cord one day, and he tied the lamp to the chair. Well, I walked by and did not see the string and knocked over the lamp. The lamp broke, and guess who paid for the lamp.

When Gene was six he heard us talking about Irish Cathey's wedding. Gene sat at the table eating, saying. "I'm not going to do it, I'm not going to do it." I finally asked him what he wasn't going to do. He said he was not going to be ring bearer for Irish. I relieved his anxiety and told him that she did not ask him.

Gene loved photography. He had his own dark room. Gene studied astronomy for many years on his own.

When the boys were little I tried to save money and give them haircuts. After the last one I gave Gene he cried for three days.

Gene never came to the table without combing his hair.

One Halloween Kent had a friend over for pizza and later handed out candy for the trick or treaters. Kent and his friend finally got tired of this, so they decided to hide behind the bushes and scare the kids when they came to the door. Gene came rushing in the back door into his room and came out all dress up in a Halloween costume. He went out the back door and around the house and walked up to the front door when Kent and his friend jumped out at him. It did not scare Gene, but the boys were mad when they found out it was Gene.

The boys always had various little jobs at home to earn an allowance. Gene was always an "A" student. When he started basketball with all of the practicing he came to me and said he could not do his chores, maintain his A average and play basketball also. I made an agreement with him: if he stayed in basketball I would do his little jobs for him. This worked fine.

Gracie and I were planning to go to Hawaii, and Gene came home from school and was upset. He said at the Friday night game the players were going to give their Mothers a rose at the game, and we were not going to be there. We went to Hawaii and cut our trip short and were back Friday night to receive the rose.

Gene had a printed place card. Every year he would set out this name card for Christmas so Santa would know where to put his presents.

We did not have room for a garden. Our neighbor Annie Flietman had some garden space she was not using and said we could use it. Gene wanted to plant a garden. He and I planted potatoes, and as they grew they got potato bugs on the plants. Gene had to go out and pick them off. One day he said he felt like the Orkin man.

When Gene started full time work at the office of Ken McDoughle, he and Gene started to pull pranks on each other. One day Gene crawled under Ken's desk and locked all of his drawers.

When Gene was working in the outside plant he thought they would not tell him what to do because he was the boss' son. Gene came to me and asked me to have the plant manager put him to work.

Gene never ran around shirtless.

One day when he was running track he tripped and fell and skinned himself. At the supper table that evening he told us about his falling. Kent teased him about being clumsy. Gene said, "I can't help if I don't know where my feet are going." His coordination was a little off because he was so tall.

Gene taught himself to play both the piano and the organ.

When Gene went to church with me I would look at him, and he would be as white as a sheet. He would kneel so still that he felt faint and I had to take him out in the fresh air.

I always told him his handwriting was awful. He said, "I can't help if my mind goes faster than my hand."

One cold night when we came home there was a small white kitten in our yard. Gene took it in and fed it. It was coughing. Gene wanted to take it to the vet. I told him I was not paying a vet bill for someone else's kitty. He took it to the vet the next day and paid the bill. He brought the kitty back to the house, and it went home.

One time when we had a litter of kittens I went to town. When I came home Gene came running out and said raise the hood. There were his kitties.

We had a large tree in the back yard near the back door. When Gracie came home in the evenings she would hear, "Hi, mom." He would be high up in the tree—said he could see so much up there.

When Kent and Gene were small, Gracie would lay out their clothes to wear. If Kent did not dress quickly enough Gene would hide his clothes. He always wanted everything to be neat.

When Gene purchased his new home in Denton he needed drapes. When pricing them Gene felt he could not afford them. Gracie told him if he wanted her to make them for him she would. He said yes and picked out the material.

Our old vault had an air hole at the bottom. When Gene was little and came to the office he would always run his car back and forth through this hole.

Gene's friends

Gene always had friends. In his earlier years it was Bob Hamric. They were constantly together. At lunch time on Saturdays they would go around to the home of Bob's Grandmother, Bertha Hamric, to our place and to Dan Hamric's house, checking at each to see what we were going to have to eat—then they would stay and eat at the place with the menu they liked the best.

I built them an 8-foot x 10-foot clubhouse where Gracie held their Cub Scout meetings. I fixed it so that they could have four bunk beds, two on each side. These would fold up out of the way in the daytime. Rain or shine, they had a place to hold their secret meetings. The walls still have some of their secret words on them.

Today this is our garden tools center and where the cat gets fed. I have fixed the door so that it opens very easily and closes on its own. Our cat that we call "Kitty" has learned how to pull the door open with his claws to get in and to press on the door to get it out. In the process of going in and out the cat's tail got caught in the door one time and skinned the hide off his tail. Dr. Tisdale, the local vet, had to cut about 6 inches off her tail. After that I fixed the door to leave a gap even when closed so that the cat's tail will not get caught in the door.

On another occasion Gene and his friends had purchased French fries, laid them in the hole they had dug in our backyard and left to get some drinks in the house. Well, our dog found the fries and ate them. When the boys came back they found the fries were gone.

Even after graduating from college, Gene and Troy Wolf continued to be good friends. They shared apartments first in Gainesville, then in Sanger and then a home owned by Troy. Later he purchased a new home in Denton. Throughout his college years a group of his friends would gather by our place after Mid-Night Mass every year, including his future bride, Kaylynn, bringing a bottle of wine. To this day, more than three decades later, some of his friends still gather at our place after the late Mass with a bottle of wine.

Gene the teen

I mentioned earlier about Gene worrying that he didn't know how to learn. He overcame that fear over time, and he learned well—better than many of his classmates. He would ride with me to school in the morning when I went to work. We would study German on the way. I would give a new word until he knew what it meant, then we would go on to a new word. He learned fast and soon had a vocabulary of German sayings and words.

He always wanted to work for what he got. When he got older he mowed the grass around the office and cleaned the toilets.

As he got older he would go during the summer with the guys working on telephones. We had him working with another person replacing protectors on the outside of the homes. He came to me and said that he could do that quicker by himself than working with another person.

He graduated in the class of 1981 from Sacred Heart High School with honors as Salutatorian of his class. Susie Felderholf beat him out as Valedictorian.

As Gene neared the end of high school, he had many offers from various colleges and had a hard time deciding which college to attend. Also he was worried about the widespread use of drugs in the schools. He finally decided to go to the University of North Texas in Denton.

College days

After graduating from high school, Gene worked for the company before starting college in the fall. We were in the process of changing out the hard wired telephones to modular phones—phones you could plug in. We had assigned one of our regular repairmen to work with Gene. Gene came to me and said that he did not need a second person with him for he could do it faster by himself then working with another person.

Our boat was getting very little use after Gene started college. I had told him I would keep the boat, but he would have to pay the expense of maintaining and operating it. I stored it in our double garage attached to my shop. Gene took it out once or twice and said he did not realize how expensive a boat was to operate. Besides keeping it in gas, he had the insurance and permits—after a short time he told me I could go ahead and sell it.

Gene was interested in computer technology and that factored into his decision to go to North Texas, but he was worried about what kind of a roommate he would have to put up with. He had heard there were so many drugs in the dormitories. On the day he moved in he met his roommate, who was from Houston, and did not know how to take him. As they adjusted to each other they gradually became good friends—a friendship that remained through his later years. Brian Bearden was Best Man at Gene's wedding and, later, sponsor of his child.

Gene joins Nortex

His favorite teacher kept telling Gene not to work for his parents so Gene just could not make up his mind to go back into the family telephone business or to go to work for some other company. He had received several good offers, so he had trouble deciding what to do. We needed a computer specialist, and he was well suited for that position. To help him make up his mind I posted a help needed notice in the college where he would see it.

His friends came to him and asked if he was going to take the job, for they would if he was not interested. He immediately called me and said he would like to apply for the job if it was still open. Of course, we would not fill the position if there was a chance he would work for us.

He said would come to work for us, but he wanted to be interviewed just like any other person. They had studied in his class how he should go to an interview. So we set a time when I would pick him up and interview him for the position. At the agreed time I drove up outside of his dormitory and he came out for the interview. He looked like a young man on his wedding day. He had on his best suit, white shirt and tie. His shoes shone brightly. We went over to Chili's by the Golden Triangle Maul for the interview. The waitress noted how dressed up Gene was and wanted what the occasion was, and I told her I was going to interview him for a job in our company. She said that she had to do the same in the near future.

Needless to say, Gene got the job.

Gene started working with the company in January of 1987 at the same age that I was when I started with the company in 1949. His first office was next to Donna Endres. His first job was to update our computer system. Later we added on the telephone office, and Gene got his own private office. Gracie got all new office furniture for his office. Gene was well on his way to become the manager of Nortex.

He worked to upgrade our computer system and spent most of his time in the computer room. He came to visit us at Christmas Eve that fall and announced that he had proposed to Kaylynn Patterson and she accepted. He then called Kaylynn's Parents for their approval.

Gene gets married

Gene and Kaylynn got married in 2000 and settled down in their new home. Gene continued to work for our Communications Company and would work late and drive back to Denton after a day's work in Muenster.

On Oct. 20, 2003, Gracie and I celebrated our 50th wedding anniversary in Sacred Heart Community Center with a dinner and dance for about 150 of our friends. Gene was MC for the program, and he announced that Kaylynn was pregnant and they would have a child next year. A couple weeks later we took Gene and Kaylynn on a cruise to the Panama Canal. Kaylynn was very pregnant on this cruise.

We had a two-way radio on the ship so we could stay in contact with of each other on the cruise. One morning we were waiting for Gene and Kaylynn on deck for breakfast. When they did not show up I called him on the two-way and asked him if he was up and ready for breakfast. His response was, "We are now."

Everyone sitting in the area could hear him and all got a laugh out of his response.

Gene wanted to earn everything he received. While in high school he started with the company mowing the grass and cleaning the toilets. He continued up through the company until he was Chief Operating Officer. He was instrumental in acquiring 10 MHz of valuable spectrum, which a few years later became the backbone of our wireless internet system. The company had a bright future under his leadership.

Until it didn't.

Gene is killed

On Nov. 25, 2003, Gracie was watching the 6 p.m. Dallas news, and I was not feeling good, so I went to bed early. It wasn't long before a local police officer came to the door and said he wanted to talk to both of us together. Not long before, all of the trees in our front yard had been poisoned, and we thought he was coming by to give us an update on the trees. He waited until I got dressed and came into the room where Gracie and the local police were waiting. Gracie had seen a story on the news about a wreck and had commented to herself, "I hope it is not anyone we know."

The officer told us that Gene had been killed in a multiple car accident at Sanger, Texas. A pickup truck was traveling at a high rate of speed. The driver, drunk and arguing with his wife on his cell phone, lost control of his vehicle, went through the bar ditch, hit the bank on the west side of the highway, went airborne and sheared off the top of Gene's car above the engine, killing him instantly. The drunk driver then continued on and hit an 18-wheel truck traveling on the side of Gene's and ended up dead on the side of I-35. The impact knocked the driver of the truck out with the truck continuing on south, then crossing into the north-bound traffic of I-35, knocking over an electric pole and ending up with the cab of the truck halfway in a room on the south side of the motel.

After experiencing the initial shock of the news, I began to wonder who would operate the telephone company. Gene had already taken over most of the operation of the company and had made a name for him in the telephone industry nationwide.

That showed at the services following his death. From Ron and Julie Strecker of Oklahoma Panhandle Telephone Co-op to John Greenberg of Brazoria Telephone Co. South Texas to Jeff Haynes of Alpine Telephone Co. of Alpine, Texas—managers and salespeople from every one of the 35 telephone companies in Texas were there for the standing room only wake service and the funeral the next day.

The funeral Mass was at the Immaculate Conception Church in Denton before it moved to its present location—the same church where he married Kaylynn Patterson, three years earlier. Fifty employees serving as honor guards formed a double line as he was brought into church and again when he was taken out of church. Monsignor King said the funeral Mass, the same priest that married him and Kaylynn. Monsignor King was good friend, for Gene was on the transitional team moving Immaculate Church to its new location. Monsignor King also presided at the internment in Muenster Sacred Heart cemetery.

Flowers filled the room from all over the United States and as far away as Attendorn, Germany. 'Gene Fuhrman Trust' was established in Sacred Heart School in Gene's honor—Gene was instrumental in bringing computers to Sacred Heart School while he was in school years earlier.

The streets in Muenster along Main Street had been blocked off for the 2003 Muenster Christmas parade, which was taking place at the same time as Gene's interment in Sacred Heart Cemetery. He was 39 years old. He had wanted to have a family by the time he was 40, but he didn't get the chance to see his son grow up.

In the reorganization of the company, I said I would not operate the company but would remain President and Chief Executive Officer (CEO) and stay active more in an advisory capacity. Gracie would remain in charge of the office and would prepare an eventual replacement. Joey Anderson volunteered to be Chief Operations Officer (COO) and was approved by the Board. Alan Rohmer remained Chief Financial Officer (CFO). There was no change in the Board, for Joey and Alan were already Board members.

Reorganization of the company left one problem. Gracie and I were getting old, and the death of Gene left the company with no one in the family to continue the company. Selling the company would be a blow to the town and to our employees. Gene's older brother, Kent is not capable and a grandchild, Conner, was too young. Gracie and I have worked 60 years to get it where it is today, and we did not want the company dismantled before our eyes. The solution seemed to be to form an ESOP whereby the employees would eventfully own stock in the company. This required us to sell stock in the company to the ESOP at a 20-percent minority discount.

As we fade out of the picture it is our hope that the company will continue to grow and prosper. We want to see the company stay in this community, continue to give employment to young people, stay on the leading edge of new technology, and give the employee's security, for they helped to make the company what it is today. We ask that as we get older they will help us so that we can stay in our home longer and help to get to doctors as needed.

At my 90th "come and go" birthday party all of Gene's friends showed up for the occasion. When they left the party they asked, "would you tell us, one more time, COME BACK WHEN YOU CANNOT STAY SO LONG!"?

CHAPTER 19

Ellen Grace Friske Fuhrman Tells Her Story

Martin Friske, my Dad, was born Dec. 19, 1901. He had two sisters, Betty (Mrs. Joe Luke, Martha's brother), so we were double cousins to their two kids, Norman and Alma Marie. The other sister was Emma, who lived in Hereford, Texas.

Dad had a brother Arnold who was 15 years younger than he was. I think Arnold was "an accident," as they say.

Martha Luke Friske, my Mom, was born Aug. 15, 1901. Mom had many brothers and sisters. I did not know all of them. I knew of Ben, Henry, Alphonse, Joe, Carl, Theresa, and Lydia.

Mom was a few months older than Dad and he mentioned it many times.

Our story was written in the days during which most Americans were struggling—the Great Depression. The effects were still affecting everyone's life. My Dad and Joe Luke, Mom's brother, ran the Muenster Mill for several years. Dad said that Joe stole from the cash register, and they went under financially. They sold the Mill to Joe Felderhoff, and then Mom and Dad moved to Hereford and farmed.

After seven years of crop failure because of no rain, Dad, Mom, Myrtle and Toni Mae, my two sisters born in Hereford, moved back to Muenster. When my parents left Hereford they were broke. They took all of their bills along with them and 12 years later returned to Hereford for a visit. They paid off all of these bills, but one business to which they owed a debt no longer existed, so they gave the money to the church.

Grandma Friske (Dad's Mom) was a petite lady and very prompt and proper. Our children never received a Christmas gift from them, but Arnold's children did.

August Friske, Dad's father, (my grandfather) was retiring, and Dad took over the farm. It consisted of about 300 acres of land three miles west of Muenster.

Highway 82 did not exist when I was born in 1933. As was usual at that time I was born at home. Joan and Jere came along later. Mom and Dad would play ball with us kids in the yard as we were growing up.

When highway 82 was built in 1936, the one farm now became two farms because the highway went through the middle of it. There was one farm south of the highway and one farm north of the highway. Dad farmed the farm north of the highway. Arnold Friske and Delores lived on the south farm the first few years they were married, then they moved to Gainesville.

On the north farm there was an old two-story house and some out buildings. I remember sitting on a long bench at the dinner table. I also remember climbing up the stairs to the second story. I was about 5 or 6 years old. They tore down this house and built a one-story home with only two bedrooms when the family really needed three bedrooms. I do not recall where we all slept (Dad and Mom, four girls and one boy). While they were building the new house we all lived in the garage.

I was about 6 years old that summer, and while Mom helped in the fields, I took care of Jere. We had an outdoor toilet. We did not have electricity on this farm. We had a wind charger to keep a battery charged to listen to the radio. We had kerosene lamps to use for lights, often used to do our homework around the kitchen table. We didn't have a refrigerator. On Sunday mornings after church Dad would buy a block of ice to put in our icebox—we had a cool icebox until the ice melted.

On this farm we had a chicken house that had a slanted roof to the cow lot where the cows always stayed. We kids would get on the roof of this chicken house and jump in the cow lot, which was soft. I guess we really smelled good with all of that cow manure all over us.

This farm had timber and a creek north of the home. We kids played in it, especially after a rain, often climbing around in the trees. The creek had a water gap between us and the neighbors' property line, and every time it rained the water would wash it out and we would have to put it back to keep our cattle from getting out.

A county road also ran between Grandpa's two farms. We would herd our cows down this road to graze. On the east side of the north farm

Dangelmayr owned the land, which featured a nice grove of trees close to the road. While the cows were grazing we would go and climb in these trees.

Coming from a family of girls I soon grew up to be my father's helper on the farm. I drove the tractor and plowed, harrowed, chopped cotton and corn—and picked cotton and corn. I helped dad combine shocked grain (sometime there were snakes under the shocks). I helped put loose hay up in the barn. Daddy never baled the hay· he hauled it in loose, and I had to help stack it in the barn. He had no hay handling equipment, and it all had to be stacked by hand with a pitchfork.

Dad kept gas in 55-gallon barrels that he used for his tractor. Someone would always steal our gas. We raised chickens and often, when they reached fryer size, someone would steal them. One morning Mom found a man's handkerchief in the chicken house. She assumed that someone had put chloroform on the handkerchief to quiet the chickens, so they then could take them. Mom put an ad in the Muenster Newspaper asking whoever owned the handkerchief to reclaim it at our home. No one claimed it.

One night, before we had yard lights, Mom went outside and thought she saw someone at the barn. Mom was handy with a gun, so she went into the house got her 410 shotgun and loaded it and shot whatever that was at the barn. It went plop to the ground. It scared her to death, for she realized she may have killed someone. She did not sleep much that night.

The next morning she went out to look at what she had done and found a very dead owl, shot between the eyes. A certain neighbor eventually moved, so we finally got to keep our fryers to eat.

This farm we lived on contained the most edge rocks in the country. We always told August Friske (Martins dad) that he bought the rockiest land available.

Myrtle and I were the workers, and Toni and Joan were the lazy ones. Toni always claimed to have a backache to get out of work.

When I was 12 we moved to the farm south of the highway. Dad began farming both farms.

We finally got electricity on the south farm, and did we think we were in heaven. We had a refrigerator and electric lights with an electric radio. We did not have a water heater. We still had an outhouse.

We milked cows, and one Sunday Mom and Dad were gone somewhere, and Toni's boyfriend, Ray Lueb, came to see her. He was being nice to her and said he would help us kids milk. We had one cow that was really hard to milk and we gave that cow to him. We just stood back and watched him and laughed.

Myrtle, my oldest sister, dated several different men—Mom and Dad never approved of her dates. Mom went so far as to buy a birthday card and send it to a boy she liked with Myrtle's name to it. Myrtle wised up to this.

Myrtle went away to nurse's school in Galveston. She came back and worked at M & S Hospital.

During WW II she met her first husband. He was stationed at Camp Howze and came to visit her, staying at at our home overnight. The next day Dad and Mom took them to the priest's house and had them get married. In those days you did not stay at your girlfriend's house. I did not like this guy. He always used "Jesus Christ" as slang words. I guess I was 12 or 13 at the time, and I did not like him doing that. So I asked him why he always said this. I never heard it again.

I always blamed Mom and Dad for this mess. They had someone local picked out for her. That would have been a disaster, also. They always tried to pick out our future husbands. They did not like Alvin, either. I don't remember much about Myrtle at home; she was nine years older than I and left home at 18.

Myrtle and Toni went to grade school at Sacred Heart. Muenster did not have a high school at that time. Myrtle went to high school at Saint Mary's in Gainesville. She rode on the motorcycle behind Bill Luke to school. Toni went to high school in Wichita Falls.

I went to Sacred Heart School High School during the time they were attempting to consolidate Sacred Heart with the Muenster Public School. Sacred Heart School's football mascot and colors were taken over by the public school. Even the water heater out of the locker room was taken. This is the time that the Tigers were born. This split my class, with about half going over to the public school. Thirty students started in first grade, and 12 graduated with me from Sacred Heart School. I stayed with Sacred Heart School, even though the tuition went up.

I liked sports. I played volleyball and basketball in school. During the summers I was on a baseball team that played teams from the Gainesville Training School and Southwestern Bell Telephone operators. When there was practice during the summer I walked three miles into town for practice and then three miles home after the practice. You can just see a kid do this nowadays. I played hind catcher when playing softball. I played basketball when the girls played half court. I played guard and never had to shoot the ball. We played the training school girls, and they were mean.

My Dad would take me to town in the evening if I needed to be somewhere. He would go over to Grandma and Grandpa Friskes home until I was finished. Sometimes I would join in the domino game. Grandpa always wanted me to be his partner.

It was during my junior year in high school that I met my future husband. I credit chickens for that good fortune. My mother always had more eggs than we could eat, so we sold the surplus to the Farmers Marketing Association in town. While my Dad delivered our milk to the association cheese plant, I took the eggs to John Herr, who was buying eggs for the association. At the same time Alvin was selling his mother's surplus eggs at the store. We exchanged greetings, which sparked an interest in both of us. He did not know who I was but saw me get in the pickup truck with my Dad, and he knew him. He learned my name by the time there was a dance in the K C Hall in Muenster. Those years the boys and girls came single to these dances. Dad took me to the dance and went to Grandma Friske's house and played dominos.

Alvin was at the dance, and we danced all evening, and he asked me for a date the following weekend. I was 15 years old. He did not take me home that night, for Dad was waiting on me at Grandma's. They lived one block from the KC Hall. When Alvin took me home after our first date, he kissed me at the door, and I knew who I would like to marry someday.

We were together from about May 1949 to December 1950. We double- and triple-dated with Alvin's friends, Ruben Sturm and Bill Miller.

Alvin was working for the local telephone company and had just bought a new car, and in December 1950 he was drafted into the army. He was stationed at Fort Hood, Texas, the first six months and came home every weekend. We spent Saturdays and Sunday mornings together before he would have to leave again.

In July 1951 he was transferred to Germany, and he left his car, and his brother Bill and I took him to Dallas to catch a train to Fort Hood. I kissed him goodbye and would not see him again for two years. It was toward the end of my senior year in school when he left. My senior prom took place after he left so I asked his younger brother, Jerry, to be my escort.

In the meantime I graduated from S.H. High and had a job at the S.H. Kress five and dime store in Gainesville. To be closer to my work I stayed with Grandma Friske, who lived on North Weaver Street in Gainesville. I sold notions at Kress Co., and theft was prevalent. To discourage theft I kept all cases full. When I sold an item, I would replace the item from stock to keep the counter full.

A local boy came around to visit, and my Grandmother wanted me to go with him, but I was not interested.

The manager of the Sears store in Gainesville needed another clerk, and the manager, Katherine Nelson, had been watching how I worked to detect theft and how I keep my area neat. She asked me to go to work for Sears. So I changed jobs and went to work for the Sears store on East California Street.

Alvin and I exchanged letters regularly, and my mail from him went to my parents north of Lindsay. My mother would open my mail, read the letters, and seal them again before giving them to me. After a while, my mother claimed that Alvin was not writing anymore and that there was no mail. I knew better and arranged for the Gainesville post office to hold my mail, and I picked it up at the Post office.

While Alvin was gone Mom and Dad tried their best to get me married to a Lindsay boy before Alvin got back. I did not want to do anything until Alvin was back and I had a chance to see what kind a person he would be after two years in service.

Alvin came back home on Dec. 10, 1952, and the first thing he did was come to the Sears store and gave me a big kiss.

After Alvin was back, my parents would not let him pick me up for a date. At the time we were double-dating with James Bayer and his date. So James would pick me up and we would go with him and his date for the evening, then he would take me back home again. Mom and Dad caught wind of this, and I decided I would have to move to Gainesville if I wanted to be with Alvin.

Alvin proposed to me in the car in the front of Marie Gerray's house, and I readily accepted. He did not ask for approval from my parents because, obviously, they did not approve.

We were married at 9 a.m. on Oct. 20, 1953, in St Peter's Church in Lindsay. We were not sure Dad would give me away.

We planned to walk up the aisle together if he did not show. He was there to take me up the aisle and give me away. When Alvin came out of the sacristy to meet us he hit his head on vigil light and he said he did not notice it hurting until the middle of the afternoon. We had our reception in the basement of the old parish hall in Muenster and our dance in the VFW hall.

When we decided to leave the dance for our honeymoon Gordon and Katherine Nelson were to take us to Gainesville where our car was hidden in their garage, to pick up our car and luggage. In those days it was traditional to do something to the car to make it difficult for the honeymoon couple to leave. When we wanted to leave we could not find Gordon and Katherine. Robert Bayer stepped in and took us to the Joe Mages farm, and we waited in their home. All the members of the Mages family were upstairs asleep, and I don't think they ever knew we were there. Robert went back to the dance and brought Gordon and Katherine out to the Mages farm to pick us up and take us to Gainesville. We then left for our honeymoon.

At that time Alvin was still working at the telephone company, and I was working at Sears Roebuck in Gainesville. Later I quit Sears and went to work for Tractor Sales as a bookkeeper in Muenster. From there I worked for Muenster State Bank as a teller.

Before we were married Alvin purchased some lots at 624 N. Cedar St. from Annie Fleitman. This land had 50 peach trees on it. Our home was finished, and about two weeks after we were married we moved in. Over the years we have remodeled three times, and now we have a very nice home with many conveniences.

We did not have much luck starting a family. Over the first few years we lost three pregnancies. Then we adopted a small baby and named him Kent. We had no problem with him until he started school. As he got older he became more difficult. He graduated from Sacred Heart High without a diploma. Alvin got him several jobs, but he worked long enough to get a paycheck and then he was gone. Finally, he left and we did not know for years where he was.

Then three years later I became pregnant again and we named our new son Gene. This time the baby lived, although he weighed only 4 pounds and 4 ounces, as he was born two months premature. He came to be the joy in our life. Alvin s wedding ring fit on Gene's little arm. Because he was premature he came up with a number childhood diseases as he grew older.

He enjoyed fishing and Alvin and Gene spent many times together fishing. First it was on local ponds and eventually by boat on Lake Texoma. I joined them, starting by camping out, then with a travel trailer, finally to owning a cabin on Lake Texoma. Gene grew up with many friends and we enjoyed teaching them how to water ski and feeding them Bar-B-Que chicken when they were old enough to go out on their own. Alvin always told them to "come back when you can't stay so long.' They loved it.

Gene joined Alvin at the phone company after graduating from North Texas State University. He had a home in Denton, Texas, and got married in the year 2000—and we welcomed a daughter into our family.

In 2003, at age 39 Gene was killed by a drunk driver. Gene's wife was four months pregnant. Today we have a handsome, 6-feet-tall grandson named Conner, and he is a joy to us.

Mom and Dad never accepted Alvin or our children. When Kent was about 5 years old, he and I were shopping in Gainesville and ran into Dad on the street. He had a few words for me and never spoke to Kent. After we parted Kent asked, "Who was that?" I told him it was his grandfather. At Christmas our children barely receive anything from their grandparents, while Joan's kids always received nice things. We would go over to the Friskes at Christmas in the afternoon, and the boys never wanted to go. We always laughed, because when we showed up Joan, Barney and the kids left. When Mom and Dad celebrated their 50th anniversary we got an invitation but were not included in any part of the formal program, and neither were our children.

About the same thing happened up in Oklahoma City when Toni and Ray celebrated their 50th. I was a bridesmaid for them. On their 50th they had Paul Nieball, the best man, come up on the altar and be introduced, but they did not ask me to come up.

Also at the reception they had Paul at the main table, but Alvin and I were just among the other guests, so we received no recognition whatsoever. Alvin was very upset over this. We never went to visit again.

I left the bank and started as a telephone operator in 1955. My pay was $1.25 an hour, and, after we purchased the Muenster Telephone Co., I became an operator. Later, when we bought the company, I became bookkeeper. As

I write this it is 2018, and my title is "Director of Administration" and the name of the company is now "Nortex."

Alvin and I both have been very active in the telephone industry. We both have received the highest award given by the Texas Telephone Association, the Neville Haynes Award.

When the present office was built I was instrumental in doing the planning, as I was with another three additions.

Some of my accomplishments in the telephone industry were:

- I served 34 years on the Independent Telephone Pioneer Association.
- I completed courses in management with the Texas Telephone Association and a supervisory training course at North Central Texas College.
- I served on the OPASTCO site selection committee from 1997 to 2005 and also was instrumental in having the Company Handbook published.
- I modeled at a Texas Telephone Association Convention style show. Outside the business arena I was secretary of the Muenster Garden Club, Grand Regent of the Catholic Daughters, the first lady president of the Sacred Heart School Board and cub scout Den Mother for many years.

My parents always said I should not marry Alvin because I would never get to travel because he had been all over. They also claimed he would never be a successful businessman. I have thanked the Lord many times that I did not listen to them. Alvin has been a very successful businessman, and we have traveled many times. Some of the places we have been to are Germany, Canada and Hawaii a number of times. We played golf in Scotland. We've been to Switzerland, Russia, Puerto Rico, Mexico and Cuba and most of the states in the U.S., some several times. We have taken four cruises on Viking River cruises.

Alvin has quite an imagination. We have more gadgets. Our backyard is low in places; he installed an underground drainage system to the garden, so the garden is watered from rain in the yard and the run-off of the sprinkling system.

When we were going on trips he wired the outside of the home to be able to watch our home while we were gone. He installed an emergency generator, so we would have electricity when the power is off. We have a very elaborate lighting control system in the home. We have a two-story second garage and shop, and, so he didn't have to climb up the stairs, he installed a lift. It sure comes in handy when we have something heavy to take upstairs.

Today, in 2018, Alvin and I are enjoying the fruits of our labor through the years. We have had our disagreements, but it is always fun to make up. We still spend some time at the telephone office. I have enjoyed all 65 years of our marriage and our life work, telephone service.

SECTION II

HE TELEPHONE

(How North Texas Communications Came to Be)

Operators were the communication center of Muenster. All local calls had to be connected by them. You could leave word with the operator that you would be visiting next door, and the operator would transfer any calls you received next door. Children could ask for mommy. Boys calling for a date could ask the operator which girl had not been called. Or if you called a girl who already had been called, the operator would tell you, "You are too late."

CHAPTER 20

Foreword:
My Fascination with the Telephone

M y interest in the telephone was born before we worked for the company.

In 1942 the U.S. governments took our land north of Lindsay to build the air force training center. We moved to our mother's ancestral home in Lindsay until Dad could find another farm. Later my Dad was able to find the John Yosten farm two miles east of Muenster. We moved to this farm in 1943. I was 16, and the telephone intrigued me—I was curious about how it worked. Little did I realize that someday it would be my life's work! I had read how a telephone worked and was curious to make one that did work. I was very limited on the materials I needed to make a telephone, but I took a Y-shaped magnet that came from the flywheel of a Ford tractor that lay around the shop and wound some very fine copper-varnished insulated wire around each end. There had to be a couple hundred feet of wire wrapped on each pole. I used wax to hold the Copenhagen box and the metal lid at the right distance from the magnet. The metal lid had to be close to the magnet but not touch it.

I made two of these, one for each end. I ran a wire from the north window of my bedroom to the washhouse a couple hundred feet away. I drove a metal rod in the ground outside of the bedroom window and connected a wire to it and ran it in the house. At the washhouse I connected a wire to the water pipe from the water well to get a good ground. On each end I connected one end of the fine copper wire wrapped around the magnet to the wire to and from the wire to the house and the other to the ground wire.

I got Jerry to talk on the washhouse phone, while I talked on the phone in my bedroom, and I was heard in the washhouse. The same was true from the washhouse to my bedroom. This telephone system did not need batteries. The metal lid vibrating from our voice close to the wire wound magnet caused a pulsating current to flow between the phones.

The current pulsated at the same rate as the pitch of our voice, so an exact duplication of the voice was generated on the far end. You would talk into the telephone and then put the telephone to your ear to listen. You would have to move it back and forth to carry on a conversation.

The first phone that we built

The telephone line to our farm on the Yosten place was a disaster. It was always out of order. It was hung on the fence on a lot of places, and the poles were falling over. So Bill and I built a new phone line. We got some old poles from the telephone company and dug new holes and built a very good line from Highway 82 to our home. This was before we worked for the phone company. Long before Muenster Telephone Co. was organized many small neighborhood telephone systems flourished and faded away. "The Way It Was" would not be complete without learning a little about these early neighborhood lines.

CHAPTER 21

The First Telephones around Forestburg

I n the early 1900s every community around Forestburg had its own private telephone system. These systems consisted of one wire strung along fences and hung in trees from one farmhouse to another. There were no power lines to create noise on a one-wire telephone system. These systems were a group of neighbors on a party line. They called each other by cranking the phone. Each party on the line had a certain ring. There could be one short-ring party—a two short-ring party or a three-ring party. There could be a longring party or a short-and-a-long ring party. There could be a mixture of these codes to accommodate 10 or more parties on a single line. Many homes had two different party lines come to their home. In this case it would be possible to connect the two lines by way of a knife switch, and a party on one of these lines could call a party on the neighboring line.

There was the Stony Point line, the Dewey line, the Hardy line, the Dye Mound line and the Round Prairie line along with Forestburg. Early settlers that had phones in the Stoney Point area included Horace Littell, P.H. (Hud) Bailey, Ernest Fanning, Sam Cook, Nina Morgan, Willie Jackson and G.W. Barken.

Those receiving telephone service in the Dewey area included Tom Reynolds, John Boyd, Owen Foster, Jim McMillion, Tip and Lizzie Reynolds and John Huddleston.

One of the earliest records of organized telephone service in the Forestburg area was in the minutes of the Round Prairie Telephone Company, organized in 1906 east of Forestburg. First officers were: W.G. Meek-President; Charlie Dunbar-Treasurer; C.C. Perryman-Secretary. J.W. Bovlers, J.M. Buck and Charlie Dunbar were Trustees.

Others at the organizational meeting were W.F. Landers, J.W. Landers, Bob Bowers, R.A. Wiley, T.D. Wilson, A.U. Perryman, J.F. Wylie, and

Edward Meek. Others receiving telephone service were Charlie and Susan Grant, Ernest Kuykendall, Mack Knox, Columbus, Grant, Jim and John Perryman and Henry.

Regular meetings were held until about 1911. The Round Prairie Community was located at the junction of the roads at the Ben Perryman place east of Forestburg. The lines were maintained by those who received telephone service along the way. A charge of 10 to 20 cents was made if a connection was made with Central at Hardy or at Forestburg. Settlement was made at the end of the month.

Mr. Buck agreed to be Central at Hardy. Hardy also had connections with the Peoples Telephone Company in Saint Jo at the time. Connections were also made with the Circle Belt line at Dutch Landers in Forestburg. Later, Central was in a two-story house in Forestburg.

It is believed to have been operated by the Youngbloods and Lydia Poynor. This house still stands in Forestburg and is owned by the Bridwell family. There is no evidence that Central consisted of numerous party lines accessible to one another at one. It is assumed to be a switching point between two or more neighborhood lines by means of switchblades.

These were single-wire lines hung on trees and fence posts. Cranking out different rings a person could call anyone else on the line. Switching points in homes along the way sometimes were used to connect you to the next neighborhood line. Telephones could be purchased from Sears and Roebuck or Montgomery Ward.

As the early settlers broke the sod and planted cotton, the land started to erode. Soon deep ravines appeared, and the people were no longer able to raise cotton, so many moved away. As they left, the phone systems deteriorated. These phones were in operation until about the mid '30s. Also in the '40s rural electric power lines rendered single-wire telephone service that was still too noisy to use.

Forestburg was receiving telephone service by a rural line from Saint Jo when the Saint Jo Telephone Company was purchased by Earl Nunneley in 1942 from the Arch Holland Estate. Texas Pearl Holland, the mother of five boys including Judge Louis Holland, was operating the Saint Jo system. During World War II she sold the system to Earl Nunneley when her boys left for service and she had no one left to operate the telephone system.

CHAPTER 22

Early Telephones in the Rosston Area

T he first telephone in Rosston was created in the early 1900s. It was a switchboard type that hung on the wall in the Harper home. At this time, no one in this area had talked over the telephone, and Fern (Harper) Forteberry said, "when it rang we would all run to answer."

There was a switch in the W.M. Vess home at Rosston and also in the Jane Hall home at Leo. According to what we can learn, the operator of the switchboard would call these homes and would be switched over to another line for conversation.

Lunford and Lulu Pane were the next ones to operate the switchboard. Mr. Payne discarded the wall type and put in a desk type, so that the person operating the switchboard could sit in a chair. In the early days, they were not called telephone operators. Since the telephone system was centrally located, they were called "Central."

People in the vicinity did all of the upkeep on their own lines. The telephone in the home was wall type, with the batteries, and a crank. One twist by hand of the crank was a "Hello Central." The lines were party lines, and some of the rings would be two, three or four longs, and sometimes one or two shorts, thus the crank on the telephone would go around and round for a long and one half turn for a short. The rates were $1.00 per month.

George Stevens owned the telephone office next. Originally, he located it in a little Red house, later moving it to the hotel.

In 1922, S.P. Durham bought the system from George Stevens, and at its peak there were about 100 subscribers. At this time telephones were in good order. When Garland Harry became seriously ill, his wife put in a call to Dr. Walter Johnson, who had left Rosston and now had a practice in Ardmore, Oklahoma. This call cost $1.

In 1924, telephones began to diminish. By this time Hill Christian had the only telephone in the area. This phone, on a line from Hood, was a part of the Bell System in Gainesville. Mr. Christian had to keep up the line, and this was quite a problem, as it was not uncommon for a prankster or anyone whose vehicle had broken down on the road, to cut the line, and take out a length of the wire for their own use. In 1930 the phone was removed, and the community was without telephone service.

In 1956, Alvin Fuhrman, manager and co-owner of Muenster Telephone Corp. made a canvass through the community asking the people to sign up for telephones, if they wanted them.

Yes, me.

After 27 years of being without a telephone, Hill Christian's signature was first. It had been 35 years since anyone else in the community had had a phone. About 50 people quickly signed up, wanting a telephone. In 1957 the first connection was made in Rosston, between the George Berry store and the Muenster exchange. The call center was Bell telephone in Gainesville. This ended a period of isolation for Rosston.

In 1971 Muenster Telephone Corporation erected a brick building in Rosston to house the Rosston exchange. The telephone lines are now buried cable, with a direct dialing system, and the toll center is in Denton, with the General Telephone Co. Rosston has now joined the 21st century in its telephone connections, much to everyone's delight.

There are a few pangs of regret, however, at the loss of the friendliness of the old party line, and fond stories are still told of some of the funny things that happened with the old-time telephones. For example, in 1915, A.P. (Ace) White, brother of Mrs. Bill Gilliland, was "wooing" Miss Florence Norman. He pulled the old phonograph up close to the telephone, cranked it up and was playing Miss Florence a record on the phonograph and giving her sweet talk into the telephone. Soon he could be heard saying, "Hello Miss Florence—Hello Miss Florence, Miss Florence, Miss Florence." Realizing the young woman was no longer on the phone it dawned on him what had happened. His brother, Dee White and Jay Gilliland, had cut the telephone line just outside the house.

Burt Moseley attended school with the Boatenhammer children, who had not been around any type of telephone system. On their way to school they could hear the telephone line humming with the wind, and said they knew someone was talking because the line was singing.

However it's off with the old and on with the new. Now, instead of "Hello Central," we hear "D.D.D."

CHAPTER 23

The Beginning of Muenster
Telephone Company

The earliest information about telephone service in Muenster comes from Mary (Mrs. J. S.) Horn, who was Muenster's first telephone operator. She told of telephone service to Muenster from about 1900 to 1909 being a single magneto line from Gainesville in the Schenk Drug store. The telephone line was strung on the telegraphs poles long the railroad tracks.

At that time Dr. Crawford came to her and her husband and said that he was trying to start a local telephone company and provide some kind of local telephone service and asked about putting a telephone switchboard in her home. This was a magneto system, the only kind of telephone service known at the time. They agreed, and a few days later he came and installed a 20-line magneto switchboard on the wall in her living room with a wooden magneto wall phone as the operator's telephone.

Muenster Mutual Telephone Company

Dr. Crawford found the demand for telephone service greater than he expected, and the first switchboard was not convenient to use. It was decided a larger switchboard was needed. So the Muenster Mutual Telephone Company was organized, and John Herr was elected the president and Henry Henscheid was vice president. They set monthly charges at 30 cents a month per telephone, 20 cents going to the operator and 10 cents to the company.

One-position 100-line switchboard

This magneto switchboard sat in the front room of Mrs. Horn's house for over 30 years as she raised her family and attended to the switchboard day and night. It was the latest in communications, a 100-line magneto board.

Each telephone line was terminated on the switchboard in a jack that a plug could be inserted in to make a connection. Each jack had a coil and gate above the jack. When a subscriber cranked to get the operator, the gate would rattle and drop down to mark the line so the operator could distinguish which line was calling.

Twelve-cord sets allowed 12 conversations to take place at one time. Each cord set had two cords with plugs—back cord closest to the jack field and front cord closest to the operator. These cords were used to complete a call from the calling party to the called party. The operator would answer a call with the back cord, find out who they wanted to call and used the front cord to plug into the line to be called. There were two control keys on each cord set. The red-handled key was used for ringing and the black key gave the operator access to the cord set for talking. Each cord set had a coil and gate similar to each line. When a subscriber completed their call, they would give a short twist of the crank, causing the gate to rattle on the cord set and drop down. The operators knew the call was finished and removed the cords from the line and was prepared to answer the next call on the line.

This was in the age of no electricity, so the operator had to crank a generator to ring the called party. There was no battery provided from the telephone office, every telephone subscriber had two dry cell batteries in their phone, which had to be replaced every couple of years.

The operator's headset hung down in front of the operator, and if she turned while talking her voice would fade in and out. The one-wire telephone lines served the community well with no electric power lines to create noise.

Mrs. Horn continued until 1914, when, because of her ill health, the switchboard was moved to Miss Ann Markowitz's home in the east part of town. In 1917, the first telephone directory was published by Hugo Lehmann, editor and publisher. The book contained over 330 telephone listings with a section listing numbers in Myra. It states that president and manager of the telephone company was Frank Seyler, with Peter Walterscheid as repairman. It mentions that if there was a "pay station" on the system in town it would be perfect. The switchboard remained maintained by Miss Markowitz for 12 years until she resigned in 1926.

First billing system

When a call was made outside of Muenster (all calls to towns outside of Muenster were toll calls), the operator made a paper ticket of the call. She recorded the calling party's telephone number and the number they were calling. She had a mechanical timer on the switchboard. The operator many times would have to go through several operators in other towns to complete a call. When the called party answered, the timing of the call would start. She would have to listen to start the timing and monitor the call to be able to tell when the call was completed. The telephone line to Gainesville was attached to the telegraph poles along the railroad track.

Each cord set used to complete a call had a drop indicator. To keep from being charged for a call longer than you talked, a short crank would alert the operator and cause the indicator on the cord set to drop down notifying the operator that you were finished.

When a subscriber was through talking and "rang off" after a call, she would look at the timer to get the length of the call. She would record this on the paper ticket.

In the event of a second call at the same time she would have to remember what the time on the timer was when the second caller started talking and when they stop talking and record this also on a paper ticket.

So these tickets had the complete details of each call. As these calls were being completed they were filed by telephone number.

During the month a statement was prepared with the hand-copied name and address and the monthly recurring charges in preparation to complete the billing at the end of the month. During the month, each day these toll tickets were posted to the statement. You notice on the sample ticket pictured here that the charge was circled—Lizzy, (Elizabeth Herr), chief operator, did this when she copied the call to the statement indicating that ticket had been posted.

At the end of the month with a hand-operated adding machine she added up the toll calls along with the monthly recurring charges. The total toll charges would also be listed on the ledger for that month. A lot of this hand work could be accomplished during the month at slack times on the switchboard.

These statements were stuffed into a window envelope that was purchased with a three-cent stamp already embossed on the envelope.

Payments were posted to the ledger sheet as they were paid, and the billing cycle started all over again. Unpaid amounts were picked up off of the ledger. This billing system continued for about 42 years until it was replaced with newer technology.

The doodle lines in the grain of the wooden switchboard shows how time was spent during the slack times.

This all happened before my time and was related to me by Mrs. Mary (J. S.) Horn, the first operator who was still living when I started with the company.

Two-position switchboard

In 1945 the war was winding down, and there was an abundance of used telephone equipment on the market. This is when Jake Horn found a good buy on two 100-line telephone switchboards that came out of a military base somewhere.

There were two switchboards exactly the same, and Jake purchased both of them. They were not designed to do the job that Jake planned to do, but they would work. They were designed to work in a large office building and the phones in the same building with no long telephone lines.

The town of Muenster would work fine on the new board, but the rural lines were too long and in poor shape and would not work. He wired in magneto jacks along the bottom of the jacks fields on the new board. This arrangement allowed the operator to interconnect calls between different types of systems. So now Jake had the benefits of two systems—Common Battery in town and magneto lines for the rural. The long distant lines from Gainesville also terminated on magneto jacks with no supervision.

Jake mounted these two WWII switchboards side by side in the front bedroom converted to the telephone office of Mrs. Horn's house. These were low-profile boards, and they had to be fitted over a hole in the floor so that the cords would go below the floor level when fully retracted. The two boards doubled the number of lines available as the old magneto switchboard was a 100-line board and each of these new boards also was a 100-line board. The hole in the floor, even though it was boxed in, caused an updraft from under the house, and the operators constantly complained of having cold feet. Also bugs seemed to enjoy the ability to appear from under the house and peep out at the operator through one of the many holes—especially crickets. Needless to say, if there is a draft there also will be dust, and this liked to get into the equipment.

This switchboard had many features that were not on the magneto board. A subscriber simply picked up the phone to make a call. A distinct click would be heard and a light would come on over the line jack wanting the operator. The Common Battery phone had no battery in it. The power to operate the phone was furnished from the telephone office. This is why it is called a Common Battery system.

The new board had supervisory lights to guide the operator through a call without her having to listen in to see if the call was still in progress. Each cord set had two lights. With a call in progress, the lights remained distinguished. When one or both parties on the line hung up, the light for one or both cords would light up, telling the operator they were finished with the call, and the operator could take down the cords making the connection.

The board had one major flaw. It was not designed to work on long local loops. In the idle condition power to the lines was fed through an unbalanced line relay—this caused a loud roar on the line until the operator answered. Also, the switchboards had seen heavy use where they previously were used, and the jacks and cords were badly worn.

This switchboard was installed in 1945 and was used continually for about 15 years until 1960, when it was replaced with a larger three-position switchboard. The Common Battery telephone system was a major improvement in telephone service in the Muenster area.

The toll lines to Gainesville also terminated on magneto jacks along the bottom also.

Twelve large, 2-gallon glass jars provided the 24-volt battery needed to operate the new system. (One of the glass jars is featured in the Gene H.

Fuhrman Museum.) They were housed in a weatherproof cabinet along with the battery charger in a specially built shelter outside on the north side of Mrs. Horn's house. Each jar was filled with sulfuric acid and a set of lead plates to produce two volts of direct electrical current. The batteries hooked up together in series produced 24 volts of power. The battery charger kept the batteries charged.

The primary purpose of the batteries was to condition the electri cal current from the charger to eliminate hum noise. Also, the batteries kept phone service going when the power was off. The new switchboard also had a ringing current generator, so the operator would not have to crank a ringing current generator to complete a call.

The Main Frame that terminated the cables from around town was hung on the wall behind the switchboard in the corner. Most lines close to the telephone office were still one-wire lines. Open wire lines that served subscribers east of town along Highway 82 were terminated on the telephone pole in front of the office, and twisted-pair insulated wire was used to terminate the lines in the office.

Long distance lines were routed along the side of J.P. Flusche junkyard to the office from the railroad tracks. Eight physical #10 copper wires strung along the railroad tracks to Gainesville provided four physical long-distance lines. By the use of phantom coils, two additional circuits were obtained, giving a total of six toll lines to Gainesville. Train wrecks would always interrupt our long distance service. The Bell equipment was mounted on the wall above our Main Frame.

It was on this switchboard in 1955 that Gracie started working for the telephone company as an operator. The other operators were the Herr sisters—Elizabeth (Lizzy), Lena and Katie. Lena was the night operator, and Lizzy was the Chief Operator. On the wooden desk and the hand-operated adding machine that are now in the museum, Lizzy would also do the billing. She hand-copied the name and address and toll calls on an invoice, which was placed in a window envelope at the end of the month and mailed. The three-cent postage was on the envelope when they were purchased from the Muenster Enterprise.

A homemade phone booth was in the southwest corner of the room behind the door with the telephone number 48. The switchboard, billing desk, phone booth—all of this was in one south room of J.S. Horn's home.

Outside the window on the east side room was an emergency generator that was used during commercial power failures. During a failure, the operator could push a button to start the generator and a double pole; a double-throw, heavy-duty switch on the wall would transfer the electric power from commercial power to the emergency generator. This generator now rests in the corner next to the Two Position Common Battery Switchboard in the museum.

This switchboard was in service in the later part of 1952, when I returned from army service. Gracie lived on a party line, and every time I called her a number of people would be listening in. So I installed a key on each of the two positions of the board that the operator would use to call Gracie. Her phone would be the only phone ringing when I called.

For the technical person, when the special key was operated, it shorted the tip and ring of the line together to prevent any other metallic phone from ringing and her phone was then rung with a ground return.

For 34 years the switchboard was the lifeline of Muenster. In 1945 new technology caught up with communications in Muenster, and the magneto switchboard was relieved of its duties. Muenster converted to a Common Battery system, which was a new technology at the time. Rural Muenster still had its magneto telephones.

Herman Younger

The company had no money when my brother Bill and I started with the company in 1949. Ice storms were sweeping the area and at the same time north FM373 was being widened and paved. We had very few tools and material to work with. Several months after we started work, controlling interest was sold to Herman Younger of Fort Worth, Texas for $20,000. This gave us more capital to work with. One of his first acts was to purchase the new black Ford construction truck. Herman was the husband of Bess, Hugh (Cotton) Jackson's sister. Cotton Jackson was J.M. Weinzapfel son in law. Herman worked for Southwestern Bell in Fort Worth and J.M. Weinzapfel of the local bank felt that his telephone experience would be very beneficiary for the Muenster system. Herman's wife, Bess became the bookkeeper.

Herman would pick up all of the old telephone pole line equipment that was discarded by Southwestern Bell in Fort Worth and haul it to Muenster. The first neoprene drop wire we ever saw came from Fort Worth. It was in pieces and had to be spliced together to be used. We spliced drop wire together on rainy days.

At first, Herman was up every weekend bringing drop wire, cross arms, insulators, transposition brackets, old telephones and old cable. When the Trinity River flooded downtown Fort Worth, Herman hauled to Muenster a pickup load of old water-soaked dial telephones filled with mud.

Many times Herman brought technicians from Fort Worth with him to work here. The first key system that Muenster had was installed in Endres Motor Company by technicians Herman brought up from Fort Worth.

Herman had two boys around 10-12 years old, and they would come up with him at times.

At other times, technicians came along to repair old lead cable and install new cables. On one occasion a new 16-pair lead cable was completed from north Main Street about three miles north of Muenster along north FM373. We had the poles and strand ready for them to spin the cable to the support strand.

When Herman purchased the company the only truck the company had was the 1929 Plymouth touring car converted into a pickup truck. One of his first moves was to purchase a new ¾ ton Ford truck chassis. I will tell you more about this truck later.

Earlier I told you about building a 16-mile, open-wire line to Forestburg. In Forestburg we installed a 10-line Stromberg Carlson automatic Relaymatic switchboard. This gave us 10 lines in Forestburg with the one line back to Muenster local and long distance service. The Relaymatic was all relays and slow to ring after you dialed. That was my first experience with dial service, and I was really sold on it. This is where my tinkering around in Dad's tool shop when I was growing up at home paid off. With no previous experience I installed the SC dial board and made it work with the operator's switchboard in Muenster.

To get supervision to the Muenster operator for her to know when callers hung up I improvised a special relay in a glass jar to protect it from dust behind the Muenster two-position, manual switchboard that made supervision on the cord set work. The switchboard was installed in an old bank vault. We had to bring 120-volt power and the telephone cables down a small hole on the top of the concrete vault. It was always nice and cool in there—summer and winter. When I had to work on the board in the evening, Gracie would come along and watch me work and knit on a sweater.

Two-positioned switchboard with 200 lines

One-position 100-line switchboard

View looking from telephone office - 1950

CHAPTER 24

Communications Center of Muenster

Operators were the communication center of Muenster. All local calls had to be connected by them. With the advent of the common battery switchboard, supervisory lights on each connection made monitoring calls unnecessary and the task a bit easier.

General call: If a farmer had a cow missing he could call the operator and she would make a "general call." Ten short rings on a line signaled all to listen to the message.

Death bell: When someone in the Sacred Heart parish would die, a certain bell on the church would be tolled. Wanting to know who died, townspeople would pick up their phones at the same time, and the switchboard looked like a Christmas tree with all the signal lights. Telephone service would come to a virtual standstill when the "death bell" was tolled.

Fire alarms: A steam whistle at the Farmers Marketing Association cheese plant was the fire alarm for the town. The operator was responsible for blowing this steam whistle. Codes were used so that firemen could go straight to the fire. A long blast followed by one, two, three or four short blasts gave the location of the fire in town and the volunteer firemen could go straight to the fire. At times the fire alarm would use up all of the steam in the plant and they would have to quit processing milk.

Burglar alarms: Alarm signals would come to the operator. She would notify the business owner and call the sheriff's office in Gainesville when she received an alarm. A burglar was caught robbing the Gulf station by this means.

Shortly after we started working for the company in 1949 Jimmy Lehnertz, who operated the Gulf service station across the street on Highway 82, was being burglarized regularly. He came to us and asked if we could wire up some kind of burglar alarm. So we wired a switch into a swinging door in the station so that when anyone went through the door after hours it would signal the operator across the street. Jimmy would set the alarm when he closed up in the evening.

One night the signal came in while Lena Herr was operator, and, looking out the window, she could see someone moving around in the service station. She called the Jimmy, and he came with his gun. He had the burglar cornered in the back room, but the criminal broke out the window and fled in his car. Jimmy chased him, caught him and caused his death. Jimmy was charged with murder. When his trial came up Lena testified in his defense. Her testimony was instrumental in having the murder charges dropped.

Cow service: Dairymen in need of an artificial insemination technician would leave word with the operator. The tech would call in occasionally to see where his services were needed.

Dating service: On Saturday nights all the guys would come to town and hang around Joe Trachta's Drug Store and makes calls for dates. This was still the time of the crank telephone. Joe had a magneto phone on the wall in his back storeroom. The guys would go to the back room and call the girls for dates. Some of the short guys would have to stand on a stool.

General calls: Ten short rings on the line indicated a general call. If you were missing a cow, horse, cat, dog . . . whatever, you could call the operator to put out a general call. After ringing 10 times on a line, she would make the announcement of the missing item. Also, for 50 cents peddlers selling peaches, apples and other vegetables used this service to advertise their wares. Once when Elizabeth (Lizzy) Herr was operating the switchboard by herself and during a very busy time, a peddler came by and paid his 50 cents to advertise his peaches for sale, then he went uptown and waited at a private phone for the call.

Lizzy did not get around to calling the line as fast as he thought she should, so he came back and demanded his money back. We gave him his 50 cents back. That was the last general call we ever made.

Correct time: Subscribers were always calling in for the correct time.

Wake up service: You could leave a message with the operator to wake you up in the morning at a certain time.

Toll service: We had some businessmen in town that would not stay on the line while the operator completed their toll calls, so they would just give her a number to call and hang up. Depending on the line used, the operator knew where the call came from and would get the requested party on the line and then call the businessman back. One time we had a new operator working, and she did not know that she was to get a customer's party on the line and call him back and did nothing. The operator working beside her noticed and helped her complete the call and got the right party back on the line to complete the call.

Voice calling: Most children could pick up any phone in town and tell the operator to call home. The operator would recognize the child's voice and know which home to call.

Call transfer: You could tell the operator you would be at the neighbors', and she would transfer your calls there until you returned home again.

Personal service: This service, especially, served me well. As I noted previously, Gracie, my wife, lived on a party line, and every time I called the neighbors would listen in. So I installed a special key on the switchboard that I asked the operator to use when I called Gracie. This way I could call her without the neighbors hearing their phones ring. For the technical person, I rang her phone using grounded ringing, while the neighbors were still on metallic ringing.

The advantages of party lines

Gracie turned me down for a date only one time. When I called, she said she already had a date, so I called another girl on her line. I knew someone in her family would be listening. She never turned me down again.

How I acquired the company

When I came back from service in 1952 I asked Herman to give me a chance to buy the company if he ever wanted to sell it. After four or five years he started to lose interest. Herman's wife, Bess, kept the books, and the only time we heard from them was when the deposit slips were late getting to her. He became more interested in the horses than he was in the telephone business.

We were able to complete the deal by 1960. I planned to get an REA loan and completely rebuild the system, for it was in bad shape. From an engineering study it was determined that we would take $450,000 to buy the company and rebuild it with a dial telephone system for the three exchanges. I could not convince J.M. Weinzapfel, president of Muenster State Bank, to loan me the 10-percent equity I needed. So I agreed to give Bill Miller half interest in the company for the collateral the bank wanted to loan the money.

We received the government loan, and we all gathered in our home to sign the papers—on our kitchen table. At the closing of the deal were Herman and Bess Younger; Herman's attorney (last name was Thorpe); Bill and Terese Miller; Robert Snakered, our attorney from Fort Worth; J.P. Paganette, REA field accountant; and Gracie and myself. Check No. 1 we wrote to pay Herman was the largest check we ever had written, and we had to redo it several times to get it correct.

Herman Younger was a great person to work for. He was patient as we worked out the financing with the Rural Electric Administration in Washington and Muenster State Bank.

We saw Herman occasionally after that. He had his horse and buggy in the Rosston parade one year. Gracie and I stopped by to visit him at his Weatherford ranch, west of Fort Worth one year—he was in a wheelchair after suffering a stroke. His first wife, Bess, had died earlier, and he was married to his high school sweetheart who was taking care of him. Herman died in 2000.

CHAPTER 25

The Mark Sense Ticket

I n the late 1950s Southwestern Bell introduced the Mark Sense Ticket. With a series of pencil marks on the front of a toll ticket, an IBM machine was able to read the details of a toll call and list the toll calls on a monthly statement. Up until this time, Lizzy Herr was still hand-copying toll calls details on statements each month to complete billing. This greatly improved the billing process.

Toll calls were timed on a calculagraph machine. To start the timing of a call the operator would put the toll ticket face up in the calculagraph machine and pull the left handle of the machine, and when the call was completed she would put the ticket back in the calculagraph machine and pull the right handle. It did not make any difference in what order the tickets were placed back in the calculagraph. The length of the call would be printed on the back of the ticket. The operator would then turn the ticket over and read on the back of the ticket how long the call was. She then would record on the front of the ticket in a series of pencil marks as depicted in the sample shown. This made it possible for the first time for a machine to read the details of a toll call and print them for billing.

In making the change, the company discontinued a system that had been used since the beginning of telephone service in Muenster, over 60 years before. Prior to the Mark-Sense-Ticket each call had been recorded on a small slip of paper (toll ticket) as the call was made, and the toll tickets were filed under the customers' names. At billing time, those calls were listed by hand on the statement. When the number of toll calls was small, the method worked fine, but by the time it was discarded, more than 6,000 calls a month were being recorded and billed by hand.

With the new method, operators recorded toll call data on IBM tickets, which were collected in the office of Southwestern Bell in Dallas. At billing time, the tickets were put into a machine that gathered, added, filed and printed them according to telephone numbers. The toll statement in duplicate, along with the tickets, was then sent to the local office.

In preparation for billing Lizzy had made all of the changes on the IBM plates and stamped the name, address and the recurring charges on snap-apart bills she was using for billing. The toll statement was then added with the recurring charges on the snap-apart bill still using her hand-operated adding machine to complete the bill. This was then stuffed in a postage-paid, window envelope and mailed.

A copy was sent to the customer, while the other copy along with the tickets were filed in the local office. In addition to being neater and more economical, this modern method freed up company employees for other office work. If there was a question about a call, the original ticket was on record in the telephone office.

CHAPTER 26

The First Computer Billing

When the Cooke County College started computer programming classes I signed up. I was fascinated by computers and what they could do. They were teaching FORTRAN IV computer programming language. Their IBM computer was a cabinet as large as two automatic clothes washers. One would build your program on special programming forms—then wait for your turn at a card punch machine and punch cards—one card for each line on your programming sheet. Then you would go over to the computer, wait your turn, (everybody was using the same computer), feed your cards into the card reader and wait for the results. The machine would digest your program and print the answer or an error code on another card. My first program was to add 2 + 2. It took several sessions for me to get the correct answer.

Taking classes with me at the college was a computer operator for a welding supply company in Denton. He offered to do our billing for us on his computer. We worked out an arrangement where he would build the billing program under our guidelines and do the billing for us, including printing our bills. I showed him what I wanted, and he built the program. For the first time our billing was fully automated.

Also listed on each bill was what the subscriber was being billed—business or residence, two- or four-multi party line, extensions—as well as miscellaneous services such as speed dialers. The subscriber could see exactly what he was being billed for.

Our mark-sense toll tickets came to this person each month by federal express. He printed a list of the calls and totaled the cost of the calls. He then combined them with the monthly recurring charges for each subscriber and printed the bill and then FedEx them to us in Muenster. We stuffed them into envelopes, put the postage on and mailed them. For the office we got a copy of the completed bill and kept the mark-sense tickets in our office to answer inquiries.

From the billing we could get all kinds of information about our billing. For the first time we could get totals for the various types of service we were providing. This was a great improvement in our billing and sure beat completing bills by hand.

This process worked fine for a year or more until the end of a month was at hand, and we did not have our billing. The freight man mentioned that our toll tickets were piling up in the hall of the welding supply company. I went to Denton to check, and the computer operator was gone and my toll tickets lay out in the hallway. It was only a few days from the end of the month, and the billing should be in the mail. My billing operator just left town without saying a word to us. We were stranded—with no billing—and we would have no income if we did not do something fast. To make matters worse, Helen Hess, the only woman we had in the office besides Gracie, got sick and could no longer work, and a lot of the billing was in her head.

Carson Gilmer of UDP in San Antonio had approached me a number of times to do our billing for us. I told him about our predicament. He flew up in his private plane the next day. Gracie and I worked late into the night with him rebuilding our billing system. Luckily, the office copy of our bills had the name and address of each subscriber and the service each was receiving, but disconnects—new and changes in the service for the month—gave us some problems.

Carson took our billing back with him and entered them into his billing system. He had a printout ready when Gracie and I flew to San Antonio a few days later and reviewed each account for accuracy. Our billing was a few days later that month, but we had learned a lesson. We were very grateful to Carson for getting us out of a bind.

1100 Datapoint Computer

There it was—sitting on an elevated platform in all of its glory—the 1100 Datapoint computer used in Carson Gilmer's new billing system by UDP. The system consisted of the keyboard that was attached to the processor and CRT and four disk drives in a handsome black cabinet. We had never seen anything like this in the past; this was the forerunner of the desktop computer. The year was about 1985 when UDP introduced the new billing system. It consisted of the following:

1. Keyboard: Data input was through a keyboard attached to the processor. This was a great improvement from the keypunch card. You still wrote your program on a programming form, but data was entered directly into the computer by way of the keyboard.
2. Disk data storage: As noted, the computer had four large disk drives. Each had a data capacity of 3.5 MB. The disks were 10 inches in diameter, and data was stored on only one side of the disk. Now we had random access to data. The disk could easily be popped out and a different one put in its place. This was a great improvement over the tape data storage system that was the only way to store data up to that time.
3. Private processor: One did not share the processor with anyone else. We had 15 MB of random access memory. We did not have enough memory to do multi-tasking, but this was a great improvement over anything seen before.
4. Data Modem: They also used a new device to transmit data over regular telephone lines between computers. They used a data modem to send information between our computer and computers in San Antonio.

The new UDP billing system was provisioned in such a way that all of our basic billing information resided in San Antonio. Programs on the Muenster computer allowed us to post payments, establish new accounts and make necessary changes in our accounts.

In the meantime, toll tickets would be accumulating at UDP in San Antonio. At billing time UDP would pick up the payments and billing changes via the data modem and update the San Antonio database. The toll file would be closed for that month and processed in preparation of billing. The two files would then be merged, and the billing would be transmitted to Muenster to be printed with a new high-speed printer that was part of the new billing process.

This was an overnight process. We would leave our computer on when we left for the night. It would download the data, process the billing and return it again. In the morning when we came to work, our billing was ready to be printed. We would then print the bills, stuff them into window envelopes, add postage and mail them.

A copy of each bill was retained in the computer so that the billing clerk would go to the computer to bring up any account to answer questions about the billing.

As we grew, the computer system was changed so that a multiple number of persons had access to the data from data terminals.

The 1100 Datapoint computer along with all of our billing equipment that we used for 95 years are displayed at station 37, 38, and 39 in the Gene Henry Fuhrman Telephone Museum.

Computer heaven

After we got our new 1100 Databus computer and after our billings were converted over to it, I was eager to build new programs. I first had to learn how to program the process. UDP had classes in San Antonio on how to program, so I spent quite a bit of time in SA learning the computer. To this day, Gracie reminds me of the time I spent at the office programming while our boys were growing up.

There was nothing like it at the time, but it was a terribly slow machine. This was before the desktop computer. It seemed like it would take it forever to perform a calculation for you. It performed only one problem at a time. If your program required the file to be sorted, the computer would have to "rollout" and clear its memory by recording everything in memory on the disks. It would then use all of its memory to sort your file. The sorting program was also slow. It would take a number of passes to perform a sort. But it was the great addition to our office, and I loved it.

A feature of the first program I wrote was that when you brought up the computer in the morning, the computer would wish anyone in the office that had a birthday that day, "Happy Birthday."

Early computers "killed a word." This had to be changed to "delete." In my early programs I had it so that if you made a mistake, the computer would call you "Stupid" or "Dummy." Paulette got so mad at me for being called stupid by the computer that I had to change that.

Looking back, I built many programs that have come and gone, but I had two main programs that I built: our cable record program and a program used in the design of CATV systems.

At the time we had no good way to keep cable records up to date. So I built a program that would allow us to locate a cable pair through many different ways. You could locate a cable pair by— cable pair.' "subscriber s name," "street address," "route number," or "location number"—by hitting enter, you would bring up the next cable pair in the selected mode in consecutive order.

The information you would receive would be the cable pair, subscriber's name, street address, cable route number and location number.

You could expand the record to find the number of load points, airline miles and route miles from central office, estimated resistance and line loss and number of joint use power poles contacted in the back span.

This cable record program was used until we changed everything to the Martin Group plant record system in about the year 2000.

My first word processor was for the Datapoint computer. It was called "Describe." My mother wrote her memories, and I entered the whole book in the computer in Describe. Describe is very powerful and unlike anything we are using today. The format of the letter was determined by imbedded instructions placed in the test as the letter was being typed. You would not know what the letter would look like until the text was processed through the computer. For instance, to start a new line you simply would simply added +nl in the text and continue typing. If you wanted to start a new paragraph you would add +np and keep typing. There was a command for every situation you needed to write a letter. You could even go to other files and include a sentence or paragraph from other files. Gene kept the Databus computer language in our computers when we went to the desktop computers. Databus went out of our lives with the passing of Gene.

When I fell off the pole and broke my leg, the company had no health insurance, so he paid the premium on my private health insurance for a month. I went back to work on light duty until I could climb poles again.

He brought up from Fort Worth technicians to install key systems, repair lead cables and put up new telephone cables. We would have the poles and strand ready, and they would come up and spin the cables on the strand and splice it in.

Two years after I started with the company I was drafted into the army in December 1950. This was during the Korean War. While I was gone, my brother Bill left the company and continued his education in St. Louis. Cotton Jackson, Herman's brother-in-law, became the repairman while I was gone. During this time telephone service was extended to Marysville, Texas. My younger brother, Jerry, worked during the summer digging rock holes and trimming bush helping to build the line.

After spending two years in Europe I returned home in 1952 and went back to work for the company. When I came back to work, Cotton Jackson left the company, and I became the manager and repairman.

Our first computer

Telephone cable and wire
on Main Street in 1950

CHAPTER 27

Construction Trucks

T his is the story of the first three construction trucks this company-
owned. Trucks are a vital part of any telephone system.

1929 Plymouth truck

When I came to work for the telephone company in January 1949, the
only truck the company owned was this 1929 Plymouth four-door car that
was converted into a truck—the cab was cut off right behind the driver's
seat, taking all of the back seat out of the car. Then they found a used
pickup bed and mounted it on the chassis behind the cab. The pickup bed
they used was a little too long for the truck, causing the back wheels of the
car to be about in the middle of the bed, which made the truck tail-heavy
with any kind of load. If you took off too fast with a load the front wheels
would come off of the ground.

It was a good-running truck, always starting, and it gave us no problem.
The ignition key was on the left side of the steering wheel just like the 1949
Plymouth car I was driving at the time. It had a three-speed transmission
and a reverse. The gearshift came up from the floor, and the starter was
a pedal next to the gas pedal. We slipped the clutch a lot, especially when
backing up to set a pole. We never had any clutch trouble.

It had a hand-operated wrench that you had to crank while pulling a
pole out of the ground.

We rebuilt the telephone system two times using this truck. We had
two ice storms about two months apart in 1949. Dynamite was carried on
the floorboard with the caps in the glove compartment.

It was like the picture shown, but we had a pipe rack on the back made
from metal pipe that held a lot of our tools and a ladder. The truck was the

only way we had to haul poles and set poles. We would hoist them on the rack, and when we drove they would stick way over the front of the cab. We set poles with it by placing the butt of the pole in the hole with the pole leaning on the pipe rack, then we backed up to upright the pole. The top of the cab was a little flat from us walking on it, and at times the pole would come loose from the hole and fall back on the cab.

This truck was in good running condition when I left for service in 1950. But when I came back two years later the truck was sitting on the south side of truck shed on East 4th Street with a cracked block. It no longer would run. No one drained the motor or put antifreeze in during winter. The last I saw of it, it was sitting in J.B. Flusche's junkyard.

The old black Ford truck

The day Muenster Telephone Company first saw the black Ford truck was during the latter part of 1949, and it was a welcome sight. This was one of the first improvements that Herman Younger made after purchasing control of Muenster Telephone. The only construction truck the company owned at the time was the 1929 Plymouth touring car made into a truck. The new Ford truck came without a bed. My brother Bill, found this oilfield winch truck bed in J.P. Flusche's junkyard. The bed was for a longer truck, so it was cut off and made shorter. Some of the wood had rotted off. so that part was covered with a steel plate. A space was made under the bed to store long-handled digging tools, crowbars and shovels. A used wench was purchased from John Bezner in Lindsay and installed on the truck. Bill did all of the welding on the truck, assembling the bed and A-frame, and installing the wench. Now, we had a construction truck with a wench andA-framee to set poles, but no boxes.

We had boxes made from oak wood and built by the Home Art Shop, a local cabinet shop operated by Jake Horn. The boxes were built of oak wood because Jake owed us for his phone bill, and this was one way we could get our money.

The truck was put to good use rebuilding telephone lines in and around Muenster.

We had to dig all holes by hand, including rock holes. We carried dynamite in one of the side boxes with the caps in the glove compartment.

Driving over tree stumps, ditches and rough terrain eventually bent up the running boards and fenders. There was no room for the truck in the company garage on East 4th Street, so it had to sit outside in the weather. One night, the truck was stolen and the A-frame was raised to its maximum height. A number of power and telephone lines were torn down by the truck before it was returned to its parking place with wires still dragging behind it.

Upon my return from the service, many new routes were built with this truck. Telephone service was extended to Forestburg in 1954 and Rosston in 1957. Most of the telephone cables and open wire lines around Muenster were also rebuilt. When we were pulling poles or moving heavy loads, the front wheels would lift off of the ground. The truck had a very handy lightweight winch truck. As the years went by, newer and heavier trucks took over the line construction work, and the old black truck was called on to do less and less. At first, it sat out in the weather by the warehouse. There the plastic decoration deteriorated, and the Ford symbols disappeared. The black paint faded, the rubber strips and tires rotted, and the glass cracked. The wooden boxes fell apart and one was removed. The manifold warped, making the engine very noisy when it ran. So much dirt had fallen off of tools thrown under the bed through the years that no more tools could be placed in the storage area under the bed.

When the new warehouse was built, the truck found a place out of the weather. For many years, it was made to run for Christmas parades. Some years, the motor would be frozen and the battery was dead. Gasoline additives gummed up the gas system.

I drove the truck in the 1993 Muenster Christmas parade. The motor was very loud and ran erratically. There were very little brakes.

The truck was a symbol of Muenster Telephone Company, and I did not like it, for the truck did not reflect well for the company. So we decided to restore it.

Also, about this time the Telephone Pioneers asked to have the truck on display at 50th anniversary of the Texas Telephone Association Convention in the Loews Anatole hotel in Dallas. Larry Eldridge of Muenster Telephone accepted the challenge of restoring the old black truck. Authentic parts were hard to find and took time. It was not sure the truck would be ready for the convention. The finishing touches to the truck were completed the week before the convention.

Larry hauled the old black truck to Dallas on first the morning of the three-day convention. Monday evening, as visitors entered the evening activities, there was the old black truck with its new facelift, standing proudly in the middle of convention activities in the Grand Ballroom of the Loews Anatole hotel.

The Bell construction truck

Not long after Herman Younger became owner he became aware of a Southwestern Bell (SWB) construction truck that was being sold in Denison, Texas. We put our bid in for the truck, but for some reason we were not being considered. At the time SWB had a young, ambitious Independent Company Relations Agent, and I complained to him about not being considered. About a day later that he called and said the tuck was ours.

Charles Cook and I went to Denison to pick up the truck, and we found out what was going on—apparently, someone working for Bell wanted the truck also.

We put a new battery in it and started the motor. It sounded terrible. It hit on about half of the cylinders. We limped off the premises and headed to a downtown repair shop. There we found out why the motor was missing so badly. The spark plug wires were changed around so that the motor would hardly run. We corrected the spark plug wiring, and it ran like new. This truck was used many years as we expanded the telephone service to the surrounding area.

CHAPTER 28

The Myra System

The Myra one-wire, manual telephone system was purchased from Don Hoskins in 1956 and modern dial service was installed there. In the '50s Myra was owned and operated by Don Hoskins. It was a magneto one-wire system. It covered areas in all directions from Myra. It had never been upgraded when rural electric lines came and was really in bad shape. In its heyday it was larger than the Muenster system. Myra once had a hospital, a pharmacy, a cotton gin and a bustling community. Four events caused the decline of the Myra Telephone Company:

(1.) The first blow occurred in 1936 when Highway 82 by-passed the town. Traffic on the highway never got close to Myra, making it a sleepy town.

(2.) In 1939 Cooke County Electric built the power lines into the countryside, and the one-wire telephone system picked up noise from the power lines, rendering the lines almost unusable. To make the system usable the one-wire line would have to be rebuilt to a two-wire line. This cost more money than the company could spare, and the conversion was never made.

(3.) In 1940 a large part of the Myra Telephone Company's serving area was taken over by the army for the Camp Howze army camp. The company lost all of its subscribers around Marysville.

(4.) Finally, in 1959, the Katy railroad went out of business and removed its tracks.

The Myra Telephone Company was purchased by Muenster in 1956 with about 30 phones in and around Myra still in service. We built a concert block building on a lot we purchased from the Black Water Company. Herman Younger found a used 30-line North Electric dial board that I installed in the new building. The only thing I remember of this board is it had a vibrator ringing current generator that started up every time a call was made. Also the relays and gang switches were extremely reliable. I do not believe there was ever a malfunction of the board.

It is now in the Gene H. Fuhrman museum next to the manual board.

CHAPTER 29

Services Returned to Rosston in 1957

I n 1957 we experimented with our first electronic pair gain device. Up until then, we needed two wires for every telephone from the telephone office to the subscriber's home to provide phone service. Electronically we can make another phone line without adding more wire. Transistors had not been invented yet, so our first pair of gain devices (carriers) had tubes to make them work.

A young company in Amarillo, Texas, called Panhandle Carrier had designed an electronic system of putting multiply conversations over a pair of wires. So I spent a week at their plant in to learn more about this new Panhandle carrier. Gracie went along for the ride. Working with Panhandle engineers we designed a system that would serve all the people along the route and the communities of Rosston and Leo at the far end. I studied how to be able to have up to 10 conversations over the same pair of wires talking at the same time without interference. This was an ingenious way to provide telephone service to an area that was too spread out for conventional phone lines.

We had 16 subscribers working off of the 18-mile physical line. Halfway to Rosston the physical line was split into two lines—a high-pass filter allowed Radio Frequency (RF) to pass freely from one line to the other. The telephone service along the line was extracted from the physical line by the use of low-pass filters. Eight subscribers were fed directly from the telephone office. Eight subscribers received telephone service back-fed from a telephone line gained by the Panhandle Carrier in Rosston. Two additional lines were used to serve people in the Rosston/ Leo areas. This proved to be so successful we used Panhandle Carrere in other areas.

This was the beginning of electronics in our telephone system. This service worked great when it worked, but the tubes continued to give problems. Finally, in 1962, we replaced the tube type system with a transistorized Stromberg Carlson system, which gave us fewer problems.

With the advent of the transistor many pair-gain systems came on the market. The Rosston system had to have electric power at the cabinet, but when the transistorized systems came along, the power could be fed along the line, making the systems much more versatile.

Cables

In 1949, the Muenster Telephone Company had only one 50-pair, non-color-coded, lead-jacketed, 22-gauge paper-insulated telephone cable in service. It ran from the telephone office, which was in the home of Mrs. Horn on the corner of Highway 82 and Oak Street. The cable continued north a half block east of Main Street to a half block south of Sacred Heart Church. From there it went over to Main Street, continuing north in front of the church to 9th Street. At that point, two 10-pin cross arms, each with 10 wires, represented the line that went west on north Main along FM 373. Five telephone lines of open wire continued north to serve the rural area.

This cable was hung on a 6,000-pound support strand and hung on cable rings about every six inches apart. The wind and temperature changes would cause the lead cables to move a little in the rings and they would eventually wear a hole on the bottom where it laid in the rings. This was before cables were lashed to the support strand; after the advent of that process the problem was eliminated.

A hole at the bottom of the lead cable would not give trouble until we got one of the summer thunderstorms that occasionally occurred. The barometric pressure would drop drastically, and the hole at the bottom of the cable would suck in the water as it rained. The paper-insulated cable would soak up the water as it rained, and all of the telephone lines in the cable would go out of order. With a cable ring situated every six inches for almost a mile we had a problem on our hands. Even if we looked at each ring we would not be able to determine which ring was getting wet and causing the problem.

Cable fault locators we had at the time would only work to find a solid short. A wet cable is not a solid short—so we had to use a breakdown transformer to try to weld a pair together at the wet place. We would give the pair a shot of high current, and then check with an ohm meter to see if there was a solid short. We had to get it while the cable was good and wet also—if we let it dry out a little, it would not weld together.

When we were successful in getting a solid short we would put a tone on the pair. The tone we had at that time sounded like a hog grunting. With an exploring coil and headsets this tone would be audible outside the cable and be present all the way to the short. At that point it would disappear or be drastically reduced. So if we went past the wet place, there would be no tone, and we would have to backtrack until we heard the tone again. If it ended in mid-span, we would have to use a ladder to get to it, or, if it was at a place where we could not use a ladder, we would have to use a "cable cart" and roll out to the fault. The lead jacket would have to be removed to let the cable dry out. Desiccant, a drying agent, would be freely sprinkled on the wet cable. If it was still raining, we would have to keep it covered.

It takes years of experience to close an opening in the lead cable with a lead sleeve and have it look like something. The lead sleeve had to be split open to get it over the cable, then, using a wooden paddle to tap it back together and seal it. After that the ends had to be tapped down around the cable to make it possible to seal the ends again. We used a propane torch to melt the lead and seal the cable. Occasionally, Herman Younger would bring a Southwestern Bell cable splicer from Fort Worth, and the crew would use a lead pot and melted lead. The lead would be heated on a propane heater until it was liquid on the ground, and, by use of a hand line, pulled up to the repairman, who would seal the lead cable. They could do a much-better-looking job sealing the cable this way. I never could master the task of sealing the lead cable, and it always looked like I used bubble gum.

Wet places were not the only problem with earlier lead cables. Lightning could really tear up a cable. This problem would occur where open wire was connected to a cable. Even though we had all of the protection that we could place on the wire, at times it would get into the cable anyway—especially during a dry spell when a good ground on the pole was not possible. The lightning would follow the open wires into the cable, and, in those days, into the cable terminal that was fastened to the pole. The terminal lead would make a 90-degree turn to be spliced into the serving cable. Damage would usually occur where the cable made that 90-degree turn. Lightning could not make the turn. The damage would not always be visible on the outside of the cable and would have to be located, as with a wet cable. A person would have to find two wires that the lightning welded together.

Plastic insulated cable

In 1960 we replaced all of our lead cables with plastic insulated cables (PIC) and thought we had solved all of our problems. Later in 1972 we converted to all-one-party service and replaced all of the open wire rural lines and lead cables with PIC buried air-core cables, as well. Cables filled with Vaseline jelly were already in existence at the time (but were but expensive), so the Rural Electric Association (REA) would not let us use them. In a jelly-filled cable, all air spaces are filled with a Vaseline-like substance that excludes all air in the cable so water could not get in. We could use filled cables on our toll lines to Myra, Rosston, and Forestburg only. The rest had to be air-core cables. According to the REA and our consulting engineers, this would be the end of cable problems.

We soon learned that PIC air core cables had problems of their own.

PIC air-core cables, whether in the air or buried in the ground, had the ends open, and there was always air space in the cable. The outer jacket would be removed at every terminal needed to serve subscribers of phone service along the cable. The cable would breathe air in and out through where the other jacket was removed as the atmospheric pressure changes. Moisture in the air going in the cables would bring in moisture. Buried cable gave us more problems than cable in the air. In the summertime, warm air enters the cable and condenses in the colder ground. In the winter, the colder outer air enters the cables and condenses in the warmer ground.

This moisture would condense into water and collect at the low places such as the bottom of a hill. In the manufacture of PIC cables designers leave tiny pinholes in the insulation around the individual copper wires. The tiny holes would let water to come in contact with the copper cable pairs and cause noise on the lines. Also, electronic equipment would not work in a satisfactory manner over cables with moisture in them.

There were many unsuccessful attempts to save the PIC air-core cables. Dry air was forced into a cable with no luck, and sealing the end did not help. We tried to force jelly into the cables to replace the moisture to no avail. The cable had to be manufactured with the jelly in it.

We eventually had to replace all of the air-core cable with jelly-filled cables. The jelly would not allow air in the cable and kept water out even if the outer jacket of the cable developed a hole in it or was damaged. It was in 1982 before most of our buried cables had been replaced with filled cables.

We finally found the solution to reliable copper cables; we now replace the copper cables with fiber optic cables, as we take fiber cables all the way to the homes. Water and lightning do not cause problems in fiber optic cables. The glass fibers do not corrode even if they are lying in water, and glass is a non-conductor of electricity, so lightning will let it alone.

There is one inherent problem with fiber cable. Since fiber does not conduct electorate current, power cannot be fed down the line—it must be provided where the fiber is being used.

Perils of the Telephone Man

A telephone man never knows what he will run into when he goes out to install or repair a phone in homes.

When most homes are built, they seldom have the phone accommodations placed in the right place, or, in an old home, you either have to move the phone they have or you add another phone. Many times people want their phone on the opposite side of the house from where the service line is. Also, they want it installed on a wall in the middle of the house. And they do not want the wire to show. Now you have your choice: either run the house wire in the attic or (in most cases) under the house. Either way, you have to run the wire in the wall to get to where they want the phone and to keep the wire concealed.

To get into the wall from the attic you have to drill a hole in the plate in the attic above the wall where they want their phone. When a home is built and before the wall studs are placed, builders sheetrock the whole ceiling of the house, and then the walls studs are placed. This makes for no visible indication in the attic where those walls are. Also about a foot of insulation covers the ceiling in the attic, making it more difficult to find a wall. Consequently, phone men measure from landmarks they know will be in the attic for the right places and go up into the attic, measure and drill. When you pull the bit out and you see daylight, you know you are in trouble. You missed the wall and you have a hole in the ceiling. Then you are lucky if the owner does not want the whole room re-painted.

In some cases the roof is too low, and you cannot drill from above. When this is the situation, you use a long bit and drill through the switchbox hole, up the wall toward the 4 x 4 plate above the wall that is also supporting the roof. Suddenly, you have a new problem: you've gone higher than you had planned. Sure enough, you go outside to look and, yes, you came out through the roof. When this happens, you are hoping you won't have to put a new roof on the house.

Now you have a sheetrock wall and nothing to screw the phone to. You have to use special expansion bolts to hold the phone on the wall. You feel pretty lucky that you did not fall through the ceiling as you've completed the job. Of course, that is when the homeowner tells you that your walking in the attic has caused paint to pop off of the nails heads and that he/she wants the room repainted.

At times you can come down in a closet, go through the wall and connect the phone that way. You drill the hole through the wall, run your wire and you think, "I've got it made. That was easy." Then you find out the closet door won't close. It was a sliding door and you drilled right through the door and now your wire is holding the door open.

Sometimes you can talk the property owner into just letting you go through the wall to put the phone on the inside where the line comes to the house. You think you have it made, so you go inside and drill a hole all the way through to the outside, when you hear hissing sounds. You go outside and, yes, you drilled right into the air-conditioning system outside the home. You have to get the air-conditioning man to fix the air-conditioning system.

All of these things have happened one time or another in my life installing and repairing telephones in people's homes. We no longer will go into an attic to run a line unless we are not responsible for any damage. In most cases, we get the property owner to run the line in the attic if he wants it concealed.

Perils of the telephone man—under floor

When you're installing a phone in a home and the customer wants the phone on an inside wall, you have two options as to how to run the wire. In earlier years we did the crawling ourselves. If the house was built off the ground on pier and beams and the procedure was done during the hot summer and the attic was too hot or the ceiling was too low, you would have to run the wire under the house. Today we ask the property owner to crawl in the attic or crawl under the house to hold down damage claims.

The telephone man never knows what he will run into when he must crawl under the house to install a phone. Years ago, I received a request for an extension to be added in a relatively new home in the east part of town. They wanted their phone on an inside wall in the middle of the house. There was no closet near to run the wire in. The only way I could get the phone where they wanted it was to crawl under the house. In those days I worked by myself. The way to get under the house was in the Master Bedroom closet on one end of the house. I got my flashlight (and discovered the batteries were almost dead), got down through the bedroom closet hole and proceeded to crawl toward the place they wanted the phone.

When I got to the place and stopped, I thought I felt something crawl on me and I shook my flashlight to get it to burn a little better to see what was going on. I realized I was sitting on top of a red ant bed with ants crawling all over me. Needless to say, it did not take me long to get back out of that hole in the closet and shed all of my clothes. Luckily the ants had been in the dark so long under that house that they did not bite me, and, luckily, nobody was in that bedroom. I do not remember how I completed that phone installation.

At another time I had to install a phone in a home south of Myra. They wanted their phone on a middle of the house wall, and I would have to crawl under the house to install the wire. I discovered there were a number of dogs living under the house, and they had plenty of pets. When I got under the house I realized that it was infested with fleas. That was another time I made a quick exit.

I never seemed to keep a good flashlight, and at another time as I crawled under a house I ran into something live and big. I had to shake my flashlight to make it work, and I found out I had bumped into a fierce looking bulldog. Luckily, he was friendly and I got my phone installed.

Of course, under the house you cannot see where the walls are so you take measurements to determine where the wall is located. You measure and then proceed to drill the hole. When you remove the bit and see daylight you know you are in trouble. You missed the wall and came out in the hallway. All you can do is drive a wood peg in the hole and move over and drill a new hole.

Because every installation needs a ground for lightning protection, you must drive a ground rod. You manage to drive a ground rod even though it seems a little difficult. You go into the house after you have driven the rod and find out the rod hit a rock which deflected it back up again, and it is now sticking up in the middle of the floor. It is not easy to remove the rod.

Then there was the time I had the Forestburg teacher who complained about getting wrong numbers when she dialed. When I dialed I had no problem. Then I asked her to dial, and she got a wrong number. She was dialing incorrectly—when she dialed she did not bring her finger all the way back to the stop. This would cause her to get wrong numbers. When I explained this to her she got mad and demanded that we buy her a new dining room set because our repairman sat in one of her cushioned chairs with a screwdriver in his back pocket and ruined a chair. I looked at the chair but could see no permanent damage, but she insisted, and we paid her for a new dining room set—table and chairs. I did not realize until then that teachers do not make mistakes.

CHAPTER 31

Repeat Coils and Phantom Lines

From the 1940s through the early 1960s the "repeat coil" played a major role in providing telephone service in the Muenster telephone system. Repeat coils, sometimes called phantom coils, have two windings around a metal core—the "in" winding and the "out" winding are identical. There is no metallic connection between the windings. So, sound going in one side comes out exactly the same on the other side, but there is no metallic connection between them. They required no battery power to make them work. The repeat coil had many uses in the early telephone systems; one of the uses was to connect unlike telephone lines to work together.

In the days before electric power lines there was no electrical interference in the air, so all telephone lines were built with just one wire using the ground return, and this worked fine. But when the Cooke County Electric Cooperative began building power lines in 1939, the one-wire phone line paralleling a power line picked up electric noise and put a loud roar on the line, making it useless.

A two-wire telephone line does not have this problem. Each wire picks up the same amount of electric noise in sync and thus cancels the interference, so that you have a quiet line again. It would have taken a lot of money to rebuild all the rural lines of the Muenster Telephone Company, and at that time the phone company had no money. So a second wire was added only where the telephone line paralleled the power line.

A repeat coil was then connected into the line where the line changed from one wire to two wires, and vice versa. The telephone lines continued as a one-wire setups where there was no power line. This worked reasonably well until the weather got dry. The ground rod would not make a good connection to the dry ground, and you could not hear. We would have to pour water on the ground rod so you could hear again. Another problem we had with a one-wire telephone line was when several lines ran parallel with each other over any distance there was a tendency to cross talk between the lines. Also electric storms would burn up the repeat coils. Early lines were magneto lines, and voice and ringing signals would pass through the repeat coil unchanged.

A modern example of a repeat coil is the connection of the sound system in Sacred Heart church to the sound system of the Muenster CATV Channel 2 during church service. Making use of the center tap of the coils, they act like a third wire from church to the Muenster headend. When a key is activated in church a signal sent over this third wire triggers the headend to change from the audio coming from KGAF to the audio coming from Sacred Heart Church. A similar arrangement puts the audio from the Muenster Baptist church on Channel 2. You will find a phantom coil at station 25 in the Gene Henry Fuhrman Museum.

Phantom telephone lines

This may be a little technical, but I cannot pass up telling about the "Phantom Coils," sometimes called "Repeat Coils," used in our early phone system. We almost doubled the number of conversations on rural lines without adding more aerial wire. Remember, this was at the time when there was no electronics. In the early 1950s, the company just did not have enough money to build more lines. Our lines where filling up with subscribers, but we had no money to string more wire.

In most cases the pole line would have to be replaced as well. We used the Phantom Coil to increase the capacity of the lines without adding more wire. I explained earlier how conversations and ringing on a magneto line would pass through the phantom coil unchanged. Phantom coils placed in the line have a center tap that connects equally to the two wires of a telephone line. For each two-wire magneto line we could get a third wire by putting a phantom coil on each end of the line—one in town and the other at the far end. A telephone line has two wires, so by doing the same on a second line on the same side of the 10-pin cross arm, we would get the two wires, and we had another magneto line with no wires—a phantom circuit.

On the other side of the cross arm were two more magneto lines. By putting coils in it the same way, we were able to get a second phantom line. When talking on a phantom line, the conversation goes over all four wires unnoticed by the other parties talking over the same wires.

We were able to get a third line over the same wires by installing phantom coils in the phantom lines. A conversation on this line would go over all eight wires on the cross arm, unnoticed by the others using the same wires

The lines in question went from North 9th Street to the first four corners about three miles north of Muenster. By the use of phantom coils we took the four two-wire open wire lines and got seven lines—all of this without batteries or electronics.

Other uses of the phantom coil

We used phantom coils to add another line going south of Muenster, as well. Where FM373 crosses FM1630 we added a line going west from the intersection. This was even a common battery line. Just picking up the phone would signal the operator. At that time this service was only available in town.

Also, a common battery line to Bill Miller's Humble gas station worked over a phantom circuit on lines going east out of Muenster. When I lived three miles east of Muenster, his phone worked on the same wires in town as our rural magneto phone in the country.

CHAPTER 32

All about Poles

Telephone poles we set over 50 years ago in 1949 were still standing until a few years ago.

When Herman Younger bought the Myra exchange in 1957 he purchased a used Ford tractor with a hole-digger. This was a big improvement from digging dirt holes by hand, but it was not much for a rock hole. For rock we had the local welding shop take a 10-inch drilling pipe to cut hardened teeth in the edge. This replaced the auger of the digger. This worked fine, but there was no weight to make it cut the rock. So we took a 4-inch x 12-inch wooden plank about eight feet long, placed it over the top of the digger gearbox (protruding about four feet behind the digger), and several of us sat on the plank to add weight. As the core bit turned in the rock it would shake vigorously.

Today, rarely used, sitting in our East Truck Center yard, is a Texoma hole digger mounted on a truck that can punch a hole in the ground through about any kind of soil. It's large enough for any of our poles and it can dig as deep as you want it. It can do this in a matter of minutes. It not only digs the hole, but it picks up the pole and sets it in the hole and holds it straight until earth is tamped around it. We would have given anything those early years for a good hole digger, now it is rarely used.

Pole climbing

I never had time to drag ladders around to work on poles. I could climb a pole to make a test or fix a problem and be down driving away before I could ever set a ladder against a pole and climb up the ladder to work. Ladders against a pole are not very safe, anyway. I would put my climbers on in the morning and take them off when I quit in the evening. We had very few good poles to climb in the earlier years. Most of he poles were Brd-d'Arc poles—hard as iron. You could not drive a nail into them. They were full of knots, making them difficult to climb. We never saw new poles. Taller 25-foot poles were used only to cross roads. They usually had not been set very deeply in the ground, so they were leaning one way or another. A leaning pole is difficult to work on, especially if you have to work on the learning side the pole.

How not to climb a pole

I had been working only about five months in 1949 when I had to fix a line on what is now FM 2739, two miles east of Muenster and about four miles north by Dry Elm Creek. My truck was the 1929 Plymouth touring car that was made into a pickup. The magneto telephone line serving the oil fields and homes of northeast Muenster was out of order. I had to make a test on a weather-beaten, 25-foot pole supporting the telephone line over a gravel road to see where the trouble was. I strapped on my hooks and safety belt, slipped the shoulder strap of my bulky EE8 army magneto test phone over my shoulder and started up the pole. I climbed the leaning side because I had to work on that side of the pole at the top. (This is not a good idea I soon learned).

As I neared the top I was thinking to myself what would happen if my spurs would cut out. Suddenly, that happened. One second I was going up and the next second I was going down. I fell clear of the pole because it was leaning. I do not remember hitting the ground, but when I came to I knew that I had messed up my knee.

I unstrapped my climbing hooks and belt and all my tools along with the telephone and hobbled on my good leg to my truck. I drove to a place where the telephone line was low to the ground and called in. Doctor Myrick was in so I came on into Muenster. Dr Myrick was a general practitioner, and I really did not want him to work on my knee. He x-rayed my knee and said it was not broken and sent me home. That night my knee got as big as a watermelon, so my brother Bill took me to the Gainesville Sanitarium emergency room the next morning. We did not tell Dr. Myrick I was going to Gainesville, but when I got there, Doc Myrick was waiting. Their x-rays showed that I had cracked the knee socket. He said it was too swollen to do anything with, and he put it into a plaster cast.

The knee kept on swelling and the plaster cast did not expand, making me miserable. I finally convinced the Doc to slit the plaster cast so it could expand. It was several days before a woman doctor came in to set the knee. She used several screws to hold the knee socket together. Some six decades years later, the screws were backing out, causing some discomfort, and now I've had both knees replaced, so no more screws.

When I went back to work I initially did light duty in the shop, splicing drop wire together and repairing the mud soaked telephones that Herman Younger hauled up from Fort Worth. After several weeks, I started repair work again. At first I used a ladder to access poles. At times the ladder was not tall enough to work at the top, so I used the ladder to get as far as it would reach, then I climbed to the top of the pole with my hooks. The ladder slowed down the process, so I went back to climbing. The hardest thing I ever had to do was to start climbing poles again from the ground up. I continued climbing poles for about 40 years, until about 1980. I slipped a number of times, and my safety belt caught me. Other times I would only fall a couple of feet before my hooks would catch again. I learned always to climb a leaning pole on the high side of the pole.

Today, most of our guys do not even own a set of climbing hooks. They use the bucket truck to work on the aerial cables and the CATV system. What I would have given those first years for a bucket truck to use to work on poles, especially the weather-beaten, knotty, leaning poles of those earlier years.

CHAPTER 33

The Three-Position Switchboard

Midway through the 1950s Herman Younger purchased a used, three-position switchboard from somewhere in south Texas and had it delivered to Muenster. I wasn't very happy with the idea of staying with a manual switchboard, for I wanted to go to dial service. I did not immediately install the manual board. The only place I had to store it was in our truck shed, where it took up two positions. The switchboard sat covered up with a tarp in the dusty/dirty truck shed for a number of years.

Finally, in the late 1950s, I decided I had to do something—the two operators no longer could stay up with traffic on our two-position switchboard. Herman Younger was not interested in investing the money that it would take to go to dial service.

I rented the Horn's east bedroom and commenced to install the three-position common battery board. We took the window out of the room on the east side to get the switchboard into the room. We partitioned the room in half. The south half contained the operator side of the switchboard. This gave plenty of room for operators to sit at the switchboard, to get around behind to get in and out. The north half was the equipment room. There was just enough room for the power board/ charger and mainframe. A new set of batteries completed the installation.

A wall was built from the top of the switchboard to the ceiling. This arrangement gave me access to the back of the switchboard for repairs. The switchboard did not stretch across the room, leaving enough room on the west side for a door to give access to the equipment room.

This switchboard was very similar to the two PBX switchboards we were using. It was still a common-battery system. But it had automatic ringing. The operator pushed a button to start the ringing, and the ringing stopped automatically when the calling party answered.

Telephone lines appeared on both of the outer positions. The center position had new number groups that did not appear on the outer positions. The center operator reached in front of the other operators to answer calls. The outer operators reached in front of the center operator to access the new number groups. Because lines appeared on both of the outer switchboards, an operator completing a call would have to test to see if the line was busy on the other position. If it was busy she would get a click when touching the tip of the cord in the jack. If there was no click, she would push the plug all the way into the jack and complete the call.

We were now completing all of the calls that went within the state of Texas. Out-of-state calls still had to be forwarded to the Gainesville operator to be completed. We had two calculagraphs mounted in the switchboard that were used to time the calls. On these machines, the clock and hands are arranged to make an imprint on the back of a toll ticket when levers were pulled. There are two clock faces and hands. One printed minutes and the other the seconds. The clock face and hands moved together, but worked independent when one of the two levers was pulled. When a call started, the toll ticket was slipped in the machine face down, and the left lever was pulled, printing an impression on the back of the ticket of a clock face without hands. When the call was completed, the ticket was placed back in the machine, and the right lever was pulled. This time only the clock hands were printed inside the clock face. The distance the hands moved from the time the clock face was printed was the length of the call. Tickets could be placed in this machine in any order In 1960, in preparation of going dial with frequency ringing, I converted the manual three-position switchboard to frequency ringing, so the new phones could be checked out as they were installed. I installed special keys on the left side of each switchboard that the operator used to select the frequency of the phone being called. Each position of the ringing keys represented a certain code ring on the old system. In this manner, code ringing was converted to frequency ringing until the cutover to dial was complete.

This switchboard was used until May 4, 1963, when Muenster converted to dial service. Charles Cook cut the switchboard into small pieces when removing it from the house. Many of the pieces were missing when we assembled the switchboard in the Museum.

What you see in the museum today is just a shell of what the board was in its prime. In the museum the three-position manual common-battery board is the last item you pass before coming to the Stromberg-Carlson dial switchboard.

We had 11 operators when we converted to dial service. They were Lizzy, Lena and Katie Herr, Elizabeth (Girlie) Fuhrmann, Elizabeth Mollenkopf, Alvina Voth, Ida Hoenig, Helen Hess, Isabella Fette, Nora Truebenbach and Mrs. Ted Grimminger.

When we built a new telephone office in 1961, Bell had installed an open-wire, tube-type, 0 Carrier to service the open wire along the railroad line to Gainesville. The railroad pulled up its tracks about a year earlier, but our long-distance service continued another 10 years on the old right of way. The open-wire telephone lines were in bad shape by the time they were replaced with a T-Carrier system in 1972. The new system was built along U.S. Highway 82 to Gainesville with buried cable. We provided the facilities within five miles of our area, and Southwestern Bell provided service to the east, some 10 miles in the Gainesville area. The new T-Carrier gave us 24 high-quality lines to Gainesville, improving our toll service.

CHAPTER 34

House Movers

The moving of the Joe Lehnertz house reminds me of my experience with house movers. House movers in the earlier years represented a high-risk business proposition. They operated with no insurance and never bothered to get permits. Their equipment consisted of an old trunk they must have found in a junkyard and a set of truck trailer dual wheels—this and two long steel skids and some heavy wood planks and hydraulic jacks; that was all the equipment they had. They never bothered to notify you when they were going to move a house and thought nothing about tearing down telephone lines to get the house moved. They would never pay for damages. In most cases, it would do no good to go to court, because they had no money, and their equipment was worthless. Because they didn't have a permit to move a house on public streets or highways, they were always in a big hurry to get the building moved before they were caught.

Moving a drilling rig routinely resulted in our lines being torn down also. In fact, that is why the company was incorporated in 1927. Someone discovered oil north of Muenster, and the members of the Muenster Mutual Telephone Company were worried that they could be sued if a drilling rig was damaged going under lines that may not be at the legal height. They formed the Muenster Telephone Company Incorporated to limit their liability from house movers and drilling rigs.

Tommy Hesse had a house mover move a house to South Walnut Street. I do not know where the house came from, but I soon got word that he was trying to get under our cables at the corner of Cross and Walnut Streets. The cable was dragging heavily on the roof of the house he was moving. I got the crew to hold the cable up walking along the roof till the house was passed the cable.

House movers II

Then there was the house mover at Forestburg that was moving a house down the highway from Saint Jo to Forestburg. He had torn down our lines a number of times before.

We had just rebuilt the open-wire line where FM 677 from Saint Jo dead ends in Forestburg and enters FM 455 to Montague. He drove right through the line without stopping. As usual, he would not pay for the damages.

He also would not show me his permit or tell me where he was moving the house. Lucky for us, Alfred Fanning, who operated a Forestburg grocery store, was driving right behind him and saw him tear it down. I got an injunction against the mover to keep him from moving more houses until we were paid for the damages, and he agreed to notify us and pay our expenses when he moved a house in the future. The trial took place in Gainesville, and Alfred testified that he was following the mover and saw him tear down the lines, making no effort to protect the wires from being torn down. I was also called to the witness stand and was asked why I asked to see his permit—was I the police or something? I told the court that I asked to see the permit when he would not tell me where he was taking the house. I needed to see if any more lines in his path would be too low for the house to clear. He had no insurance to move the house on the FM highway.

The company received its damages, and he did not tear down any more of our lines. I believe I finally got his attention.

Just like today when we locate our buried cables to keep them from being cut, in earlier years we gladly worked with the movers to clear our lines rather than get our lines tore down.

Three position switchboard

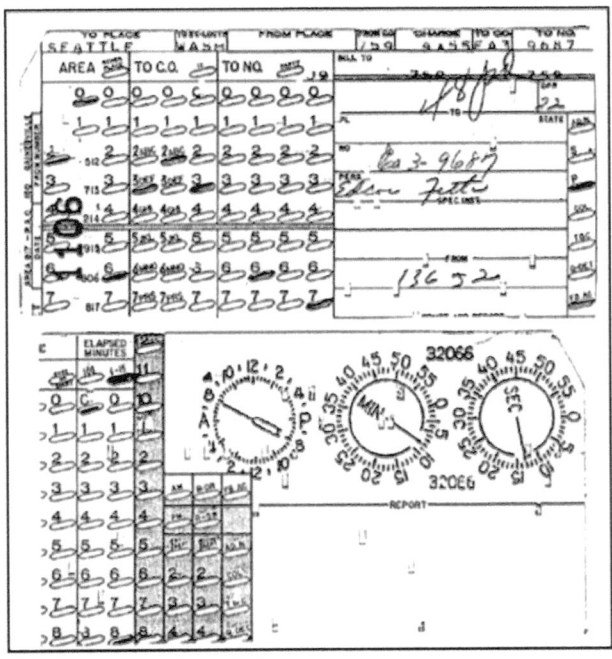

Mark Sence ticket with Calculagraph markings

CHAPTER 35

Improvising Became a Way of Life

I mprovise (v): To fabricate out of what is conveniently on hand In the earlier years, the success in operating a telephone system depended more on your ability to improvise than on your financial ability. Growing up on a farm, where you must improvise almost daily, was good training for maintaining and expanding a telephone company in the 1950s. There were no engineering firms that you could go to for help. Even if there were, we had no money to pay for them.

From the time I started working for the company in 1949 until the time we went dial in 1963, I had to design and build from parts cannibalized from retired equipment without blueprints or instruction manuals, and to build circuit plates to make different systems of different manufacturers (magneto and common battery, manual switchboards and automatic dial systems) work together.

Forestburg's first switchboard

This was during the time that Herman Younger of Fort Worth owned the company. All of the telephone equipment that Herman purchased was used equipment and did not come with installation manuals. In 1955 he brought me a 10-line Stromberg Carlson relaymatic dial switchboard to be installed in Forestburg. I installed it in an old concert bank vault. There was an air hole in the ceiling that I used to run the cables into the vault. I built a wooden bench and painted it blue to set the switchboard on. I also built a two-tiered battery rack also painted blue to hold the 24 battery cells that made up the 48-volt power system. You did not need much of a main frame for 10 lines and one trunk line back to Muenster. The trunks lines used simplex dialing with hi/lo supervision. No textbooks gave instructions on how to make this work with a manual switchboard.

On the Muenster end I had to interface this with the two-position Kellogg manual board and have it so the both operators could dial numbers in.

In Forestburg, the operator needed supervision to know the condition of the call. She needed to know whether the called party answered, when he/ she was still talking and when he/she hung up. Experimenting, I found a relay that would follow the hi/lo condition of the simplex trunk line, sealed it in a pint fruit jar to keep it clear of dust, wired it into the system— and the operators got supervision. Our operators completed calls between Forestburg and Muenster and long distance service.

Years later, the 10-line switchboard in Forestburg was replaced with a 50-line Kellogg Relaymatic. While I had prints of the circuits, I still had no instructions on installation or how to make it work with the manual switchboards we were using in Muenster. I had to improvise.

Instrumental in getting service

Before 1972, when there was no Public Utility Commission (PUC) in Texas, I was instrumental in getting many of Southwestern Bell (SWB) customers' telephone service very quickly. No state entity set the boundary lines between telephone companies. There was a lot of area around us in Cooke and Montague Counties that were not served by any telephone company. Whoever served the area first would claim the area. So I claimed as much territory as I could.

The people living on the Wolf Ridge and Silvell's Bend area north of Lindsay were not able to get SWB to serve them, so they came to us. We studied the area and figured that with the use of power line poles we could serve the area. Even though it was marginal profitable for us to serve them at the time, we expected that to improve in the future. We planned to follow county roads all the way east to the Silvell's Bend road (now FM 1202) and serve all of the area. Today this would be all of the Moss Lake/ Sivells Bend area back to about three miles north of Highway 82. When we prepared to build the line, we found that almost overnight Bell had plowed a cable into the middle of the county roads to cut us off. This is a rocky area, and they plowed a cable into the gravel road bed. Some places you could see the cable on top of the road. For many years, the people received very poor service because the cable was cut every time the county graded the road.

The same situation existed between Forestburg and Bowie. In 1970, there were people living along the Sunset /Forestburg FM road wanting service. This was considered to be in the SWB area. They were not able to get SWB to serve them out of Bowie. They came to us requesting service. We ordered cable and contracted with Roy Keeling out of Mineral Wells to plow in the cable for us. When he came out to plow in the cable, he found that Bell had plowed a cable down the road to serve the people. Again, almost overnight SWB plowed in a cable to serve these people to keep us out.

Leo, Texas

We had a different situation east of Leo, Texas. A ranch had one-party service about 10 miles out of Gainesville along Highway 51. The husband had died, and his wife was running the ranch. They were paying a lot of money a month in mileage charges for one-party service and came to us for less expensive service. At the time we were plowing cable east of Cogburn Cemetery by Leo and were getting close to the ranch. We could only give her party-line service at the time, so we could not help her.

New Harp

And then there was the New Harp area south/southwest of Forestburg in the late '50s. The REA program had just been extended to include telephone service. Central Telephone Company headquartered in Decatur, Texas, had its loan approved before we had approval of ours. They were in a vast expansion program and had staked service out of Alvord to within a few miles of Forestburg. Mr. Anderson and Poteet were in the skunk pet business, shipping skunks throughout the world. If you had a skunk under your house, they would get it out, de-scent it and ship it out. They lived in New Harp about seven miles south of Forestburg and they wanted our service.

So we laid about 36,000 feet of new drop wire on the ground to provide service before Decatur could. At first you could hardly hear through that much drop wire, so we added load point every 5,000 feet, but they could hear much better. Right after we got the drop laid, wildfires driven by a high wind raged through a heavily wooded area south to Forestburg. My drop wire was in its path, so when the fire got close I cut both ends free and hooked one end to my pickup and pulled it out of the way of the fire. After the fire passed, I pulled it back and spliced the ends back together, and they had service again.

Galen Force, REA field representative at the time, was also instrumental in making Decatur relinquish the area to us, for they would not loan money to two companies to provide service to the same area.

When the PUC was formed in 1972, each company was assigned an area and had to have their approval to change the boundaries.

Just one year later came Myra

In 1956, just a year later, I had to improvise again when we purchased Myra. Herman Younger found an older-model, 30-line North Electric automatic dial switchboard for Myra with three trunk lines to Muenster. Again I had no manuals on how to install this switchboard. Nothing was made to work together. I had to modify the trunk circuit plates in that board so the operators could dial into Myra and get supervision.

We continued to have problems with some long-winded persons tying up our trunks lines between Muenster and Myra, so when we installed the three-position manual switchboard in Muenster, I cannibalizes one of the switchboards we took out of service for relays and designed timing into the trunk lines so that after about 10 minutes they would get a warning tone and be disconnected one minute later.

During those earlier years, you would have to do a lot of improvising to provide basic services. Without this ingenuity we would not have been able to provide most of the services that we provided in those earlier years. We would be like the hundreds of companies that no longer exist today because they could not make do with what they had. They did not have the ability to improvise.

Saving Forestburg

Early in the 1960s we had our loan application in with REA, and we were waiting for approval to start construction. Central Telephone Company in Decatur was about a year ahead of us in getting a loan approved and was very active in gobbling up territory. Before the time of the Public Utility Commission, if you had service in an area, other companies would not come in and over build you. Before I knew it, Decatur had staked lines out of Alvord that came within a mile of Forestburg. They were planning to serve all of the New Harp and Uz areas.

The Forestburg people did not want service out of Alvord, and I did not want to give up the area either. We were already serving the town of Forestburg, and it would be a toll call to call neighbors served out of Alvord. So I purchased about 10 miles of neoprene drop wire and laid it on the ground. We had this line loaded with about 10 subscribers all the way from Forestburg to New Harp. By this time, we had a 50-line, Relay-Matic Kellogg dial board serving Forestburg. The first year it worked well, except for the fact you could not hear well on the far end. I added load points about every 5,000 feet, and that seemed to help. Rodents started chewing on the wire, which later years gave us problems. We used this line for about three years until aerial lines could be built.

After the line lay on the ground a number of years it started to give us problems to keep it working, and we were still waiting on loan approval. We decided to go ahead and build the line to New Harp—after all, it had already been staked out. So we just used the line as staked by Decatur to build the line all the way to New Harp.

Galen Force, the REA Field Representative, was also very instrumental in causing Decatur to abandon the territory south/southwest of Forestburg. He told them that a loan was being made to us for the area and REA would not loan money to two companies for the same area. Decatur then pulled back to the Denton Creek in Montague County.

The great grass fire

The spring of 1960 was very dry with high winds. Wild fires broke out north of Forestburg and swept south around the west side of Forestburg and threatened the area where we had laid a telephone line on the ground. The fire jumped roads and burned everything in its path. The fire could not be stopped, so firemen would gather around a home and, as the fire swept through, wet it down with water. Buildings and everything else burned. There was a heavily wooded area along the Alvord road about a mile out of Forestburg, and as the fire approached I prepared to pull the line out of its path when I had a flat tire on my truck and had to drive on a flat tire to get out of the way and find a safe place to put on my spare tire.

When the fire got close, I cut both ends of the line free, tied it to the back of my truck and drug it down the road out of the path of the fire and waited for the fire to pass. After the fire passed through and a few hot spots were distinguished, I pulled the line back and put it into service again.

I left home for Forestburg before noon when it was still warm without a coat, and then a cold front came through.

Gracie was at a volleyball game in Nocona, during which people kept announcing how bad the fire was around the Forestburg area. When she returned home, she called the operator and asked if they had heard from me. They had not. She knew I did not have a coat. There were no cell phones at that time. So she asked her brother-in-law, Gilbert Endres, to come with her to look me up to give me a coat. It was dark, and she could see the fires light up the sky on her way to Forestburg. I do not know how they found me, but I was west of Forestburg by the Rex Anderson's two-story home by the time they caught up with me. The coat really felt good.

Forestburg's 50-line Relaymatic switchboard

The 10-line Stromberg Carlson Relaymatic switchboard that we installed in the Pryor McGee old bank building vault in 1955 was too small from the beginning, and we soon needed a larger board.

I learned of a 50-line Kellogg Relaymatic switchboard in Yell County, Arkansas, that was for sale so Gene Walterscheid and I drove our black Ford truck to Yell County Telephone Company Arkansas and picked up the board. It was much larger and taller than I had anticipated.

Also, it was raining steadily as we loaded the board. Omar Saunders and his crew helped load it with the aid of a crane they had. They loaned us tarps and blankets to cover the board from getting wet. We chained it down the best we could, with it sticking off the back of the truck. We drove through a steady rain all the way back home. We had no apparent water damage to the board.

I installed it in a new concert block building on land we purchased from Pryor McGee, which is located right behind the old Forestburg Bank building. Today, this bank building is now used as the Forestburg museum.

A much larger, brick building was built in 1961 to accommodate the new Stromberg Carlson equipment when the whole Muenster system went dial.

The Kellogg Relaymatic dial equipment was sold to another telephone company in south Texas, which had it combined with an identical system that had become too small, making a larger system.

The concert block building became the Pryor McGee Barber Shop in 1964. After about 10 years, Pryor McGee died, and the barber shop closed and we eventually tore the concert block building down.

Improvising—Rosston

Rosston wanted telephone service 1957, but it was too costly to build open-wire circuits 18 miles and keep no more than eight subscribers on a line. About this time, the first electronic pair gain devices came on the market. This was before the transistor. It was known as the Panhandle FM carrier system, with tubes instead of transistors. I saw this as way to serve the Rosston. I spent a few days at the factory in Amarillo, Texas, learning the system. I used what I learned at the factory and designed the system. With one pair of #14 copper weld wires, I created a way to serve 32 subscribers and not have over eight on a line.

Subscribers along the line to Rosston were served on two lines. Eight were served on the physical line from the telephone office. A high-pass filter by Jim Christian halfway to Rosston split the line to Rosston in half metallically. This allowed high-frequency RF to pass on through and continue on to and from Rosston but blocked voice and DC on the physical lines. A cabinet with three channels of carrier was mounted between stub poles in Rosston. Two of these served subscribers in and around Rosston; the third channel was fed back on the line coming from Muenster and served the subscribers along the last half Service in the '60s.

CHAPTER 36

Financing the Buyout in 1960

S hortly after I went back to work for the telephone company after coming out of the army in 1952, I asked Herman to give me a chance to buy the company if he ever wanted to sell it.

We had outgrown the three-position manual board that was providing service. He said he would sell it for $150,000 dollars. The price sounded reasonable to me, and I went about the task of getting financing. The REA loan program had just been opened up for telephone companies, and I applied for a loan.

I planned to replace all of the rural lines, build a new headquarters building and go dial. Our engineering study showed we would need $450,000 to build a new headquarters building, rebuild the system and go dial.

With the aid of our first REA loan we were able to purchase the company in 1961. We completely rebuilt it with open wire lines and cut to dial in 1963. Open wire was used because the REA would not approve buried cables.

A big thank you to Herman Younger

Herman was a great person to work for. He was patient for his money, as we worked on our loan for over a year. He allotted funds to operate the company while we completed our financing, and I returned half of this back to him when we closed the deal. If it were not for Herman, we would not be here today.

At the time, REA would only make a 90-percent loan. I would have to have 10 percent equity—or $50,000. I did not have that kind of money.

I had to take in a partner. Rudy Hellman wanted half interest in the company for the Relax Theater building for our headquarters. He wanted $25,000 for the building. The theater had discontinued operation and was vacant. That was not what I had in mind. Robert Bayer was interested, but I never got a proposal. Muenster State Bank would loan what I needed, but the bank wanted equity, which I did not have. I knew that this would a good deal for Dad to invest in—for both Bill and me—but I would not ask him.

Bill Miller was operating a fleet of milk trucks at the time and the bank would accept his signature to give us the money needed. We agreed to a 50/50 partnership after Alfonse Hoenig agreed to remain on the board to break any ties that may develop. Partnering with Bill proved to be a stormy relationship, as I was interested in improving the company and Bill was more interested in making him instant money. Alfonse fell out of a pecan tree, breaking his back, and was bedridden when we closed the deal to purchase the company. We had our organization meeting at his farmhouse west of Muenster.

Bill agreed to become Chairman of the Board; I was the President; Gracie was Secretary; Therese Miller, Bill's wife, was Vice-President.

Alfonse gave stability to the board and had to break quite a few ties. The success of the company is due a great deal to the dedication of Alfonse, who took a lot of abuse from Bill when Bill did not agree with decisions made by the board.

Alfonse continued as the fifth director for many years until he fell off a stool while washing his pickup truck and broke his hip. He never made another meeting after that accident.

We continued without the fifth director for many years until Therese died suddenly, and Robert Miller, Bill's son, took her place her place on the board.

Bill thought he could always do things better and for less money. I had made a deal with Alvin Hartman for the land on which to build the telephone office when Bill Miller became a partner. He told me he could get the land a lot cheaper and went to the Hartman's and told them to forget about the deal I made with them. He wanted to negotiate a new, cheaper deal. Joan told him fine, they had sold the land too cheap, and now they wanted twice a much as previously. So we paid twice as much for the land. Bill also wanted to finance the purchase of the land and sell it to us at a much higher price. Needless to say, we did not go along with any of his deals, but we did have to pay more for the land than if he had stayed out of it.

Bill sold his interest in the company in 2000 for $6 million dollars to Gracie and me, which made us the sole owners of the company.

Alvin cutting over to dial service - Watching Cecil Cole, Pete Brazile, Jarel Haley - 1963

Here I am,

3 Position Switchboard 1960

Last Operators

CHAPTER 37

Cutover to Dial Service in 1963

The cutover to dial in 1963 ended the era of the telephone operator in the Muenster system. Muenster Enterprise editor R.N. Fette wrote of the momentous occasion:

"The wand of modern living touched Muenster on May 4th and brightened the lives of all the citizens with a new dial telephone system, but it also has left an atmosphere of nostalgia. The community is going to miss the cheerful competence of the operators who said 'Number Please' . . . for the last several years and before that 'Central.' For more than 50 years the telephone girls had been at the beck and call of the community on a 24 hour basis, serving in a capacity far more extensive than that of a city telephone operator."

"Now, telephone subscribers must make their own calls by dialing a number. And there will be times when they will be a little homesick for those helpful and efficient girls who said, 'Number Please." But time and progress marches on."

We had a very busy year after cutting the system to dial service on May 4, 1960. I told you about starting wireless dial phone service in 1964 and CATV service in 1968. Also, in 1965, we buried five miles of cable to Leo, Texas, and added five more subscribers on the way. The tube-type Panhandle Carrier was replaced with a Stromberg Carlton transistorized open-wire carrier.

But there were smaller events during the '60s that kept things interesting. Soon after we cut our system to dial service, some problems we did not anticipate came up. We wanted to give Cooke County Electric an easy number to remember, so we gave them 759-2211. With the Stromberg Carlson mechanical switching it was not necessary to dial the 759 to complete a local call. One would just dial the last four digits—in CCEC's case it was 2211. With all new lines this was not an issue right away, but as the trees grew up in the open-wire lines we had a problem.

Trees would slap the lines together and tap out 2-2-1-1 and ring the Co-op's phone. There would be a loud noise on the line in most cases when you answered one of these calls. This was not so bad during the day when it would ring in the office, but when Leo Sicking was taking night calls and the wind was blowing, he would not get any sleep. We did not come up with a good solution to this problem until we buried all of our rural cable in 1972. Even then, a faulty cable could somehow tap out 2-2-1-1 occasionally.

When we first cut to dial service we gave the fire number as 759-2222. We soon found out that is not a good number to use for the fire department or any time. When people start to dial a 2200 number and get interrupted or forget what they dialed, they tend to start over again and dial 2222 instead of the number they intended to call. Also, again when the wind is blowing, and there is a tree in the line somewhere, it could tap out 2222. This was not a good number to use to call the fire department. It is an easy number to remember but too easy to cause a false alarm. I finally changed the number to 759-2235 to stop the false alarms.

We still had lead cable and party lines when we first cut to dial service. We used frequency ringing, so you would not hear your neighbor's phone ring, but there was a buzz in the phone when your neighbor was called. Some who liked to listen in on other people's calls soon found out that if you put your phone on a metal pie plate you could hear better when the neighbor's phone rang.

After we had converted lines to frequency ringing and before we cut in the dial switchboard, subscribers were still working off of the manual switchboard, and there were several lines that were constantly going off hook then hanging up again. They picked up just to see if someone was talking on the line so they could listen in. This made for a slow response by the operator, for she would wait to see if they were going to hang up again. If she answered too soon, they would hang up when she answered. This caused an unpleasant noise in the operators ear.

Trees were always a problem with open-wire telephone lines. The telephone line to a farm east of Muenster went through a lot of trees in the fence line along the road from Highway 82 to the house. The homeowner's neighbor would not give us approval to cut these trees. These trees were putting the line out of service with a lot of noise. I moved the farmer who owned the trees with his neighbor to the same party line. Later, I was driving down Highway 82 past the place with the trees, and the neighbor, who, it turns out, had just one arm, was cutting down the trees in the telephone line along his place. I stopped and told him he did not have to cut the trees, just give us permission to cut them—we cut the trees.

A problem caused by a contractor

REA Field Engineer Hollis Beane would not approve placing conduit from the east /west alley behind Rohmer's Restaurant the one half city block north to the telephone office. Without the conduit, we would have to go aerial with a number of large cables. This caused us to need an anchor behind Rohmer's restaurant. Emil Rohmer gave approval for us to place the anchor in the fence line. After construction was complete, and we had cut the system to dial, Emil came to the telephone office all upset because the contractor did not place the anchor behind his restaurant in the fence where it was staked. I did not blame Emil for being upset, for he wanted the anchor in the fence—not about a foot outside his fence.

I had the contractor come back and dig up the anchor and move it over, to the fence where it was staked. Apparently, it was easier to dig the anchor hole away from the fence than to dig it where it was staked.

CHAPTER 38

Mobile Telephone Service

I n 1965, we did not have a good way to contact our repairmen once they were out in the field, and I was looking for the best way to do this. Operators of drilling rigs in the area had been asking me to establish some kind of wireless service. I could have put in a two-way system similar to the one used by SWB, but we had just converted to dial service and no longer had operators. This service would have required operators to switch calls from wireless customers to the land phones.

About this time Motorola came out with a push-button, two-way radio system that subscribers could use to dial the numbers they wanted to call without the assistance of an operator. Lee Felts was the Motorola salesman, and together we worked out a system that I felt we could live with and maybe make money from, and satisfy the demand for wireless service. It used the regular Motorola two-way radio but had a control head that converted it to an automatic two-way system.

I worked out a deal with the city to install our antenna on the water tower. So we started Motorola push-button dialing mobile telephone service so that we could reach our repairmen in the field and at the same time offer this service to our subscribers. We soon had about 20 subscribers using our service, besides our own trucks. Now we had a way to contact our men in the field.

When we turned on this service we immediately ran into a problem with a very vocal Leo J. Haverkamp of Haverkamp Oil Well Services Company. It turned out that we were operating on a frequency range that was close to Leo J.'s two-way radio systems, and our systems cross-talked. He blamed the problem on us, because he had not had the problem before—no one else was using phone service in his area prior to our arrival. We had to figure out what was wrong. It turned out that his radios were driven over the roads for years, and the screws came loose. We tightened all the screws on his radios, and the problem went away.

The system worked great initially, but some problems soon became apparent. There was only one channel (JR Channel), and only one person could talk at a time. There was a busy light that came on when the radio was busy to let you know the line was busy. When the busy light was on and you picked up the phone, you could not hear anything. It was supposed to be a private system and no one else was supposed to be able to listen to conversations going on. However, one could go into the manual mode and listen to any conversation. The ringing system was supposed to be foolproof, but at times two or more phones would ring at the same time.

At this time Southwestern Bell was providing two-way radio service from a tower north of Saint Jo. They had a pair of open-wire lines that ran along the railroad from Gainesville to Saint Jo. They still had operators in Gainesville that completed all of the calls. The system had the same problems as ours. Only one person could talk at a time, and there was no privacy—anyone could listen in on the conversations.

This constituted the wireless telephone service in our area until around 1967 when SWB came out with Improved Mobile Telephone Service (IMTS). They erected a tower right behind the telephone office in Gainesville and moved their antenna there from Saint Jo. We were going into CATV service about this time, so we saw a chance to improve our mobile radio service and provide TV service.

We erected a 250-foot tower on three acres of land from Leo Haverkamp's place two miles northeast of Muenster and mounted our mobile radio antenna on the top of the tower. This raised the height of our antenna about a hundred feet and greatly improved the coverage of our service. We also changed to IMTS mobile service at the same time.

The IMTS radio was huge and would not fit anywhere in the car except in the trunk. The control head was mounted on the floor by the driver. It had a rotary dial on which to dial your calls. This system worked very well, but the same problem existed that we had previously: only one person could use the system at a time and the privacy of your call could be compromised with the manual mode.

Another flaw the system had was that the power transistor that was used to turn the radio on/off could short out, and the radio would not turn off. If the radio stayed on through to the next morning, you would have a dead battery. Also, if the radio stayed on, no one else could use their mobile telephones. In addition, all neighboring telephone company systems around about a 75 mile radius on the same frequency were also locked out. For radios mounted in cars this was not a major problem, for the battery in the car would run down and free the system for others to use.

But when the radio was in a drilling rig and would not shut off, we had a major problem. A rig drilling day and night would keep the battery charged, and the battery would never go down. All subscribers within about 75 miles could not use their mobile phones. Our JR channel was being used by other telephone companies around us—Dallas/Fort Worth, Sherman /Denison, Wichita Falls and north of us in Oklahoma. Anyone of these could be putting our system out of order; it did not have to be one of our own drilling rig radios. The rig with the problem could not receive calls, so the operators wouldn't know they had a problem, because their radio could make calls. This happened to us.

With a makeshift radio directional finder I was able to determine the signal was coming from Oklahoma. Pioneer Telephone Company was the only company using the JR channel in southern Oklahoma. They had drilling rigs operating in the south part of their serving area. I was able to reach their radio repairman, but he said I was possibly closer to the rig than he was. The faulty radio could not receive calls, so a trip to the rig was necessary to manually shut it off. I was able to get the radio turned off, and our radios worked again, but when a new crew came on in the morning, they turned the radio on again—and we had our problem once more.

At one time we had up to about 20 radios working on our system, but when cellular service came along, we soon lost all of our subscribers.

Subscribers in the 1980

In the beginning of the 80s we had 1,466 telephone subscribers in six exchanges. Muenster had 1,012 subscribers with 32 mobile phones; Myra had 111, Rosston 101, and Forestburg 242. At the same time, the Valley View system had 619 subscribers with 421 in the main office and 198 in the Valley View East exchange. It was at that time that the City Council renewed our telephone franchise for another 35 years.

Cozy addition

In 1983, plans were finalized to add 2,500 square feet of office space in the Muenster office. During the remodeling of the business office, beginning in August of 1983, all office personnel were set up in the large conference room, even the computers. We were kind of cozy at times, but all managed to live through it. The new offices were ready for occupancy in April of 1984. With 11 building and ground locations to maintain and the enlarged headquarters building, Gene Vogel started that year as Building & Grounds Maintenance Supervisor.

The transistor started to be widely used a number of years later, and many new pair-gain systems came on the market. As soon as we received funds from our REA loan in 1960, we replaced the tube-type carrier system with a transistorized Stromberg Carlson system that gave us less trouble. Also, we added more channels and extended service six miles to Leo, Texas. Pair-gain devices worked well and were used for many years until an exchange in Rosston was established, and copper cable plowed along the route.

The mobile phone has come a long way over the years

CHAPTER 39

Modern Day Service

In the early 1980s we established the Rosston exchange. We built a brick building and installed a Stromberg Carlson XY automatic switchboard. This allowed us to serve the area with one-party service and no party lines.

Special T-screened cables were buried with digital T-Carrier to provide trunk lines back to Muenster.

In 1982 the XY mechanical switchboard was replaced by a Stromberg Carlson Digital (DCO) remote switch. The XY office was donated to Texas A&M College to be used in their telephone training classes.

Internet service introduced

In 2007, the DCO switch was retired and replaced by an AFC digital system that also provided high-speed Internet DSL service to our subscribers. DSL service and telephone service ride the same cable pair and can be used at the same time. Today service in the area is provided by a Calix system, and all subscribers have high-speed data service.

Service in the '70s

In the '70s, we continued to have ice storms. Gracie took great pleasure in teasing me when it was raining and the temperature was 28 degrees. We usually had one or two ice storms each year. We could offer only-party line service in the rural areas. The wind blowing would always cause some lines to be out of service because of wind felling trees. Trees and open wire lines do not go together very well. We had a lot of electrical storms, and the lightning would really put a line out of order in a big way.

Time and again, the lightning would burn down the heavy galvanized steel wires right out in the middle of a span. Lightning has weight. It does not go around corners very well. On a house, if there was not a good ground, the lightning would jump from the ground wire several feet to another wire or water pipe that had a better ground. Where open wire is terminated into a cable lightning will destroy the cable where it made a corner even if the corner in the cable was not very sharp.

At a house in Forestburg the lightning came in the back way and blew the protector to smithereens off of the house. The lightning hit a tree out in the yard and followed a pipe in the ground to the house. It demolished a water faucet in the yard on the way to the house. In the house, it blew out all the light bulbs and fixtures, blackened the electric wall outlets in the house, came out on the telephone house wire, and destroyed the protector on the outside of the house. It then burned up the bridle wire on the pole that connects the drop wire to the house to the open wire. I always felt the lightning that struck the tree and then followed the water pipe to the house.

When the '70s came around, we were well on our way to replacing all the open wire with buried cables and going all one-party service. Hollis Beane had suddenly died of a heart attack, and his replacement was more sympathetic to the problems caused by the open wire lines. We received an $828,000 loan from REA to replace the 254 miles of open wire with buried cables and were able to give one-party service to everyone.

We had some people who did not want to leave party lines and go to a private line. Some of these subscribers where heavy phone users—gossipers. We did not want to force anyone to go on a private line. With the new system, we could keep the party lines filled. When one subscriber on a party line decided to go on a private line, leaving the others persons on a party line, I would move the remaining subscriber to a vacancy on another party line.

Some subscribers thought that they could get the two-party rates with no one else on the line with them. I had one gossipy housewife who would not go on a private line. I used her to get all of my other party line subscribers to abandon the party line for private service. I kept moving her around until there were no more party line subscribers.

Going all one-party service required installing a great deal of additional Central Office equipment. The equipment room was not large enough to accommodate the additions needed so we enlarged the equipment room and added the large conference room. B. J. Construction Company out of Gainesville was the successful contractor. He was also constructing a major addition at the Muenster Cheese Plant at the same time.

Arnold Wimmer was the construction foreman on our job. He was terrible. He was asked not to dig in the back of the building because of our Central Office Ground was there, and we did not have the new grid completed in the front yard. Before I knew it, he had a backhoe in the middle of our grounding grid pulling up the ground rods, tearing up our grid system in the backyard. The equipment room was being enlarged, and a wall needed to be removed. The plans called for a plastic barrier to be put between the existing equipment room and the new addition to keep the dust out of the dial equipment. Before I knew, it Arnold was knocking out the wall and the dust barrier was still not in place. Dust got all over the dial equipment before I got him to put up the barrier. He was insensitive to the need to protect the dial equipment.

T-Carrier

We installed our first T-Carrier and filled T-screen cable between Muenster and Forestburg and Rosston. We started from Muenster with a 25-pair cable, and at Freemound Hill it split and 12-pair went to Rosston and 12-pair to Forestburg. ITT was awarded the T-Carrier contract, and K and B Construction Company out of Tulsa, Okla., was awarded the outside plant contract.

New toll facilities were established with Gainesville. We plowed a 50-pair t-screen cable along East Highway 82 about five miles to where we met SWB at Dry Elm Creek.

This replaced SWB open-wire toll facilities along the railroad to Gainesville. This line was plagued by splices going bad, trees growing in the lines, and poles rotting off and falling over. The train tracks had been removed, and the SWB did not maintain their pole line along the old railroad. This line was torn down many times by train wrecks—the tracks were so bad that the freight trains would derail.

One morning, I came into my office and had the police waiting for me. Someone had stolen miles of the copper wire along the railroad track. The license plate number reported of the vehicle used to steal the copper matched my pickup number. I told them I did not know anything about it, and I knew that my son Kent did not have the pickup. They examined my pickup but there was no sign of it being out in the brush. It turns out that they transposed the number and decided that it was not my vehicle used in the copper heist.

SWB had a tube-type O-carrier working on this line that put off a tremendous amount of heat. Our air conditioner for the equipment room could not keep it cool. I finally took out the ceiling panels above this equipment and let the heat go right out the roof vents. Our equipment room stayed cool after that.

The Rosston exchange was established by moving some subscribers from Forestburg and putting them with the subscribers from the carrier system from Muenster. The Rosston exchange served the Leo, Glascock area of south part of Cooke County. Corrin and Crow built the Rosston building.

In 1976, the Texas Public Utility Commission (PUC) was formed and signed into law by Governor Dolph Briscoe. We had to build a comprehensive tariff that explained all of our services and the cost. We tried to cover every aspect of our service, because to come back later and add a service we would have had to have extensive studies made to justify the charge for the new service. We started off just using GTE's tariffs that were on file and approved by the PUC.

In 1977, we purchased the Valley View Telephone Company. It fit in well with our operation, for it was all one-party service with buried plant. The central office equipment was Stromberg Carlson, the same as we had here in Muenster.

Central Telephone Company out of Decatur, which owned Sanger at the time, was also bidding on Valley View. We were on the TTA board together and I told them I put in a bid for Valley View and they kind of backed off after that.

When Lake Ray Roberts came into being, it isolated a half dozen of Sanger subscribers from Sanger by a fork in the lake. Sanger would have to lay submarine cable to serve them and drive up into our area to get back to them. I worked out a deal with Sanger for us to serve them. Since by then we had a PUC, we had to get their approval to change the boundary lines between Valley View and Sanger.

A hearing in Austin was required to change the boundary. We had one complaint—Ralph Banks—he would have to pay a toll charge to call Sanger. The PUC approved changing the boundary. Most of that land is in the State Park now. It was not long before there was no charge to call between Sanger and Valley View East.

In 1978, Ken McDougle joined the Muenster staff as resident engineer, and his wife joined as service order clerk. She filled a vacancy caused when Helen Wimmer had to quit because of poor health. June came to work while we were on a trip to Germany.

Muenster was serving 1,466 subscribers in six exchanges in Cooke, Montague and Denton counties at the end of 20th century.

Purchase of the Valley View Telephone Company

On Oct. 1, 1977, Muenster Telephone Corporation purchased the Valley View Telephone Company from the son, Robert H., and R. E. and Callie Solomon. Service continued under Valley View Telephone Company name with local installer/repairman Karl Totzer getting assistance as needed from Muenster. Billing and administrative functions were moved to Muenster.

The Valley View system consists of 645 subscribers in two exchanges; 484 at Valley View and 161 at the Valley View East exchange, about 12 miles east of Valley View near Pioneer Valley. The two exchanges covered about 100 square miles in south central and southeastern Cooke County. Included in the service area were all of Pioneer Valley and the northern part of the proposed Lake Ray Roberts.

Robert E. Solomon had started in the telephone business in Hebron, Texas, in 1913. Seven years later, he sold the Hebron system and bought the Valley View system, which at that time had a 100-line magneto switchboard. The system outgrew this switchboard by 1944, and Solomon purchased a 200-line unit from Muenster Telephone Company. Muenster had just replaced ours with a common battery unit. The Solomons still have their switchboards.

In 1957, Solomon's son, Robert H. Solomon, took over management of the system and used an REA loan to convert the magneto system to dial with new cables in town and aerial wire and eight-party service in the rural areas.

Further improvements were made in 1971, when all rural lines were replaced by buried cables and one-party service and Direct Distance Dialing was introduced system-wide. That year, the Valley View East exchange was established and cut into dial service. The system, with 633 telephones in service, had become one of the finest rural telephone operations in the nation with Bob Solomon at the helm.

Over the years, the Solomons encountered many unusual incidents in the phone business. One, the devastating ice storm of 1949, knocked their 200-phone system down to one working phone overnight. Solomon simply shut the board down and went to Dallas to pick up the supplies needed to rebuild the system.

The tower debacle

In 1987, the year our son Gene started working for the company, we had a problem with the City with a tower in the West Truck Center yard.

The lease on the land on which our CATV tower rested was expiring and had to be renegotiated. Al Haverkamp, who owned the land, wanted more money than I wanted to pay. Also, I wanted to get all of our Headend equipment together at one place. The off-air electronics were on the tower two miles out of town, and the satellite equipment was in the building in the West Truck Center yard. This was not a very good arrangement to keep the two systems balanced.

The reason I did not want to put the satellite equipment out at the tower was because we were having so much trouble with people shooting out the light on the tower. We would have to put the satellite receiving dishes on the outside of the building, exposing them to the heater.

City Secretary Celine Dittfurth gave me a permit to erect a 199-foot tower in the southeast corner of our West Truck Center yard. Before I released the purchase order for the tower, I caught Joe Fenton at the City Hall and told him I was going to release a purchase order for the tower in our truck center. He asked if I had a permit, and I told him that I did so he told me there should be no problem.

When the tower was erected and before I could mount the antennas on it, the owner of the lot next door, Emil Rohmer, objected to the tower and demanded that the city have it removed.

You learn who your enemies are and who your friends are when a controversy comes up. Your enemies come up with the dumbest statements, and your friends rally around you. Remember, this tower was on our property and not on the street. Some of the accusations made were that if we had an ice storm, ice falling off of the tower would injure a handicapped person walking by on the street . . . a mayonnaise jar falling off of the tower would break someone's windshield . . . on the country road north of town the telephone cable was not buried deep enough in the ground.

When I heard that Emil Rohmer was complaining about the tower I visited Emil to see what his objections were and found out the reason he was objecting was that 27 years earlier he had given me approval to install an anchor in the fence line behind his restaurant and when it was installed it was about 14 inches from the fence. The contractor, who did the work, did not install the anchor exactly where it had been staked. At the time Emil brought it to my attention and I had the contractor dig it back up and move it over into the fence line, and Emil seemed to be satisfied. I was unaware of lingering animosity over the incident.

Because of Emil's objection, the City took us to court to have the tower removed. The presiding judge made a statement at the beginning of the trial that he would never rule against a city. Dick Stark was our attorney, and we had him on a retainer.

The City voted 4 to 1 that Celine Dittfurth, the city secretary, did not have the authority to give me the permit, and I was ordered to remove it. Al Hess was on the City Council, and he said he ruled against us because I cut a tree on the road along his land north of Muenster and lowered the value of his farm, which he had already sold to the Meadows family.

This did not set well with me, and I contested it in court. We did not prevail and we removed the tower. The sustaining vote was by Mayor Richard Grewing, who was the only councilman that bothered to look up the cancelled check I gave to the city for the permit and it clearly stated a 199-foot tower.

We could have moved our satellite dishes out to the tower, but they would be too close to the road and would have sustained damage from vandals with rifles driving on the road. Having to removing the tower made me mad, and I went out and purchased a new Cadillac.

After that I drove a Cadillac for years.

The first T-Carrier Turnk System

First dial switchboard in Forestburg-1955

CHAPTER 40

Truck Centers

I n 1949 our truck center and store room was in the middle of East Fourth Street. We had a galvanized steel building large enough for two trucks and an office. Above the trucks old equipment and parts were stored. Along the front of the trucks on the east side was a workbench. When the wind would blow it would go right through the building. Dust was everywhere. When it was raining we would splice drop wire that Herman Younger would bring up from Fort Worth. Our trucks sat outside in the weather. At first all we had was the 1929 Plymouth car converted to a pickup truck, and we had room for it. When the 1949 Ford truck came along, the Plymouth sat outside. Our trucks were vandalized while sitting out. One night someone took our Ford truck with the A-frame on the back pulled up high and drove around town. They brought it back dragging electric lines behind them.

In 1975 when the city wanted to open Fourth Street we had to get our building off the street.

Show building: We moved all of our supplies to the old show building on Main Street and tore down the old building. The floor in the old show building was sloped to the front. Upstairs in the projection room we found parts from the projectors they once used. We found some tickets to the Relax Theater for 15 cents. At the time we were in the process of going all one-party line, and we stored all of the dial equipment in the showroom until it was installed.

There was an old Sinclair copper telephone line that went north and south through the Kreiss brothers' yard west of Muenster. We purchased the line for the copper wire. We rolled this wire up and placed it in this show building warehouse. That night someone broke in and stole all of this copper wire. The lock was not damaged—it sounded like an inside job.

Tractor sales building: When Emil Rohmer bought the show building we moved our supplies to the old Tractor Sales building in the east part of town. We used the north round roof part of this building, and Gary Fisher opened The Green Door Tavern in the south flat roof part. There was a big, sliding door that connected the two buildings at one time that was closed and locked on our side. There were some holes in the door so that you could look through to the other side. Gene peeked through one of these holes one day and got paint sprayed on him. Gary used old cable reels for his tables and hung his signs using drop wire. Our trucks sat out at night, and tools that were missing from our trucks were found in The Green Door tavern next door.

West truck center: Across the street south of the telephone office were a couple of old buildings; one was the old Muenster State Bank building that had been moved there. The other building came from Main Street as well. I was able to buy this land for our storeroom. I sold the buildings to Jackie Reiter, and he moved the buildings. The south building had a basement under it that we had to fill in. We went back and forth with the digger truck to pack the dirt as we filled the old basement.

The company finally had its own truck shed and outside plant office when Red and Kyle Kuhn built the metal building with an upstairs area over the office, restroom and the parts storage area. The east side is an open shed to garage the trucks. There was a nice pecan tree along the west side that we tried to save, but eventually had to be removed. About the same happened to another tree on the northeast side of the yard—it had to be removed as well. The tree made it hard to park a vehicle in the north parking spot of the building. This building is now known as Nortex West Truck Center and contains all of the CATV supplies and vehicles.

East truck center: In 2000 the Muenster State Bank repossessed the Wilde Chevrolet building on the east city limits of Muenster, and this became available to us. It consisted of the glassed-in show floor on the south side along Highway 82—a large shop area ideal for us to bring our trucks in and work on them. There was also a large spare parts room in which we could store all of our parts, an upstairs over the parts room that is a large area to store equipment, and an area that has been used as an apartment to live in. Outside we have half a city block to store equipment and supplies; it's paved and has a tall fence around it.

We were able to buy this from the bank for a reasonable price. This has become our last and final warehouse to store parts and garage most of our trucks. This building is now known as the East Truck Center.

Today, we have replaced the glass around the show room with a stone wall. The Gen Henry Fuhrman Telephone Museum now occupies the showroom. Office space and a ready room were added in part of the showrooms.

I believe we now have the final resting place to store our equipment and garage our trucks.

CHAPTER 41

The Evolution of Telephone Service

T his is to recap the evolution of telephone service in the Muenster area.

In the beginning only one wire was needed for a telephone line. The ground was used for the second wire. That worked fine until Cooke County Electric Coop built power lines along the side of the telephone line, making telephone lines too noisy. Then two wires were needed to quiet the noise. Ice storms required steel wire and heavier poles to withstand the ice and wind. Copper weld wire came along, making greater distance possible with less loss. Then fiber came along and revolutionized telephone service and made all wire obsolete.

The first switchboard was small enough to hang on the wall. The service proved to be so popular that only a few years after service was started a larger switchboard was needed for the operator to be able to handle the calls. There was not electricity in those early years of telephony, so magneto service was all that was available. This service continued for 36 years. You cranked the phone to attract the operator, gave her the name of the person you wanted to talk to, and she completed the call. When you were finished, you gave a short crank to tell the operator you were finished. If you did not do this the operator would have to listen when you were finished. The common battery phone came along in 1945. You no longer had a battery in your phone, for a common battery in the central office served all the phones.

This was the golden age of telephony. The operator knew everything that was going on in town. She would forward your calls when you went next door. She would speed dial if you just gave her a name. She would tell you who died when the church death bell rang. She knew which girls had a date Saturday night and which ones who did not have a date yet. She blew the fire whistle when your house was on fire and called the police if she received a burglar alarm. She always had the correct time. She knew who was cheating on whom and where the poker games were in town.

In 1962 dial service was introduced, and the golden age of telephony started to fade. No longer did you have an operator to help you make a call. When we changed to digital service you gained back some of the conveniences you had with the operator.

Today, the main frame in all of our central offices sits idle. Just when we got our plant built with the finest buried cables that gave us very little trouble we replaced it with fiber.

First, we replaced the manual switchboard with a Stromberg Carlson dial Electro-Mechanical automatic switchboard, then we went to a digital board and finally to a soft switch. Cables have gone from lead-cover, paper-insulated cable pairs to PVC plastic-insulated, jelly-filled cables—and finally to a fiber cable.

Galvanized steel wire first replaced the soft iron wire of the early telephone lines, and finally a copper clad steel wire was used before buried cables replaced open wire lines.

Just the way the traffic circle became obsolete in our road system of today, the main frame is no longer used in the telephone central office. It is sad to me to see it go—we believe we lived in the golden era of the telephone.

CHAPTER 42

Hello, Texas!—
History of Telephony in Texas

Brad Smith, who was executive secretary of Texas Telephone for many years, retired before being able to complete his history of telephone service in Texas. I knew he had accumulated a great deal of material for a book. So I visited him in his home in Austin and picked up all of the material he had about the topic. The TTA board made me chairman of a committee to accumulate the data from the various companies. On the committee was A.M. Chappell from General Telephone, John H. Greenberg of Brazoria Telephone, Robert Digneo of ALLTEL, and Dave Lopez of SWB. The board then hired Jerry Hall to take all of the material and add the history of Southwestern Bell and material of his own to publish a history of telephony in Texas. For my effort in publishing the book I was awarded the Outstanding Achievement Award at the 1999 TTA Convention in San Antonio.

In 1999, after serving 23 years on the TTA board, I was awarded the highest honor Bestowed by TTA: the Neville Haynes Award in 1999.

At the 2009 convention in San Antonio Gracie received the Neville Haynes Award over the telephone. Gracie and I were in San Antonio, but I got sick and we drove home early. We were not present for the banquet. We were home by that time, and Gracie received the award over the telephone. Joey and Alan brought the award home when they came back

More history: Gene's take on North Texas Communications
This is from a local newspaper article that spotlighted our company from Gene's perspective:

Headline: North Texas Communications provides cable, cellular service
Subhead: Nearly a quarter of a century old North Texas Communications
evolved along with Cooke County's communications needs in both the
personal sense and the business sense.

With offices in Muenster and Gainesville, North Texas Communications
provides cable television service to Muenster and Valley View, and business
phone systems and cellular phones throughout the county, according to
Gene Fuhrman, assistant manager of the Muenster office.

North Texas Communications was established in 1967, and is owned
and managed by Alvin M. Fuhrman. It began with the idea of providing
cable TV to Muenster. Since then it has branched out to Valley View. That
is where it is involved in the personal sense.

In 1984, the company became involved in the business sense—business
phone system sales. July of 1990 marked the beginning of a new era, the
selling of cellular phones.

North Texas Communications is an authorized agent for Southwestern
Bell Mobile Systems.

"We offer a good variety of models," Fuhrman said. "We have Motorola,
Panasonic and Oki models."

Fuhrman said that the message he wanted to get across to residents in
the county was NTC is a full-service communications company that stands
behind its products.

"We're customer driven, and we give the best kind of service," Fuhrman
said. "We want people to feel secure in doing business (with us)."

In the cellular phone business in particular, Fuhrman explained that
there seemed to be a number of fly-by-night companies, but that was not
the case with NTC.

"We hope to increase the company's profits through communication
network efficiencies," Fuhrman said.

In examining the future of the communications industry, Fuhrman said
it is increasingly headed to cellular, wireless types and fiber optics.

"Cellular offers more mobility and fiber optics carry more volume and
are more reliable," he added.

And, speaking of reliable, Fuhrman made mention of the employees
of the company. Don Hellman is a salesman at the Gainesville office and

Larry Eldridge is involved in sales and as a technician. They are aided by Secretary Doris Koesler.

"Our employees try to put in the extra effort to make customers happy," Fuhrman said. "All of them are very knowledgeable and well-trained."

NTC sends its employees to seminars periodically so that they can keep up with any possible changes.

In the coming year, Fuhrman said that NTC set goals to continue to provide the best service it possibly can, and to remain at the forefront of the newest development in technology.

Thus keeping up with Cooke County's communications needs.

Outstanding Achievement Award—1990

The Neville Haynes Award—1999

Gracie has been beside me every stepof
the way at the telephone company

CHAPTER 43

Fifth Generation of Telephone Service Is Here

An evolutionally new method to compete telephone calls is here: Voice over the Internet (VoIP). Since I started working for the telephone company, this is the fifth major change in the way telephone calls are completed. We started with a switchboard hanging on the wall, and now most of our VoIP calls go over the Internet with everything else.

In a nutshell, here's how far we've come:

(1.) 1909 to 1945: When I came on the scene in 1949, the magneto telephone was the major way to make calls. The wooden wall phone was the most popular telephone. Each telephone had its own battery. Each phone had a crank to signal the operator.

The operator would have to monitor the call to know when the call was completed. Everybody on the line knew when a call was made and listened in. One wire was all that was needed for a telephone line.

(2.) 1945 to 1962: Next, the common battery telephone came along. This was a big improvement in telephone service. No longer was a battery needed at the telephone. One large battery at the telephone office provided power for everybody in town to talk. You no longer had to crank the phone to get the operator. All you had to do is just pick up your phone, and the operator would answer.

Lights on the switchboard let the operator know the condition of your call. She no longer had to monitor the call. By this time, there was divided ringing, and you heard only half of the phones ring. It took two wires to make a telephone line.

(3.) 1962 to 1982: Then came the Electro-Mechanical dial phone system. Now you had a dumb machine. You had to do everything yourself, but you did not have to wait on the operator. You had to have the number to complete a call. You did have privacy.

There were still party lines—but no one else heard your phone ring— that is, unless you listened really close; then you could hear the phone buzz when someone else on the line was called. It was even better if you put it on a tin pie plate. Then we went one-party service, and you could not even do that. It was necessary to dial only the last four digits of the telephone number to make a local call. You still needed two wires for a telephone line.

(4.) 1982 to 2014: This was the introduction of digital telephone service. This machine was not so dumb anymore. We got some of the services back we lost when we went dial: speed dialing, call forwarding, conference calling and call waiting. Now you had to dial all 7 digits to complete even a local call.

Calls went through faster, even when you had nines and zeros in your phone number. You still needed two wires for the telephone line. The Internet rides the same wire to the house, but they are not mixed together.

(5.) 2014 to today: This is the era of VoIP—voice over the Internet. Everything is mixed together on a data line. The voice packets look and handle the same as data packets. You can plug your computer and your phone into the same high-speed data line, and each will know what to do. Your phone will divide your conversation into little digital packets, slap an address in front of it and send it out. Your voice is now a group of ones and zeros with a one and zero digital address. Your voice packets are mixed with millions of packets as it goes to its destination.

By checking the address in front of each packet, routers route each call to its destination. When it gets to your phone, the little packets are reassembled in the right order and changed back to voice so you can hear what was said. Of course, all of the features of digital service are included with the VoIP. Still to be completed is E911 service. While you are listening to the other party talk someone else will be talking or sending data over the same path. Thousands more calls can be carried over the same facilities. No longer is there a dedicated wire or path for each telephone conversation.

CHAPTER 44

My 80th Birthday Party and Another Party of Note

The 80th birthday party caught me completely by surprise. I was not expecting a party, and my friends did not have to go through all of that trouble. I know a lot of hard work went into making it possible—the unique gifts for an 80-year-old, the food and cake, the drinks, the decorations, the skits, the pictures and songs . . . everything about the party. All of this took a lot of work and was greatly appreciated.

I thoroughly enjoyed the evening and I want to thank all of my friends for thinking about me. Here are some remarks I made during another party, the annual company Christmas Party on Dec. 12, 2009 in the Muenster meeting room:

Since it was our centennial year I thought I would reminisce some on the switching systems used throughout the 100 years.

TELEPHONE SERVICE STARTED WITH MAGNETO SERVICE

The Company was founded in 1909 using the only technology known at the time. It was a Magneto service that was used for the next 36 years. The battery was in each phone, and one would have to a crank a current generator to get the operator. It was a party-line service, and the intelligence was through the operator. There were no power lines, so there was no power failure to cope with.

COMMON BATTERY SERVICE

Before my time in 1945 Jake Horn converted the town of Muenster to Common Battery service. The service was operated from one big battery at the telephone office. One would only need to pick up the phone to signal the operator. We still had party-line service; the intelligence was still with the operator.

We had 12 operators giving around the clock service.

DIAL TELEPHONE SERVICE INTRODUCED

In 1962, we went to an electro-mechanical dial system. You picked up the phone and dialed after you received a dial tone. We still had our eight party lines. No intelligence in the system. It was just a dumb switch that completed calls if everything was right, without the help of an operator.

ALL ONE-PARTY SERVICE

By 1972 we got tired of the party-line complaints and went to one-party service. All open wire lines were replaced with buried cables. You picked up the phone and dialed. No more party lines. Still, we had no intelligence in the system. It was just a dumb switch that would do nothing if the numbers you dialed were not correct. It completed calls without the aid of an operator.

CHAPTER 45

Company Milestones and the Future

I t was in 1982 that Digital Switching was introduced into our system and some intelligence was returned. The technology advanced so that we introduced Custom Calling features with call forwarding, speed dialing and other features. One big battery still served all the phones and kept the system working when there was a power failure. The digital switch returned many of the features we lost when we went to dial telephone service, notably speed dialing, call transfer, selective call forwarding, and three-way calling.

Fiber to the home

We went back to the future in 2009 when we replaced our ageing aerial cables and poles lines in Muenster and Valley View with buried fiber to the home (FTTH). Glass fiber does not conduct electricity, only light—so batteries had to be added at each phone to keep the phone working when the power fails. When I started working for the company in 1949, one of my first duties was maintaining batteries in telephones—well, we are back to having batteries in the phones again.

The soft switch

From 1982 to 2010, the digital switching system was used. Beginning in 2010, the soft switch was installed to provide all the above features, plus many more. Phone service has been extended over the CATV system to Collinsville, Lindsay, Saint Jo and Lake Kiowa. Calls are dispatched to multiple phones simultaneously, and we've added many other new services. The intelligence of the soft switch mounts in a relay rack. Most of the switching now is performed in small cabinets scattered across the countryside. The call comes to these cabinets via the fiber cables. Most of our equipment room sits empty. It is expected that without heat-generating equipment we will have to add heating to the equipment room.

The loss of Gene

As I noted in the family section, a tragic blow happened to the telephone company in November 2003 that shook it to its foundation—the loss of Gene in a tragic car accident.

The tribute to him following the accident was very moving. Flowers from all over the country and as far away as Attendorn, Germany, filled the room at his funeral service. The "Gene Fuhrman Trust" was established in Sacred Heart School in Gene' honor—Gene was instrumental in bringing computers to Sacred Heart School while he was in school years earlier.

The streets in Muenster along Main Street had been blocked off for the 2003 Muenster Christmas parade, which was taking place at the same time as Gene's interment in Sacred Heart Cemetery. He was 39 years old. Gene Henry Fuhrman born on March 27, 1963 and died Nov. 25, 2003.

Reorganizing

As I noted earlier, after Gene's death, I said I would not operate the company but would remain Chief Executive Officer (CEO) and stay active more in an advisory capacity. Gracie remained in charge of the office and is planning to groom her replacement. Joey Anderson volunteered to be Chief Operations Officer (COO) and was approved by the board. Alan Rohmer remained Chief Financial Officer (CFO).

The formation of an ESOP, whereby the employees would eventfully own stock in the company, required us to sell stock in the company to the ESOP at a 20-percent minority discount. We want to see the company stay in this community. Employees will have control of the company when we are gone as long as they are employed. If they are good managers and make the company profitable, their retirement will be greater. Poor management will lead to them getting less. Each year they get stock based on their salary for retirement. When they retire, they will sell this stock back to the company at its valuated worth for their retirement funds.

The future looks bright

We wish to see the company pass through numerous generations. As we fade out of the picture it is our hope that the company will continue to grow and prosper. Who knows, our grandson Conner may even be one of these generations. As we hand this company over to the next generations the future looks bright for the company. The past networks lie worthless, no longer used, buried in the ground because they cannot carry the bandwidth needed. Nortex fiber optic cables now are carrying voice, Internet and television service to the homes and businesses.

Large communication companies are abandoning the rural areas for the more-lucrative large cities. We are now servicing homes and apartment in all the cities and towns around us. This includes Forestburg, Rosston, Myra, Valley View, Gainesville, Lake Kiowa, Callisburg, Tioga, Pilot Point, Decatur, Nocona and Saint Jo. We are serving all the schools.

In conclusion

Technology has come a long way in the past 100 years. One wonders what the future holds for the communications of the future. The future well being of this company is based on how well future generations take up this challenge.

SECTION III

At times we had to guard prisoners when they were taken out to do work.

We carried a shotgun that did not have ammo in the chamber. These were pump-action guns, so we could easily place a round in the chamber. We had about a half dozen prisoners at a time. They had been confined for minor offenses and did not give us any significant problems.

If we were threatened in any way, I placed a round in the chamber, and they got in line in a hurry.

CHAPTER 46

The Early Days of My Service

In January 1940 I started working for Muenster Telephone along with my older brother Bill. Not long after we started working, Herman Younger bought controlling interest in the company. We had taken the company from disaster to a thriving company with the aid of the financial help from Herman. I had started dating Gracie Friske, and this was starting to get serious when I received my draft notice. I was ordered to report for duty a week before Christmas. It is customary for the army to quarantine new recruits for a week when men from all parts of the country suddenly must live close together. This caused us to be quarantined during Christmas, and we could not leave to spend Christmas at home—we could not even call home.

We were taken to Fort Sam Houston in San Antonio for our shots and to take tests. I had broken my leg in a fall from a telephone pole about a year and a half earlier, and it was still giving me some problems—I was hoping I would not pass the tests. However, they were eager to fill the 2nd Armored Division, and the examining rooms were empty when we walked through them. I soon discovered that if we could walk through their examining rooms we could serve in the army.

They then bussed us to Fort Hood for basic training. We were taught to march by cadence by a surgeon. I had to do guard duty and do KP duty. One exercise we went through was keeping our gun clean while crawling under machine gun fire. This was real fire. Their guns were blocked so they could not shoot too low—at least, that's what I was hoping. We had target practice with our worn out carbines. Our rifles were so dilapidated that the bullets would tumble on the way to the target. By the paper target you could see that the bullet was going sideways when it hit the target.

We were there six months. I was coming home each weekend to be with Gracie. Huge Perry, Ewald Fuhrmann and Phillip of Gainesville rode with me and helped pay for the gas. We would buy a case of beer for the way home. I did not drink, for I was driving. By the end of six months, the case of beer was gone by the time we got home each week.

One morning we have to fall out and stand in formation and we got our assignment—some of our group went to Vietnam and some of us went to Germany. Robert Beyer, my brother–in–law, went to Vietnam. I went to Germany.

So it was that on July 1951 I took my car home, spent a final date with Gracie, and they took me to Dallas to catch a train to Fort Hood, Texas. It would be 18 months before I would see her again.

USS William Mitchell

It was the last day in August 1951 when I brought my car home from Fort Hood, kissed Gracie goodbye and took a train back to Fort Hood. I was assigned to the 14th Armored Field Battalion of the 2nd Armored Division that was ordered back overseas to Europe. Every tank, artillery piece, truck and trailer of the division had been loaded on railroad flat cars for the trip to New Orleans to be loaded on ships. All 10,000 of us were boarded on Pullman railroad cars for an overnight trip to New Orleans, as well.

As the train moved through the night you could hear the clang, clang of railroad crossing warning signals on the way to New Orleans. Our train crossed over the Mississippi on the Huey E. Long Bridge the next morning and came to a stop on New Orleans' waterfront at the edge of Canal Street. This bridge carries the railroad, along with automobile traffic. In the middle of the river the auto traffic comes up on each side of the railroad to give a maximum height for ships under the bridge. To get the height over the river, the railroad starts about a mile from the river so as not to rise too quickly.

We carried our duffel bags with all of our belongings on board the troop ship the USS General William Mitchell, and were assigned a place to sleep. The Mitchell was designed to carry 8 000 men at a time. Our hammock-like bunks were slung between superstructures eight bunks high—one on top of the other in the hole of the ship. I was lucky—I got a top bunk. Can you imagine being in the bottom bunk as someone got sea sick above you—and there were plenty of guys getting sick. We were fortunate that only about 4,000 of us were on the ship, which meant that there was only one shift of men. We did not have to share our bunks in shifts.

We watched as dock and ship cranes together picked up the huge tanks. The dock crane would pick up the tank into the air off the railroad car—as the tank moved through the air toward the ship, the weight of the tank was transferred to the ship crane, then was dropped down in the hole of a transport ship along the dock. The weight of the tank was all that the dock crane could pick up. The tanks were placed in the bottom-most part of the ship for stability.

Our departure from New Orleans

During the middle of the summer of 1951 in over 100-degree heat, the entire 2nd Armored Division, over 10,000 men, marched up and back down Canal Street to our waiting ships. We passed the reviewing stand on the way back to the ship. The street was wet like it had rained from the men sweating from the heat. We were all soaking wet. There were ladies handing out cool lemonade when we stopped.

As soon as we were aboard the ship again the ship departed. A military band was playing, and the girls were waving. Tugboats pulled us away from the dock, and we started down the Mississippi river to the Gulf of Mexico. We wondered what lay ahead for us. The Cold War was at its height. Our mission was to prevent the Russians from invading Germany.

The hole in the ship was so hot that I slept on the deck the first night. We sailed around Florida the next day and headed for the open sea toward Europe.

The Storm

The first day of the 12-day journey to Europe was very pleasant. It turned cold the second day, so we could no longer sleep on deck. It got cold and windy on deck and you had plenty of time to loaf around and visit with your buddies. We got our coats out to stay warm.

About the fourth day out we ran into a vicious storm that would last for several days. The ship would go over a wave and crash down on the other side. It seemed to stop at the top of a wave and shudder as the top of propeller came out of the water, then it dove into the swell of the next wave. Water would gush across the deck, and no matter where you were on deck you got wet.

The troop ship had all of the latrines in the front and back of the ship.

You got quite a ride when you "sat on the throne" during a storm. The ones in front were the closest to me. When the ship went up over a wave you sailed into the air. The ship would shudder when the propeller came partially out of the water at the top of the wave. Then you would hang on as you took a nose-dive as the ship came down between waves. I had to hang on to make sure the throne stayed under me.

When eating during a storm you had to hold your tray with one hand to keep it in front of you, as it would slide back and forth as you ate. If you did not, you risked having your tray slide down the table to the guy on your side, who was sick. He would throw up in it, and then the tray came back again and slid to the guy on the other side, who was also sick. (I told Gene this story many times.) I remember one time there was a 100-pound sack of sugar on a table that was sliding back and forth. The storm sure made a mess—and I know why they called it the Mess Hall.

My job during the trip was to keep sliced bed for the men during my shift. I had to get the bread from the bakery and run it through a whole loaf slicer and put it in the food line for the guys to eat.

Trying to walk during a storm is also a challenge. The bulkheads came over and hit you as you walked around the ever-swaying ship. You sure enough walked like a drunken sailor.

Manipulating the stairs was interesting. If the ship was going down— you just stayed put and hung on for dear life in one place and waited for the ship to bottom out. When the ship was coming up—you stepped really fast to stay up with the stairs as they came up with the ship. This went on for three or four. I had about three sets of stairs to and from my bunk in the hole of the ship.

Sleeping at night was also interesting during a storm. The ship moaned and groaned and shuddered each time it went over a wave. The sealed portholes kept going under and out the water. You rolled from side to side with the ship, strapping yourself in so you did not fall out while you slept. You heard the sick guys groan with the ship. Then you were awakened by something biting you—bedbugs. They did not smell very good when you squashed one. Some guys never left their bunks the whole 12 days it took to cross the Atlantic.

After the storm passed it became a beautiful day again, but it was cold out in the north Atlantic.

Our ship passed through the English Channel between France and England into the North Sea and ended up along a dock in Bremerhaven, Germany.

Immediately after our arrival in Bremerhaven tugboats moved the ship against the dock. German longshoremen came aboard and started moving us out. We moved our duffle bags with our belongings on deck, and a crane moved them on shore. I tried to speak to the German workers but they talked so fast and used words I was not familiar with, so I did not have much luck.

Our tanks were lifted back out of the holes of the transport ships and again placed on flatbed railroad cars for the journey south.

CHAPTER 47

Germany

We were loaded into Pullman railroad cars again for the trip south to the suburb of Mainz Germany—where our temporary camp was set up.

Our train moved silently through the night as we passed through the countryside. There was no clanging of bells as we crossed roads. I noticed that every road crossing of the railroad track, regardless how remote the area, had a guard gate located across the road when we passed. The people lived in villages except by these railroad crossings. It seemed like there was a home near every crossings for the gatekeeper, who lowered the gates as the trains passed.

Going through Aachen, a larger city, there was a Yard Master, who oversaw the passage of the trains through the yard. He sat in an elevated office overseeing the trains as they passed through. Steel wires ran along the tracks from his office to all the switching locations in the yard. He controlled the tracks as our train rolled through the town. The trains were always on time and moved silently. They never blew their whistle, as all of the railroad crossings were guarded. The town of Aachen lay in ruins. It is on the main railroad line that runs from Bremerhaven to Mainz and south.

Our train also passed through the small town of Finnentrop. Passing through this town reminded me of the story my mother told many times. Her mother, Augusta Steinmetz Flusche (my grandmother), returned to her hometown with her youngest son Max in 1916. She took the same route I was on from Bremerhaven to visit her hometown of Attendorn and had to change trains in Finnentrop. Finnentrop is about 10 miles from Attendorn. She had taken the cheapest fare they had from Bremerhaven to Finnentrop. To make a big entry into her hometown she planned to change to first class for the short trip to Attendorn. To her surprise, a large delegation of her friends, along with a band, was at Finnentrop to greet her. Everyone watched her get off of the fourth-class train car, much to the embarrassment of the mother and son.

We arrived in Mainz on the Rhein River, and trucks took us to a tent city called Camp David. Our permanent barracks were being renovated and were not ready, so we lived in tents. It got quite cold at night, so we asked for and received more blankets. The camp was set up in an army airfield.

Up the street from our tent was a German national who had a Pepsi-cola stand, which I visited regularly. He spoke good English, and I soon found out his name was Emil Schwarz. He lived in a suburb of Mainz called Ingelheim, located along the Rhein River. He told me about being a POW during WWII war in a USA army camp north of Dallas. When he was asked where that army camp was, he said it was close to Gainesville, Texas. He said he worked in the harvest among the farmers in the area. When I told him that I was from that area, he would not believe it. I had a letter from Gracie with the postmark Gainesville, Texas, and he finally believed that I was from that area. Upon further conversations I found out that he had worked on a threshing machine for the Arend family, our neighbor back at home. He was highly complementary about his treatment as a POW.

While I was stationed in Mainz, Richard Arend, who was working in the oil fields of Saudi Arabia at the time, came to visit Emil Swartz. Emil told Richard about Ewald Fuhrmann and me being stationed close by, and he came over to the camp to visit us. I happened to be on leave and did not get to see him, but he visited with Ewald.

It just goes to show how you must always behave—you never know when you might run into someone who knows you.

Nuremberg

During the summer of 1951 I was separated from our unit stationed in Gonsenheim, Germany, and sent on a special assignment as a prison guard in Nuremberg. Nuremberg is where the Nazi criminals were tried, and most of them were hung. I arrived in Nuremberg after the trials were over and justice had already been handed out. Alger Hess was the only Nazi remaining, for he had received a life sentence. The area where he was kept was a sealed off wing of the Nuremberg prison. We never got to see the inside of that wing.

It was summertime when I arrived in Nuremberg, and streetlights came on at 10 in the evening and went back off at 3 a.m. They were gaslights, and someone would have to go around in the evening to light them. Nuremberg had lots of damage from the war. The big castle on the hillside overlooking the town was severely damaged, with the roof caved in on one end.

When I was there the old prison was being used to hold GIs who got in trouble with the law. It was our job to see that they served out their sentence.

I remember the old prison at night. It was heated by steam, and when the steam was turned on the pipes cracked and popped, making all kinds of funny noises.

The main event that took place while I was a guard was the army trial of an American soldier accused of killing several German nationals during a crime spree. The trial took place in the same courtroom where war crime trials took place. There were headphones at each seat, so you could select the language you wanted to hear the trials in. We had to guard the soldier while he was on trial and move him back to solitary confinement when he was not in the courtroom. We had to make sure he did not commit suicide.

At other times we had to guard prisoners when they were taken out to do work. We carried a shotgun that did not have ammo in the chamber. These were pump-action guns, so we could easily place a round in the chamber. We had about a half dozen prisoners at a time. They had been confined for minor offenses and did not give us any significant problems. If we were threatened in any way, I placed a round in the chamber, and they got in line in a hurry.

Two other GIs from other units joined me in Nuremberg: Pectrul from Connecticut, and a GI from Massachusetts.

The Great Operation

The winter days in Germany were bitter cold. It was not unusual for the temperature to fall below zero. We spent more than 50 percent of our time out in the field during both summer and winter. My bedroll was made up of a sleeping bag, in which I had two blankets inside to keep me warm. I usually slept inside the covered bed of our wire section ¾-ton army truck.

On each side of the covered truck bed was a bench for us to sit on while on the move. It was wide enough for me to unroll a sleeping bag and sleep on. It was not safe to sleep on the ground, for trucks drove without lights, and you could easily be run over if you were not careful. When it was bitter cold, we slept on the ground by a tree or an object covered by a heavy tarp. You would have to come out from under the warm tarp to dress in below-zero weather in the morning. Portable showers would come around about once a week, and you could take a hot shower—but there was no warm place to dress.

One time it was announced that we were going to have to go out into the field during bitter cold weather, so we would all try to find a way out. I had a cyst on my back and decided it would be a good time to have it removed. I went on sick leave and reported my request.

A few days later I found myself in the back of one of those big army trucks along with a dozen other persons wanting out of the coming field trip, including a sergeant from my group. They were taking us to a medical facility about 30 miles away to take care of our medical needs.

When we got to the hospital we had to get in a line in which they were doing minor surgery. The sergeant from our group was right ahead of me in line, and I watched as a surgeon removed an ingrown hair on the back of his neck. He sat in a chair and leaned forward, and they started the procedure by deadening the area with a local shot. It was quite bloody as the doctor cut around the infected hair and then completed the job with some stitches and a patch, I was next.

I took my shirt off and lay down on a cold table. The doctor told me to point where the cyst was. I reached around behind me and pointed to the lump on my back. He then went about his job of removing the cyst. He deadened it and cut in the area where the cyst was—keeping the blood to a minimum and was soon putting in stitches to complete his work. He then put a patch over the area, sat me up and moved to the next person in line.

I got in the back of the truck for the trip back to my barracks. On the way back the deadening was gone, and my back was really hurting.

I soon found myself in the back of our wire truck as part of a convoy with our self-propelled, 105 Howitzer on the way to an artillery range for maneuvers. We were fortunate this trip, because we got to stay in tents at night. The weather was below zero. Each tent had a pot-bellied stove and coal. We were given a cot and several blankets, so I set my cot up as close as I could to the stove.

My back was killing me, and I went on sick call to have it looked at. The stitches did not hold, so the medic put a bandaid over it and sent me back.

Today I have a lump on my back with a wide scar right though the middle of it.

Attendorn visit

While in the army in 1952, I was standing outside the Post Office in Mainz, Germany, struggling with the wording of a telegraph I planned to send to our distant relatives in Attendorn. I planned to visit them that weekend. It cost by the word, and I wanted to get the message across with few words. Karl Michael, a young German man, approached me and asked if he could help. With his help I completed my telegram, which said: "Ankommen Attendorn Samstag am 1300."

The translation in English: "Arriving Attendorn Saturday at 1 p.m." Karl helped me send it off. In Germany, the Post Office handled telegrams, telephone service along with the mail service. Before Karl left he asked me to visit his home in Mainz sometime, for he had something he would like to tell me.

When I got to Attendorn, Hildegard and Celli met me at the train station. They lived in a nice two-story house.

The house next to them was an adjoining home that had a common wall between the houses. The backyard was separated by a high hedge between them. There were two boys, Theo and Heinz, and one cousin, a girl named Thea—they were about 12 years old. They lived in a neighboring village. Attendorn did not have a sewer system yet, and you could access their toilet at the back hall of the house. There were three or four married sisters living in the town of Attendorn. One had twin girls.

I had a nice bedroom on the second floor, and it had a feather blanket on it. That was the first time I slept under a feather blanket. As it was a Saturday night you could hear the guys walking home singing "She'll Be Coming around the Mountain When She Comes" at the top of their lungs.

CHAPTER 48

Where Is My Cu zhild? (More Memories of Germany)

After Karl Michael sent the telegram to Attendorn he asked me to come to his home sometime for dinner. Remember: he had a story he wanted to tell me.

I was leery of any more help, for I had just been fleeced out of $20 dollars by a man who was going to give me a better rate of exchange for changing my dollars to marks for the trip. I was naïve—I gave the man $20, and he said he would be right back with my marks. Of course, I never saw him again.

Somehow, I felt Karl was sincere, so several weeks later I got a pass and looked up his home in the suburbs of Mainz. A streetcar dropped me off not too far from his home. He lived in a nice home, not very large, with his wife and a small son. She served a typical German meal, and he opened a bottle of wine.

After dinner with the table cleared of the dishes he brought out pictures and documents and told me this story.

It was during the war, and he and his wife were going out for the evening. They left their five-year-old daughter with a babysitter. When they came back, the babysitter and their daughter were nowhere to be found. Because of the war people were disappearing all the time. Karl went to the police, but they were not much help. At times the police came with pictures of girls the age of their daughter that had been found dead. He claimed that they were not his girl. He showed me pictures and documents of the missing child. He thought that she had been kidnapped and somehow ended up in a orphanage in Frankfurt, about 30 miles away. Because of the war they were not allowed to go there to check on her. When they finally could go to the orphanage, records were vague because of the war. They felt that she had been adopted by a couple in the United States. Somehow they were hoping I may be able to help them find their daughter.

In 1978 I returned to Germany with Gracie and Gene, and we were to be met at the airport by Karl Michael. Gracie, Gene and I landed in Frankfurt in 1978 after an overnight flight from Chicago. There were no direct flights from DFW to Germany at that time. There also was no advance seat selection, and the seats left when we got to Chicago were the least desirable seats on the plane. They were the center seats in the middle of the coach class section of the airplane that had five seats across—with two persons on each side of us. We were seated one behind the other in the middle of the coach section.

It was 26 years since I last had seen Karl Michael, and I had no idea what he would look like. Likewise, he had no idea what the GI he made friends with in 1952 would look like. We got off the plane and went through customs, and I started looking for Karl. I soon heard my name being paged, and I went to the place designated. No one came forward to meet me. So I went to the announcer and had Karl paged. Again no one came forward. In desperation, the announcer took my hand and led me to a bald-headed gentleman standing nearby. In this way we finally got together after 26 years. We went to a nearby restaurant to get reacquainted and to get a bite to eat. Here he told us what he had learned about his kidnapped daughter since I left many years ago.

The orphanage would not give out the information on the whereabouts of his child. He was sure that she had survived the war and had been adopted by a family in the United States. He had worked for the German railroad, and they helped him find his daughter. The employees of the German railroad contacted railroad workers in the United States and working together finally found where she was. She had been adopted by a family in North Dakota.

They started corresponding with the family and their daughter. Karl wanted to see his daughter again, so her adopted family sent money for Karl and his wife Erika to come to North Dakota and see their child. They had a very enjoyable visit with her, and when they prepared to leave for Germany, all agreed that it was best for her to stay with her adopted family in North Dakota. She was now happily married, still living in North Dakota. The

Michael family had exchanged visits with her adopted family a number of times.

We went on with our trip, taking our train to Attendorn, where my grandmother left in the early 1900s. Later we visited in Kaifenheim, the town from which my great-grandfather, Peter Fuhrman, came in 1868. We came back to Mainz, and we went sightseeing with Karl and Erika before returning to the U.S. We also met his son, Karl Jr., who was running a fast-food restaurant a short distance from the main railroad station in Mainz.

Gracie and I have been back to Mainz several times since our first visit in 1978. We learned that both Karl and Erika had passed away and that Karl Jr. was still operating the fast-food restaurant not far from the main railroad station. We always looked him up when we were in Mainz to eat, and he never would let us pay for our meal.

Karl accompanied us on the train to Mainz, where we had to change trains. He stayed with us until we were safely on our train to Attendorn.

To catch a train at the airport we had to go down a number of escalators to the train station under the airport. Luggage carts are taken on the escalators, and a lady behind us with a small child in her arms was coming down the escalators and lost control of her cart, which jammed at the bottom of the escalator—and she with the child kept on coming down. We had to move quickly to un-jam the cart to keep them from getting injured.

The train took us to Mainz, where we would have to change trains.

We needed to use the restroom, the "Toilette," which was in the basement of the station. The ladies went down stairs on one side and the men went down stairs on the other. To our amazement when we got below, it was a rather large open area, and you could see all the way through. The men could see the ladies waiting for a stall and the ladies could see the men standing along the walls in full view. The men had no stall, just a trough along the wall on three sides of the room. Gene did not have to go after he saw that, and Gracie made me stay close by.

Karl got us on the right train, and we were on our way to Attendorn. We would visit relatives in Attendorn and Kaifenheim for about 10 days before we would come back to Mainz and spend more time with Karl and learn more about his lost daughter before catching our flight back to Texas.

By then it had been about 24 hours since we had slept in a bed, and we were very tired. As soon as the train started Gracie and Gene were fast asleep and I was struggling to stay awake. I was afraid if I went to sleep, too, that we would miss the town where we had to change trains and end up at the North Sea. The conductor announced each stop as we went along, but in German.

He finally announced the next stop to be Finnentrop, which was where we needed to change trains to get to Attendorn.

As we were changing trains I remembered again the story my mother told us many times about when her mother came back to visit her hometown after coming to America to get married. I mentioned earlier that she was accompanied by her youngest son, Max Flusche.

Ocean liners were the only way to cross the ocean at that time, and one came into Bremerhaven on the North Sea. Then she took a train south toward Frankfurt and then had to change trains in Finnentrop to get to Attendorn.

Here's some more "meat' to add to that story: Prestige was everything in those days, and she had made folks in her hometown of Attendorn believe that she had married a wealthy man in America. She planned to ride the lowest fare train available from Bremerhaven to Finnentrop, then change to first class and arrive in Attendorn in glory. However, to her surprise they met her at the train station in Finnentrop. A large delegation with a band from Attendorn was there to greet her and watched as she crawled off of the lowest fare car and fouled her plan to arrive in style.

No such delegation greeted us as we changed trains. The train to Attendorn looked more like a streetcar—it was one car, and we were the only ones on it. It was a short ride to Attendorn, and we arrived late in the afternoon. We got off the train, and I went looking for a telephone to call our relatives to pick us up while Gracie and Gene waited at the train station.

They felt strange as I left them on the train platform, in a strange country. They did not know where anybody was, couldn't speak the language, and they were all alone by themselves.

I could not find a telephone, so I asked the train depot attendant where one was. He did not understand what I wanted and called a taxi.

We made it to the home of our relatives, who were a little perplexed that we used a taxi instead of calling them, but we were received with open arms. Of course, Gracie and Gene could not understand a word they were saying. I knew enough to be able to get around. We were so tired that we dozed off while talking to them over the dinner table.

We got acquainted with feather blankets on our bed. They are really neat. If you are hot, you just spread out the feathers so you have fewer feathers over you. If you are cold, just bunch them up.

They had a full morning of sight seeing planned for the next morning, but we would have slept all day if the youngest grandchild (Julia) had not awakened us playing outside our door at noon.

After our visit to Attendorn we continued on the train to Koblenz on the Rhein River where we were to meet relatives of our great-grandfather. At Koblenz the Mosel flows into the Rhein River.

Treis on the Mosel

Stationed with me in Germany was a distant relation of mine, Ewald Fuhrmann. He is a descendant of Peter Fuhrmann of Kaifenheim, Germany, just as I am. One weekend we decided to go to Kaifenheim and visit our distant relatives. We took the streetcar from Gonsenheim, where we were stationed, to Mainz to catch a train to Kaifenheim. We went along the Rhein River to Koblenz, where we changed trains that would take us along the Mosel River toward Trier in West Germany. We would ride this train to Karden, where we would catch a bus to Kaifenheim about five miles away.

This is in the middle of the Mosel wine country. The high hillsides that dropped off down to the Mosel had grapes growing in rows. The slopes were steep, so they used carts riding cables from above to bring the grapes down. You would need strong legs to work in these fields.

It so happened that when we got off the train, Tries, the sister city of Karden across the Mosel River, was having its annual Winzer Fest. We got a room in a house to spend the night. The parade was in full swing, and a girl who was older than we were was running a store along the parade route. She took us upstairs over her store, so we could look out of a window and see the parade better.

The parade showed all the stages of making wine, from picking grapes off the vine to crushing them in huge vats by trampling on them with their feet. We saw how the juice is extracted into a huge wine barrel to hold the wine until it is ready and, of course, the finished wine. Marching in the parade were about a dozen good-looking winzer matchen in their drendel dresses with grapevine hairpieces on their heads. They were having a ball, waving at all the people along the parade route. It was a very joyous occasion for the town.

Later we met the winzer matchen, and we bought them a glass of wine. They were all young girls, only a few years younger than me, I noticed they all had big legs—I guess from working in the hillside fields. There was one dark-haired girl who caught my eye, and I called her the "Swarza-Katz." We met the girls later in the evening at a dance, and I danced with her. She was a little on the heavy side with the big legs but a good dancer. In the course of our conversation I mentioned "katzen yammer' which she got a kick out of, and I had to repeat it to a friend of hers. I did not get her name.

Gracie and I have been back in Karden several times in recent years, but we never did cross the Mosel River into Tries to see what it looks like today.

Kaifenheim

The next morning we caught a rundown bus to Kaifenheim. The bus left us off at the road, and we walked down into Kaifenheim. We passed a farmer with a cow pulling a wagon as we continued on our way to the Nick Kaiser home on Hamp Strasse. We heard that the army had confiscated all horses for the war. All they had left to pull the wagon was a cow. Ewald had been to Kaifenheim once before, and he knew the way to the Nick Kaiser Home. Upon seeing Nick Kaiser's wife, you could tell that she was a Fuhrmann.

Like all of the homes in Kaifenheim, Nick's place consisted of a large courtyard with all of his buildings around the cobblestone courtyard. They stored hay in the loft of the barn in which they stored their agriculture equipment and had a way to lift the hay up in the barn with a sling powered by an electric motor. They had about three acres of land on the side of their place where they could keep a cow. There was a place to milk cows, raise pigs and chickens. The rainwater from the roof of his buildings ran into a pit where they kept their manure from the livestock. Periodically, they would pump this liquid from the pit and spray it in the fields for fertilizer. There were no screens on the windows, and there were flies everywhere. All the windows had shutters that could be cranked closed in case of an air raid.

This was right after the war, and you could tell they were very poor, but they shared what they had with us. The house was built sometime around 1860. It was built out of native stones. It had a basement under it. The two-story house featured a stairway to the second floor and attic. The attics were used for additional bedrooms, with the dormers in the roof.

Nick's daughter Maria was married to Hans Gerson, who was killed during WW II on the Russian front. They had been married only a few months before he was killed. Maria had a five-year-old daughter, Beatrix, who was very quiet around us. We gave her a stick of gum and were able to pick her up and hold her. Years later, we learned Beatrix married Alois Wagner, and they lived for a long time in a beautiful home next to Maria. The Alois Wagners have five sons and about three grandchildren. Maria passed away sometime in late 2015.

When I paid my first visit, the family had stacked their wheat in a grain stack, and they were threshing grain when Ewald and I were there. The threshing machine was set up next to the stacked grain and pulled by an electric motor. There was a 220-volt electric line on poles close by, and they just reached up with a long, wooden pole and hooked the motor to the line. The motor was connected to the threshing machine by a large, flat belt just like we do, except we use a tractor for power. There probably was no gasoline for a tractor if they had a tractor, so they used electric power.

The grain was caught in sacks as it came out of the machine. The straw went into a hay baler and was baled.

They lived a short distance from St. Nicholas Catholic Church, and they took us to church with them that Sunday. We had to go with Nick upstairs to the choir loft to sit right down in front along the rail, so we could see well. This was during lent, and the doors covering the statues on the altar would normally be closed, but because Ewald and I, descendants of Peter Fuhrmann, were in church that morning, the doors on the altar were open to allow us to see the statues.

We learned that Peter Fuhrman left Kaifenheim in 1868, just two years after he built a new home. Peter was born in Gamlen, and his wife was from there, as well. The story goes that a note on a loan that Peter signed for a family member was defaulted, and Peter had to sell his house to pay off the note. He came to America in 1868 with his five sons and eventually settled close to St. Joseph in Kossuth County, Iowa. Two sons died from pneumonia after arriving in America.

In 1912 Joseph Fuhrmann, one of Peter's sons, went back to Kaifenheim and visited friends and relations in Kaifenheim and Gamlen, the town he left in 1868 as a child. He planned to return to the USA on the Titanic, but it was booked full.

It was in 1920 that the church received a new high altar. The altar cost 40,000 marks, and the church still owed 20,000 marks. Joseph was so thankful for being spared from the Titanic that he paid off the 20,000. Because we were descendants of Peter, church members opened the doors on the altar during lent so we could see the altar Joseph gave to the church.

We walked everywhere with Nick. Several miles from Kaifenheim is the Schwanenkiche, built in 1825. This is a beautiful church with no homes around it. This church was used by all the neighboring villages until they could build a church of their own. I have been told it is now used for weddings and other special occasions only.

Nick took us to a Benediction Monastery and the famous Maria Laach's Abbey Church, many miles from Kaifenheim. He took us on a bus, and you could see that he was counting his pennies for the fare. This Monastery is by a large lake that formed inside of a dormant volcano. It has a beautiful church by it. Geese used the lake for a resting place on their migration south for the winter.

In 2008, about 56 years later, Gracie and I visited Kaifenheim and Wolfgang Wagner, a grandchild of Maria. Wolfgang and his family took us to see Maria Laach. It was greatly expanded into a tourist attraction and was much different than it was at the time we visited it with Nick Kaiser.

2009 visit to Nuremberg

In the summer of 2009, Gracie and I took a Viking River Cruise that took us from Amsterdam to Budapest. A-100 mile canal took us to the Danube, which flows through Nuremberg before coming to Budapest. A guided tour of Nuremberg took us past the old prison where I had spent three months of my life while in the army in Germany. There was only one wing of the old prison left. It lay idle with a high fence around it. We assumed that it was being preserved because of the history of the war crimes trial that took place there at one time in the past.

Revisting Germany where I was stationed in the Army.

CHAPTER 49

Army Life

We spent over 50 percent of our time out in the field away from our barracks. When it came time to go into the field we went—no matter what the weather was. It seemed like the weather was always bad when we were out on training exercises.

I played in a golf tournament here at "home." When it was raining it would get sloppy in a hurry around camp. We all wore boots, and mud would be six inches deep.

I was in the wire section of "B" battery of the 2nd Armored Division. Our 105-millimeter canons were mounted in an open-top armored tank powered by two Cadillac engines. We would set up behind our front lines and shoot over the heads of the infantry in front of us. The wire section's job was to lay army field wire between the different batteries of "B" Section. Sometimes we would have to lay a line to the forward observers. They are the ones that directed our fire. All wires were run from a switchboard to the different battery of guns and a line to headquarters section. I had the job of switchboard operator, and I set up my switchboard while the rest of the section was laying twisted-pair army field wire to each of the A, B, C, and D batteries. I would have to take my army-issued folding spade and dig a hole deep enough to hide the switchboard and me (the operator). Coming with a telephone background, I was in the army one day, and I learned everything I would learn in the army about telephones.

Inspections

When we got back from a field trip, the first thing we would do is clean up our equipment. We then had inspection. We would have to lay out all of our equipment—all cleaned up. We would have our boots shined, all clean uniforms, buttons all buttoned. When the captain got around to us we would stand at attention while we were being inspected. We would be "gigged" if he found something wrong. This usually meant we would get extra KP or have to pick up rocks on the parade field on Saturday.

Once in a while they would go around and inspect the rooms. You would have to stand at the foot of your bed. You would be checked on how neat you made your bed, how your shoes shined, how all buttons were buttoned. The inspector would open your footlocker and see how neat the contents were.

Guard duty

Once a month we would get guard duty. You would eat an early breakfast and fall out into formation at about 6 a.m. for inspection. The Sergeant of Arms inspected you for a clean and neat uniform then would take your weapon and inspect it while we all stood at attention. We were then given our area to guard. You could be the guard to check persons coming and going from the base at the gate. You could have been assigned to watch the outer perimeter of the base. Or you could have been assigned to be sure no one messed with the tanks and trucks in the motor pool. You had four-hour shifts—four hours on and four hours off. The young boys would like to slip through a hole in the fence and get in your trucks or whatever you were guarding.

KP duty

About once a month you would get KP duty. You would have to report early to the mess hall. We did not have to peel potatoes—they had a machine in which we put the potatoes that used water and electricity. The potatoes were ground down to where there were no peels.

Mail call

About once a week we had mail call, during which the mail orderly came by with the mail. He would call out your name when you had a letter. I usually had a letter from Gracie. Toward the end of my tour of duty, those got a little less frequent. The last one was a "dear John" letter about a couple of months before I came home. As I noted before in the family section, things still worked out fine between us and for us.

Coming home

The last names of those leaving to go home were called out each day. I waited until my name was finally called. A train took us back to Bremerhaven, where we caught our ship back home. Our ship stopped in South Hampton, England, and we all got passes to go ashore. I got some "Fish and Chips" at a local pub and went back to the ship. I do not remember getting a drink of English beer. Eleven days later we landed at New Jersey, where all returning troops were processed. A two-engine Army plane few us to Fort Hood, Texas. The first thing I did when I got back was to go to the Sears store in Gainesville and kiss Gracie.

This was the last thing I did when I left and the first thing I did when I got back.

Beatrix home

1000 Jahre

Our hotel in Kaiserslauten

SECTION IV

Just five years after we went to dial service in Muenster, two years after installing Motorola Push Button mobile service, we got into CATV. I had no problem getting a franchise from the city in 1967. The main reason I built the system was because the Cowboy football games were usually blacked out of Dallas, and I wanted to be able to show them to our customers.

CHAPTER 50

The Beginning of CATV

In 1967 after we had converted our telephone system to dial service, and our mobile telephone service was established with its antenna on the city water tank, it gave me time to look toward cable television. We had our push-button mobile dial telephone service on the Muenster city water tower, and I needed the antenna to be higher to get better coverage. I saw a way to kill two birds with one stone: build a CATV tower and put the mobile phone antenna on top of the tower and use the tower to mount the CATV antennas.

About this time Dallas received a NFL franchise, and football became very popular. A reasonable signal could be received off the air from Dallas/Fort Worth. When the game did not sell out and was blacked out, we could always get the game on Channel 12. However when the Cowboys played on Monday Night Football we had a problem. They played on ABC, and the only ABC station that did not come out of Dallas/Fort Worth was Lawton, Okla. This station could not be picked up off the air in our area.

Also, ABC Channel 8 did not always have a good signal when received off air antenna. Weather conditions could interfere with good service. This, and no football when played on Monday night and blacked out of Dallas when the game did not sell out, caused us to receive many requests for CATV service. FCC also mandated that power and telephone companies could not refuse to allow CATV companies from putting their cables on our poles. I did not want anyone else to be climbing on my poles and putting up cables that could possibly compete with me in the future. There were no restrictions for telephone companies to provide CATV service at the time.

CATV is unlike anything in the telephone business. There is no resemblance between the ways the two operate, except that they are up on poles. Telephones are a low-voltage direct current system, while CATV works in the radio frequencies, and there is no resemblance between the two. I did not have the electronic background that would have made CATV easier to learn. They did not teach it in high school, and I certainly did not learn it in the cotton patch.

Jerrold Electronics had just come out with a new transistorized system, the Starline One. They sponsored technical seminars on these systems throughout the United States with many in Dallas. I attended everyone that I could. Also I read every magazine and literature I could get my hands on to understand how the systems work. I attended the 1965 United States Independent Telephone Convention in Chicago to learn more about CATV. CATV was the main topic of the convention. Gracie stayed home taking care of our young family.

Finally, I felt like I knew enough about the Jerrold Starline One system to build the Muenster system.

The first system

Ed Dart was the Jerrold salesman at the time, and he helped me get started. First we had to run a spectrum study to see what channels we could expect to receive at the Headend site. The survey showed we would need a 250-foot tower to get satisfactory signals.

At 250 feet in the air and with a large antenna system we were able to receive a satisfactory signal—that is, all except channel 6 from Wichita Falls, Texas. The lower the channel number the larger the antenna has to be. All of the antennas were huge, but the Channel 6 antenna array was a monster; it was 4 yaggi antennas on a special mounting. Picking up Channel 6 from Wichita Falls, this antenna was looking parallel with a heavily loaded Cooke County electric power line with ancient glass insulators that caused static interference. We never did get a good picture, but it was better than nothing.

The next year, after we put our system into service, the FCC ruled that telephone companies could not provide CATV service in the same area in which they had telephone service. We received orders that we must get out of the CATV business. Nobody wanted our small system, and we would have to shut it down if we could not get dispensation from this rule. We could provide CATV service under an affiliated company but not Muenster Telephone Company—so North Texas Communications Company was born.

Designing the new CATV company

Lotus123 proved to be a valuable tool in designing CATV systems. I used it to build new systems and to redesign our older systems. After I had the distance between poles entered into the computer, along with the cable loss at the highest frequency, we were ready to design a system. These were not two-way systems, so I did not calculate the return path loss.

Just five years after we went to dial service in Muenster, two years after installing Motorola Push Button mobile service, we got into CATV. I had no problem getting a franchise from the city in 1967. The main reason I built the system was because the Cowboy football games were usually blacked out of Dallas, and the only station carrying the game was Channel 6 out of Wichita Falls. When they played on Monday night on ABC the only station within range was out of Lawton, Okla.

Jerrold Electronics held seminars regularly on the electronics of a cable system. They were usually held in Dallas and I made everyone of these I could. Everything about a CATV system is up on the poles. We had no bucket truck, and the meters with tubes that I had to use needed 110 volts to operate. I had to carry a bulky meter strapped over my neck and climb the poles when working on the system. I stole power wherever I could get it.

I had a battery-operated inverter in my truck, but the meter would not read right with that kind of power. We spun the CATV cable on 2 M strand. Charles Cook and Gene Walterscheid were working for the company when we built the cable system. The first subscribers we connected to the system were Bernard and Delores Swirczynski over on Hickory Street.

I got a lease on three acres northeast of town on Al Haverkamp's pasture and purchased a tower from Fort Worth Tower Company.

Earlier systems were hampered by the limitation of the amplifiers—there were only 12 channel systems.

I took an old washing machine transmission and built a bulletin board around it. By mounting a camera on it I was able show weather dials and a number of events taking place that week in Muenster. You can see this system in the Gene Henry Fuhrman Telephone Museum.

Locally originated programming

Almost from the beginning we were carrying announcements and weather information on Channel 2. We had more time than money, so I built a device that allowed a camera to scan two levels of information posted in the system. It would move along the bottom showing weather and time, move up on the left end to the upper level, then scan across announcements to the right side before moving down again to pass across the weather. It did this day and night.

The gear works came from an old automatic washing machine I picked up at Walterschied Appliance. Under my direction the Fleitman welding shop three miles east of Muenster did the welding and cutting to make the system work. The electric motor came from a spare interrupter motor out of our XY dial CDO equipment. You can find this information system today in the Gene Henry Telephone Museum.

Remote broadcasting

For remote broadcasting we set up a studio in a Ford van/truck. Whenever the van was connected to the local origination cable I also had telephone service in it. I used a channel of Panhandle Carrier to provide telephone service. One end was in the telephone office and the matching end was in my van.

This was very useful when we televised a live program from the Knights of Columbus Hall in Muenster during a violent thunder strum. I was able to talk to Gracie, who was at home to make sure the family was all right.

CHAPTER 51

Cablecasting in the 1970s

The first programming we carried live on our cable system was shortly after we completed the cable system in 1968. We had an Open House to show off our new service—also it was Elizabeth Herr's retirement party. Herschel Tyler of Olney, Texas, brought his TV camera and recorder to Muenster to help us celebrate the occasion. We had the camera set up so that everyone in town could see who was coming into the front door of the telephone office. At first we could not figure why no one was coming to our open house. Then we realized everyone was camera shy, so we moved the camera into my office, and we had more people coming to the open house. I have the videotapes of this first program, but the equipment it was recorded on no longer exists, so it cannot be played.

We established a studio in a vacant room in the "Tin University" at Sacred Heart School, where we set up our first equipment. The building was the old high school building that had tin siding, so it was called the "Tin University." The local news and announcements were posted on the homemade machine that now is in the museum. Every Friday I would go to the Tin University and post the new announcements for the week. A telephone pole set on the east side of the building held the weather sensing equipment. We had rainfall, wind speed and direction, outside temperature, along with the time of day.

I showed several of the junior/senior boys, Mark Schmitt and Doug Yosten how to run the cameras for students who were in Brother Thomas' Speech and Drama classes. They would read their poetry over the cable system. Their parents could watch them from their home. Occasionally, the boys would chase the girls with the camera as the girls tried to hide. Someone broke into our TV studio one night and posted pornographic pictures in front of the camera. Our police chief at the time was Helen

Tompkins, and it did not take her long to find out who did the act and made him pay for damage.

From this same studio during the 1970s we carried the "Fr. Bede's Program." It was an hour-long program every Monday at 8 p.m. We had heavy competition from the Monday Night Football game. Fr. Bede was the assistant pastor at Sacred Heart Church and enjoyed interviewing anyone he could get before the cameras. He provided the guest, and we produced the program. I had my two sons, Gene and Kent, operating the cameras. I was on the console, selecting cameras, and by means of an intercom system I directed the boys to which shots I wanted from the cameras. This went on for close to 10 years until Fr. Bede was transferred away from Muenster. I believe that everybody in town had been on the program at least once.

When we built our cable television system we included a local origination cable that ran from the public school in the north part of town to the telephone office. I could tap into this cable anywhere along the route and carry a program live on our cable system. This cable was also extended over to the Baptist Church on 121 N. Pecan Street, as well. Utilizing this cable numerous times we carried programs live from the public school, Sacred Heart Church, First Baptist Church and the KC Hall.

I used a company van to establish a mobile studio. I would move the control console and all equipment needed to broadcast a program live on the cable into the van. For a number of years I carried the graduation ceremony live from the Muenster public school auditorium, as well as from Sacred Heart Church for the graduation ceremonies of Sacred Heart High school.

I also had it arranged so that when I was connected to the local origination cable I would also have telephone service in my mobile studio. One time we were cable casting the Jaycee annual banquet live that was taking place upstairs in the KC Hall. I had the mobile studio on the north side of the Hall. I had two cameras set up upstairs, operated by Mark Schmitt and Doug Yosten. I was in the mobile studio directing the program when one of those vicious Texas thunderstorms came up. I used the telephone to check with Gracie at home to see how she was making it through the storm. This was our first telephone service over the cable television system. For this I used a channel of Panhandle Carrier, which operated in the upstream spectrum of the cable system. No return amplifiers were needed to get back to the telephone office. This was a carrier we had retired from providing telephone service to Rosston earlier.

When they tore down the old parish hall and built the new Community Center I moved my equipment to a special room that they had included for this purpose. Not too long after we moved Fr. Bede was transferred away from Muenster. I continued programming after he left. One program that I still have is Teddy Trept and his Schammel Kapella Band from Dallas. Teddy played the Thither, Gary Nelson played the accordion. There was one other member of his band, but his name escapes me. Also I have Sister Genevieve s first grade students of the '70s in a play, "The Lady of Lourdes.' These were recorded on a tape recorder and later transferred to cassettes.

Soon after I moved to the new Community Center the church started receiving complaints that I was using the church property for private use, so I moved all of my equipment to the telephone office. We had just completed the addition to the telephone building, which included the large meeting room that, among many other uses, could be utilized for television programming. The control room is now Brian Hess's office. At that time video cameras needed very bright lights to operate in a satisfactory manner. The pipe railing along the ceiling in the telephone company's large meeting room and in the Community Center Snap meeting room at Sacred Heart Church was used to hold the quartz lighting fixtures.

As we continued to broadcast through the years we accumulated quite a bit of equipment. Some was purchased and some was built out of old parts. We had two black-and-white cameras (there were no color cameras at the time) on tripods with wheels, a control console that had three preview sets and one master television set built in the console. From the console we could select which camera shots were sent into the system. We had an intercom system between the camera operators and the console operator. We had purchased a 16-millimeter Sony video tape recorder (there were no cassette recorders). From old parts I made a crawl to give credits and a horizontal wheel to attach pictures to be shown. We had quite a studio but made no money for the company.

We continued to carry live programming from the telephone office for about a year when it was discontinued and all of the equipment taken out to make room for an office.

CHAPTER 52

Distant Learning in the '90s—
The North Texas Educational Network

W hen we plowed a fiber cable from Forestburg to Valley View and from Valley View to Muenster, I saw an opportunity to provide distant learning to the schools. This included the Forestburg School, Era School, Valley View School, Muenster public school and Sacred Heart School. When we plowed a cable and it passed a school, we would include a fiber cable to the school. All schools were glad to try out the exciting new method of teaching—except Valley View. They asked us not to complete the fiber cable into the school. We left it rolled up, buried outside the school, and it was never used.

Our first system consisted of a teachers' console and three cabinets made of wood by Rudy Koesler in the home-ag department of the Public School. The teachers' console held four small televisions on which the teacher could view classes in four other schools. Also, the students in the class could view the four other schools on large monitors in front of the teacher. One camera showed the teacher, and one showed the students in the teacher's classroom. We built large cabinets to hold the television monitors in the remote classrooms.

We demonstrated how the system worked by setting up in three classrooms demonstrations at North Central Texas College in Gainesville. A senator and several legislators from Austin attended the demonstration. We had the teacher console set up in one classroom, and we set up two other classrooms as a setting like taking a course. The participants could see and hear all that was taking place at the other classrooms on the system. It was quite impressive.

From that demonstration, the teachers' console with the televisions and cameras were installed in a classroom at the Muenster public school. The system was designed for classes to be originated from any school. In Sacred Heart, Forestburg and Era we had a large cabinet that held three 20-inch monitors. Each classroom was designed to see the teacher and two other schools.

English and computer were taught from Era, Spanish was taught from Muenster. The teacher in Era liked to move around in the classroom while she was teaching, so we experimented with a camera that would follow her around.

The program seemed highly successful, so we applied for and received a $150,000 grant from the REA to install five classrooms with all new equipment. A fiber cable was extended to the college in Gainesville, so we had four schools and the college on the network. Valley View never did come in to join the system. We used special cameras that would zoom in on a student that wanted to talk. The student would push a button to talk, triggering the camera to zoom in. We had four 20-inch television sets suspended from the ceiling with a camera that followed the teacher in each classroom. The teacher also had a document camera on which she could show documents and write instructions as she would with a blackboard.

We had a classroom all set up in the Forestburg School when it burned to the ground about two weeks before school was to start. The telephone company owns an old bank building close to our telephone office so a classroom was set up for the student to receive the NTEN classes there.

The new system with the college operated about five years. Spanish and English and Math were the main subjects taught on the system. The college offered a number of dual-credit courses. We had a classroom set up where the Internet room upstairs is now so we could watch how the classes were coming along. I was amazed at the lack of discipline in the classrooms. The students did not show any respect for the teachers. They did not change what they were doing when the teacher came into the room. Some slept through the class. The teacher never did call on a student by name. Soon teachers got to where they did not want to teach certain schools for lack of discipline in the school.

Era had a change in superintendents and discontinued using NTEN. The college taught classes with only a few students taking the course.

College administrators finally said they no longer could justify the classes and discontinued participating in the educational network. When the college quit, the NTEN program ended.

The schools kept the camera and television equipment, but we recovered all of the American Light wave equipment we used to transport the class information between the schools.

With all of the equipment idle, we started using some of it to televise the Church service from Sacred Heart Church on the cable system. Today the light wave equipment is being cannibalized to transport channels 2, 55 and 70 from Muenster to the Headend east of Valley View. Some of the classroom equipment is used to televise the 9 a.m. church service from Sacred Heart Church on channel 2. Normally three areas have their own Channel 2 announcements, but when the camera equipment is turned on in church automatically all areas of the cable system are switched to the church service. This includes Valley View, Lake Kiowa, Collinsville, The Ranch, Pioneer Valley, the Shenandoah trailer park and Saint Jo.

Eventually we were asked to cablecast the funeral of Gary Johnson from Windthorst, Texas, who was killed in the war in Iraq. Their church would be too small for the people that would attend the funeral. The service was cablecasted from St. Mary's church into the parish hall across the street from the church and in the school gymnasium. Thanks to Wylie and Floyd, who set up the system, everything worked fine. We cablecasted the wake service Saturday evening on Feb. 2, 2007 and the funeral service the next day. The ladies of St. Mary's served dinner to the many visitors that came to the funeral. We left for home before they started to serve, so Gayle and Mike Humpert give us a plate of sausage and cake to take back with us.

Gary Johnson was buried next to his uncle in Archer City who was killed in the Viet Nam war. Along the funeral route, a distance of 11 miles, an American flag was posted every 300 yards along the highway.

CHAPTER 53

The First Satellite-receiving Dish

It was in 1982 that satellite television came to Muenster when we installed a six-meter earth station dish in the northeast corner of the West Truck Center yard across from the telephone office. This dish received signals from satellites 22,000 miles above the earth located over the equator between Hawaii and South America. This is the same earth station you see in the yard today across from the telephone office that is no longer being used. The reason we installed our satellite dishes in town and not at the tower was to prevent them from being damaged by kids with rifles from the road. The red light at the top of our 250-foot tower was continually being shot out.

Lenis Perkins was our TV tech at the time when we poured the base in preparation for mounting the big dish. After getting the dish mounted we laid a large coaxial cable over to the ready room in the West Truck Center, where we located the electronics. We had to add air-conditioning to keep the equipment cool. We had to learn how to line up the dish to the satellite to get our best signal. When we built the original cable system we included a cable that allowed us to feed programming from downtown to be carried throughout the system. This cable fed our satellite channels into our cable system.

We had to upgrade our cable system with a new technology for the amplifiers to carry up to 23 additional channels of television. Our original amplifiers were not designed to carry more than 12 channels and had to be modified. Superior Electrics out of Florida developed a transistorized modification that I installed in each Starline One amplifier that allowed us to carry the additional channels without the new channels causing interference on the system.

The operating frequency of these additional channels falls in the frequency range of airline communications with their control tower. A strong enough radio signal at the right frequency leaking out of our system would interfere with airliners flying overhead. We had to monitor our system constantly for leaks. The FCC gets all upset when pilots complain to them about interference.

Later we moved into a prefabricated concrete building in the West Truck Center yard and moved all electronics to it. A second dish was added when desired programs were on a different satellite.

One problem I had was with telephone men working on cable television. Charles Cook was my main outside man at the time, and he did not understand television technology and had it in his head that a telephone man could not learn CATV. He indoctrinated every person I hired to work with the same idea.

When we received the Valley View cable franchise we built the head end building with its tower and satellite dishes about three miles east of Valley View. We built it far enough off the road to protect our dishes and tower equipment from being damaged by random gun fire. We extended CATV east from our Valley View Head End across Lake Ray Roberts to Pioneer Valley and the Ranch subdivision.

In Pioneer Valley our cable service would go out at times and we would find that the electric meter powering our system would be stolen. Many times the Electric Co-op would find their stolen meter at a place they had disconnected for lack of payment.

As more and more television became available on different satellites we kept adding more dishes and more receiving equipment in the concrete building under the tower, so that we finally had to add a second building.

In about 1990 fiber cables replaced the T-Carrier systems for long distance service and about the same time started to be used to transport television. Fiber optics revolutionized television service. Fiber optic cables can carry an unlimited number of channels of television for great distances without the needing to be amplified.

Fiber optics allowed us to acquire cable systems in Lake Kiowa, Collinsville, and Lindsay, and later on Saint Jo. It gave us the ability to combine all of our systems on one Head-End at the Valley View Head End.

We can serve all of our towns from the one location. It did away with head-end equipment in Muenster, Lindsay, Lake Kiowa, and Saint Jo. 8.

Today, our system carries 68 channels of regular television, 20 channels of high-definition, 29 channels of stereo music and 40 channels of digital home theater channels. If you cannot find a channel you want to watch you can always go to Video on Demand (VOD) for more television.

The television system today

As this book was going to press our television system has been extended to Saint Jo, Gainesville, Lake Kiowa, Callensville, Tioga Sanger and Nocona. With fiber to the home and with the relaxing of the regulation of CATV, it was possible to expand our system to levels that were unthinkable a few years ago.

Today all the different services that Nortex provides are carried into the home on the fiber cable. The two-way traffic is carried on one thin fiber. Perfectly good copper cables filled with a jelly like substance that provided telephone and Internet service in our system now lie in the ground unused. Coaxial cables provided hundreds of channels of television into the home, but they all lacked the high-speed Internet capability and reliable service of the fiber cable.

The old tower

The idea was to cut the guy wires on the north side and let the tower fall south. The guy cables were cut—but the old tower stood defiant. It teamed with a good south wind to keep standing. Like a steer to be slaughtered it resisted to the end. While I was waiting for the tower to fall I heard the tower mumbling:

I did every task they asked of me for 44 years, and now they are getting rid of me. Earlier years I had a heavy CATV antenna load with mobile service on my top. When the wind blew, it caused me to rock—back and forth I would rock. For over 25 years I rocked. At first I enjoyed it, but then I got tired of it, and I got weak in my joints and I was afraid it might cause me to fall down. Then there was that kid with his high-powered rifle. Every time I got my pretty red light fixed up, that kid came along and shot it out again. I was sure glad when he grew up and my light was safe again. With my light out I was afraid an airplane would come along and fly into me when they could not see me at night.

Then I was sure glad to get rid of those CATV antennas. Those new-fangled wireless Internet antennas came along. They were not as big or cumbersome as those TV antennas—and in my old age I kind of liked that.

Then this young, self-supporting tower comes along. My boss knows I am getting old and suspects that I am getting a little weak in some of my joints. Besides, he can buy the land this young whippersnapper sits on and does not have to pay rent. They believe that I do not have too many years left and the chance to get rid of me for this young guy was too good to pass up.

I remember like it was yesterday, the day I went up in 1967. I had a new white and orange paint job and was ready for work. Halfway up they put two pretty red lights and topped me off with a huge red light that went on and off all night. I sure was proud of it. I was built a section at a time. A wench truck out of the way on the west side with a block at my base pulled my sections up—one at a time. To keep from having to climb, the tower men would catch a ride on a section as it was pulled up into place. At times a strong wind would cause them to sail out a ways from the tower as they went up.

Then they hung those big ugly antennas on my side. Little ones at the top and huge ones down lower. I did not mind it at first but 25 years is a long time.

There was my neat little concrete block building under me to house electronic stuff. It had that concrete flat roof with an asphalt finish to keep from leaking. They put a concrete roof on it, so that when ice fell off of me during an ice storm it would not damage equipment in my little house.

There were a great many requests for CATV service to bring in the Dallas Cowboy games when blacked out. My boss saw an opportunity to solve two problems by putting the mobile radio antennas on my top and my sides to mount the CATV antennas. This is when I came to life. I really had to work to get professional football out of Dallas.

Ed Dart of Jerrold Electronics helped my boss design the system. Jerrold Electronics had just come out with a new transistorized CATV system. A signal survey showed that I would have to be at least 250 feet high to get a decent signal out of Dallas. For the Cowboys, when they were blacked out, we would have to go to Channel 6 out of Wichita Falls. As a young franchise, the early games would not always sell out, and the game would be blacked out of Dallas, and that is when I had to go to work. That high ridge by Saint Jo and the adjacent power lines made it difficult for me to bring in that Wichita Falls station.

OH, OH . . . they are pulling on my guy wires—I feel shaky. I do not want to go; I still have a lot of life in me. I can do this job. Come on wind hold me up. Stop pulling on my guy wires.

Oh, Oh, here I go—Goodbye, everyone.

SECTION V

OUR TRAVELS

The room started trembling, and Gracie asked, "What's happening?" I told her, "I believe we are having an earthquake." (You don't think it really can happen).

CHAPTER 54

We Survived the Great Earthquake

I n 1989 Gracie and I traveled to California to attend the U.S.T.A. National Convention. Upon arriving in San Francisco, site of the event, we checked into the San Francisco Hilton. The Hilton is a multi-towered hotel in the heart of San Francisco. I requested a non-smokers room as close to the ground as I could get. I had been hearing that San Francisco was due for an earthquake. We were assigned to a room on the 12th floor of the 47-story tower No. 3 (the oldest tower, we later found out).

The afternoon meetings were over, and I had returned to my room and planned to relax a while before the evening events were to start. Gracie had just returned to the room from another meeting and was lounging in her slip (Gracie says she would never be late for work if she dressed as fast as she did that day). I was watching the World Series Baseball Game with my shoes off. The room started trembling, and Gracie asked, "What's happening?" I told her, "I believe we are having an earthquake." (You don't think it really can happen).

The room then began to violently shake back and forth. We could hear the building groan as it rapidly swayed.

Gracie saw the walls by the window moving in and out. I pondered for a moment as to what might be the safest spot in which to be—in our room or in the basement with a 47-story building above us. I turned to put on my shoes, and Gracie told me to catch the television set.

It had come all the way out of the cabinet and was about to fall. It still had a picture on it as I pushed it back in and closed the doors on it to keep it in. I looked back and the screen was still lighted, but blank (the television station had gone off the air). I opened the doors again and turned the set off and closed them again.

The hotel fire alarm system started sounding in the hall. A voice came on the intercom and advised us the fire alarm had been activated and we should stand by for further instructions. The power was off by the time I opened the door to the hall to see what it looked like out there (to see if the rest of the hotel was still there), and a few people were already moving toward the stairways. Gracie caught up with me, and we vacated the room moving toward the fire exit.

The stairwells were illuminated by battery-powered lights, and more and more people joined us as we moved down. The fire alarm kept sounding, and a voice kept telling us to stand by. An elderly lady moving slowly in front of us kept stopping each time the alarm sounded, and we urged her to continue. One section of the stairwell was dark, as the emergency light did not work. In a number of places the plaster cracked on the walls.

We emerged at the bottom into the garage entrance and found a person with a battery-powered radio. We huddled to find out how extensive the damage was.

The damage was extensive

Reporters told of a section of a double-decked freeway that had collapsed, and I understood it to be on the San Francisco end of the Bay Bridge to Oakland. They also told of fires in the Marina area. They reported the quake to be of 6.9 intensity, which is a pretty good quake, centered some 40 miles from us. We could not see any damage around us. We moved out onto the street to get a better view and were told to stay inside the hotel, that it was the safest place to be since it was "earthquake proof."

Upon moving back into the hotel lobby, some women were crying, some people were barefooted and some were in nightclothes. An aftershock of equal force was expected at any time. Aftershocks did occur but were not of sufficient intensity for us to feel them. Glass was on the floor from broken chandeliers. We moved to the AT&T hospitality room on the third floor, where food and drinks were available.

The payphones I checked immediately after the shock did not work but 1+ dialing could be completed from the AT&T room when we got there. I called our son, Gene in Denton, Texas, and told him we were all right and asked him to tell that to our family and friends. It was not long before AT&T ran out of drinks.

The hotel gave out boxes of fresh fruit, free food and free soft drinks. All we had to do was stand in line to get these. It took an hour and more at times to get food. Many people went back to their rooms and picked up blankets and pillows and slept in the lobby of the hotel. Mixed with the crowd sleeping in the lobby were street people, who came off the streets to seek shelter and slumber. After the first night, there were security guards at the entrances, and you had to have your hotel key to get into the hotel. About midnight they announced that an elevator was working in each tower if anyone wanted to go back to their rooms.

I felt as safe in the room as in the lobby of the hotel, so we decided to go back to our room for the night. Gracie wanted to walk up but I could see no need to be wary of the elevators, they had security guards operating them. We found our room in good shape; the ice bucket was about to fall on the floor and Gracie' s cosmetics were in disarray in the bathroom, but there were no major problems. The bathroom floor was wet from water that sloshed out of the commode.

The hotel fed us an evening meal and dessert at 10 p.m. Food remained free until we left to go home Friday. Wednesday we walked with a group of friends through San Francisco looking at the damage. The convention had stopped at exactly 5:04 p.m. Tuesday, and the airport was closed. Rental cars were not available.

The I. Magnum building nearby had all the windows broken, and crews were knocking out the glass that remained. Elsewhere, we found scattered broken windows, cracks in buildings, steel exposed in some building supports, cracked window ledges and buildings damaged at the tops from bumping together. Besides providing free food until Friday, the hotel did not charge us for the last two days in the hotel. The hotel staff was just super and seemed to do a great deal more than what was really necessary.

Stories within "The Story"

Everyone had stories about the quake and their personal experiences. Those on the 47th floor got quite a ride as the building swayed quite a few feet back and forth. They could not stand and fell to the floor—all the dishes broke, and water sloshed out of the commodes. One man was knocked out when his television set fell on him. Lamps fell off the tables.

Others reported stepping over their broken TV sets as they left the room. One elevator jammed on Fisherman's Wharf, and crews had to cut through a wall to rescue them out of the top of the elevator. John Fisher, head of AT&T, and his wife were about to board a yacht in the harbor when the quake hit. She fell into the water—and could not swim. John jumped in to save her and dislocated his shoulder and ended up in the hospital.

Gordon and Ava Lou (friends of ours) tried to get under the bed in their room, but they would not fit. They stayed in their room a while after the quake and felt some of the aftershocks. Friends staying in other hotels had no power or lights, and their buildings were dark.

Our folks back home were aware of the damage caused by the quake long before we knew how extensive it was. With no power or television stations we only had scattered radio reports to tell us of the damage. From our location there appeared to be very little damage. We were fortunate to be in an earthquake-proof building. While it rocked and shook, it sustained very little damage.

Would we go back to San Francisco? It would not bother me to go back, but Gracie says she has had enough for a while.

CHAPTER 55

Nova Scotia

It was a warm summer July day when we left Muenster to meet our Collette ride to DFW airport. We stopped at McDonald's in Gainesville to get breakfast before heading over to the First State Bank parking lot to meet our ride. I had on a long sleeve shirt, and we had packed warm clothes, for we were going to a cool climate. In the parking lot we met several persons who would be on the tour with us. There was a lady from Gainesville—her husband dropped her off, kissed her goodbye and left. A couple from Edmund, Okla., also joined us after spending the night in Gainesville so it would not be that long drive from Oklahoma early in the morning. The husband was a retired fireman from Dallas. We enjoyed being with them at times on the tour.

Our van driver was from Fort Worth. He took us on to Denton, where we met more people who would be on the tour. The driver, not familiar with Lewisville, drove past the shortcut through Lewisville and went on up to Highway 121 then back over to the airport.

After claiming our luggage from the van we headed inside to get our boarding passes and got rid of our checked luggage.

I always have a hard time getting through security, and this time was no exception. There are two ways to get through security. There is a booth that you step into with your hands over your head (and, bingo!, they tell you to go on). I was directed to go through the metal detector, and that is when my trouble started.

That metal detector did not like my replaced knees. It sounded off when I walked through, and the attendant called for another attendant with a wand to check me out. The wand was not bad, but I did not particularly cherish him putting this hands down inside my belt and feeling my butt—before going just as far in the front. He said the next time I should go through the booth. We went through security about three more times on the trip, and all had metal detectors that did not like my knees.

Our airplane was one of those small jets that make you have to stoop to enter. It had rows with one seat on the left side and rows with two side-byside seats on the right side.

When we got on the plane, my seat was not next to Gracie s, and a gentleman next to her readily exchanged seats so we could be together. I struggled to get my carry-on items in the overhead bin, and the same gentleman put my and Gracie's carry-on bags in the bin for us.

About five hours later we landed in Toronto Canada. We went through customs, then claimed our checked luggage and took it to a conveyor belt for our flight to Halifax. We had to go through security again, and that metal detector did not like me either—I had the same problem as in Dallas.

After another four-hour flight we arrived in Halifax, Canada's Maritimes Region. We were on a much larger plane for this flight, and all seats were taken. Here we met our tour guide and bus driver who would be with us throughout the tour. We also met others on the tour from parts of the U.S., Canada and the U.K. Halifax was about a one-hour bus ride to our first hotel, the Westin Nova Scotian. We were scheduled to spend two nights there· in fact, we always stayed two nights at every place we went. Dinner was on our own the first night.

On Day 2 we explored Halifax's charming downtown during a scenic tour of the city, highlights of which included the waterfront, Public Gardens, Spring Garden Road and the famous Citadel. After lunch we enjoyed a visit to one of the most picturesque spots in all of Canada: beautiful Peggy's Cove. Its historic lighthouse overlooking the Atlantic Ocean provides one of the most memorable views one will ever see. That evening we had dinner along the waterfront.

We always had good breakfasts—in fact too good. They made it hard for me to stay with my normal bowl of oatmeal. The next day we traveled to Cape Breton, and enjoyed a visit to the Glooscap Heritage Centre to learn about the Mi'kmaq heritage and Glooscap legends; we saw artifacts, including stunning quill and beadwork. And the locals tried to teach us some words from the Mi'kmaq language—with not much luck. We continued on the Canso Causeway to stunning Cape Breton Island. There was a lot of bus riding throughout the trip, and this day was no exception. We drove along the shores of Bra d'Or Lakes, Canada's only inland sea. Something I did not expect to see in Canada was the Alexander Graham Bell museum in Baddeck. We saw the first telephone, first phonograph and the many other gadgets he invented.

Nova Scotia has lots of water (oceans and lakes) and lots of trees—it was hard to see the countryside because of the trees. They should not run out of trees for a while. Everything was built out of wood. Not many buildings were constructed of bricks. The people were very friendly, for tourism is a great part of their economy. The hotels/motels were always nice and clean. The food was great—with lots of seafood. Prices for food and gifts were reasonable. We made no effort to get Canada currency. We paid with U.S. dollars and got Canadian dollars back in change. The U.S. dollar was slightly stronger than the Canadian dollar, which was 90 cents to our dollar.

We were in Nova Scotia when a cold front came through north Texas. In fact, we had the same temperature in Canada as was being recorded at home in Texas—66 degrees. My long sleeved shirts proved to be too warm, and I kept them rolled up.

Saint Peter's Church

We got up at 6 a.m. and had our luggage outside our door by 6:30 a.m. Our luggage was still outside our door when we left our room for breakfast at 7 a.m. Again we had a great breakfast: made-to-order omelets, boiled eggs, smoked salmon—the works, with plenty of fruit. I tried to block out all the other food and filled my bowl with oatmeal. I had to slip in one piece of sausage and I had to have some of that smoked salmon.

After breakfast we boarded our bus to explore the Cabot Trail with its rugged terrain and spectacular view along the Atlantic Ocean. When we entered our bus that morning we found our name on seats two rows farther back than they were previously. Every day they moved us farther back in the bus. The guide explained that this was done to give us the opportunity to visit with all people around us by the end of the tour.

While we knew the Atlantic Ocean was out there, it was mostly hidden much of the time by high trees.

Our first stop of the day was Cheticamp. Cheticamp is a busy fishing village in Cape Breton, Nova Scotia with a thriving Acadian culture. It was said that visitors will often hear the lively sounds of Acadian being spoken in town and in restaurants, where visitors could sample typical Acadian food. Cheticamp is a center for rug hooking and many other fine crafts.

Our bus pulled up to beautiful Saint Peter's Catholic Church in Cheticamp. It reminded me of Muenster's old church that had to be replaced in 1950 because it was no longer safe. The Canadian structure featured the same gothic design; this church was an immaculate white inside with an altar like our old church. In the choir loft was an old pipe organ identical to the organ that was in our church 60 years ago. The organist sat with his back to the altar, using a large mirror over the organ to see the altar and follow the priest while playing the organ. I looked on the right side and sure enough there was that large wooden lever sticking out of the organ that is used to pump air to the organ when the power was off. I had to pump the organ in our old church as a member of the choir when the power was off during Mass.

The downstairs in this church was not much larger than how I remember the Muenster Church downstairs area, but, unlike the Muenster church, there was lots of room on a second floor for persons to attend Mass. There was room for about 10 persons deep on both sides of the upstairs. They sat facing the center of the church. Almost as many persons could attend Mass on the second floor as the first floor. It must have been a large congregation when the church was built. Unlike the Muenster church that had a winding staircase in the back of the church—this church had a broad staircase in the center back of the church to provide access to the second floor.

While talking to the church representative I learned that church attendance was way down—only about 150 persons were attending services each week in this beautiful church.

This was Acadian country, and I knew that Acadians had settled first in this area first many years ago and had been deported to many places, mostly in the United States. I do not know about my readers, but I am interested in history, and I wondered why they were deported, so I looked up on the Internet to learn a little more about the Acadians.

They are the descendants of the 17th-century French colonists who settled in Acadia, Brunswick and Prince Edward Island. Although today most of the Acadians are French-speaking Canadians, Acadia was a distinctly separate colony of New France. It was geographically and administratively separate from the modern-day Quebec. As a result, the Acadians developed two distinct histories and cultures. Since the Acadians were separated from this council, their French language evolved independently, and Acadians retain several elements of 17th-century French that have been lost in France. The settlers whose descendants became Acadians came from "all the regions of France but coming predominantly directly from the large cities." Prior to the British Conquest of Acadia in 1710, the Acadians lived for almost 80 years in Acadia. After the Conquest, they lived under British rule for the next 45 years. During the French and Indian War (the North American theater of the Seven Years War, British colonial officers suspected the Acadians were aiding the French. The British, together with New England legislators and militia, carried out the Great Expulsion of 1755–1764 during and after the war years. They deported approximately 11,500 Acadians from the maritime region.

Approximately one-third of the Acadians deported perished from disease and drowning. Acadians migrated to Spanish colonial present day Louisiana, where they developed what became known as Cajun culture. Another reason they were deported was that Acadians were Roman Catholics, and when the British conquered the area, the Acadians would not convert to the Church of England and they were deported.

Through the years many of the Acadians migrated back to the region of their ancestors. This is why, despite being the deportations in earlier years, today the region is a thriving Acadian community.

Prince Edward Island

After we left Saint Peters Catholic Church we enjoyed a picnic lunch in Cape Breton Highlands National Park located in the valley along MacIntosh Brook. We stopped at the famous Cape Cod lighthouse to take pictures and again at the Gaelic College, where we watched a historic show of the region. They showed us how the Scottish kilt is made. I was amazed at the number of yards of material that were in the kilt. They had the most talkative guy in our tour group model their kilt. It did not really do anything for him—his western clothes were better. A man in a dress did not look great to me.

That evening we savored a dinner featuring local flavors. Later there was a so-called, old-fashioned bonfire where we roasted marshmallows and listened to music that was not up to its billing.

The next morning, after breakfast and an hour-long drive to a ferry (and a two-hour wait), our bus was loaded onto a ferry to Prince Edward Island. We all went up an elevator to the lounge area for this portion of the trip. We ate lunch on the ferry. After about a three-hour ferry ride we got back on our bus and rode to Charlottetown, where we took a walking tour along its narrow streets lined with quaint homes and hidden treasures. That evening we had a four-course meal featuring fresh, island products. The meal consisted of mussels, island berries and local tenderloin.

We were pleasantly surprised in Baddeck to be able to visit the Alexander Graham Bell National Historic Site. The museum features artifacts and memorabilia associated with Bell's experiments. The building was full of his inventions, but I was most interested in the telephone. His first telephone was on display, along with the gradual improvements made to the telephone over time. Mr. Bell also invented the telegraph, and he called his first telephone "talking telegraph." We would spend the next couple of days in and around Baddeck.

That reminded me that I once built a replica of Alexander Graham Bell s first telephone for a science project for our son Gene—of course, mine did not work. Mr. Bell worked late into the night experimenting to find the right combination to make things work. Earlier years when I was still at home I would piddle around in Dad s shop. Mom would see me in Dad's shop, and she would always complain, "Always doing something that ain't nothing." But the experiments I played with then helped me in later years when I got into the telephone business. I had to improvise to make things work, for there were no guidelines to go by in the early years of telephony.

Later in the day our bus came upon the cemetery where the victims of the Titanic were buried. These are the passengers of the Titanic who did not go down with the ship and who couldn't get on the few lifeboats available—they froze to death in the water.

(I have to tell a story related to the Titanic. My great-grandfather, Peter Fuhrmann, left Kaifenheim, Germany, in 1868 to come to the United States with his four sons. In 1912 the oldest son Joseph, went back to Germany to visit. When he got ready to come back home he tried to book passage on a new passenger ship making its maiden voyage from England to New York. Well, there was no room on the ship, and he had to book passage on another ship. The ship he missed was the Titanic. He was so grateful for being spared that he completed paying for the main altar in Saint Nicholas's church in Kaifenheim. The congregation had just purchased a new altar in the church and lacked about 45,000 marks paying for it. The doors that cover the statues are usually closed during lent, but when I visited Kaifenheim with Ewald Fuhrmann (also a descendant) in 1951, the doors were open. We were in the U.S. army stationed in Germany at the time. They had opened the doors to honor us as descendants of Joseph Fuhrmann.)

As our bus rolled on, we came to know the rolling landscapes of Prince Island, the backdrop of the acclaimed novel, "Anna of Green Gables." We visited Rustice s celebrated wharf dotted with fishing boats and lobster traps. We arrived in Cavendish and visited Cavendish National Park's picturesque beaches, where we visited Anna of Green Gables house. We were able to go through the house and ended up in the gift shop. (Almost every stop ended in a gift shop). At Prince Edward Island Preserves we tasted local berries blended with a "secret" ingredient to create a unique island taste.

Our last days in Nova Scotia

On the sixth day of our tour, we crossed the stately Confederation Bridge opened for traffic in 1997 and left Prince Edward Island. This bridge is across 10 miles of open water from Prince Edward Island to New Brunswick. After a long bus ride we arrived in the market city of Saint John.

We traveled along sea-sprayed shoreline to the amazing Hopewell Rocks; they are a New Brunswick icon. These flowerpot shaped rocks carved by the Fundy tides seem to rise four stories high at low tide only to disappear into tiny islands when the tide is high. The tide was out when we were there, and we went down a long, outdoor stairway to the sea floor. The guide took us along the ocean floor, pointing out interesting sights as we walked. It was a bit spooky, as you could see caves that the water carved into the shorelines. We would be swept away if the tide came back while we were on the ocean bottom. We came to another stairway that took us back up on shore again.

Back on the bus, we stopped at Daniels Flats for a lobster lunch. The only thing that was on my plate was this lobster. It was the grossest thing I ever tried to eat. An expert showed us how to eat lobster. The lobster I have eaten before was streaming hot and ready to eat with the meat in the tail turned out and cooked so you just had to use a fork to pick up a piece and dip it in hot butter and eat. This lobster was ice cold and all in one piece—I thought I saw it shiver. I believe he was dead, but he looked at you with his beady eyes and had long whiskers, as if to say, "Don t you dare.' The expert showed us how to pick up the lobster and twist its tail off to eat. I ate very little of that "cold" lobster s tail.

Then he showed us how to eat the body of the lobster. With the tail gone, you had to reach in with your fingers where the tail was and you came out with some green stuff that looked like his last meal. That did it; I had enough lobster to last the rest of the trip. I never got to the claws.

The next day we explored the awe-inspiring Fundy Trail, marveling at the spectacular views of the famous tides. At one of the stops we sampled Fundy seaweed. It may be nutritious, but it's not my cup of tea.

We journeyed to Hearst lodge, a remote fishing lodge accessible only by 4x4 vehicles, for an exclusive salmon barbeque complete with fiddleheads. I tried to find out what a "fiddlehead" was, because I did not recall eating anything out of the ordinary. It appears that a fiddlehead is salmon sliced thin and then sautéed until it looks like a potato chip. It turns green in the process. I still don't remember eating anything like that.

To get to this lodge we left our bus and took a minibus a few miles and then switched to a four-wheel-drive vehicle to make the last mile. We crossed a creek that was dry while we were there. The lodge was back in the woods along a stream too small to be called a river and too large to be called a creek. We enjoyed the salmon dinner out in the open.

On the way back to Saint John for an evening at leisure we viewed some of Saint Martin's famous covered bridges. I looked on the Internet for covered bridges in Saint Martin and counted over 300 of them. We experienced local life in the celebrated Saint John City Market, which comes alive with the aroma of fresh food. We shopped for maritime crafts and witnessed local artists at work. Later in the day we boarded a ferry bound for Digby, Nova Scotia. Upon arrival we strolled along the beach on Oak Island, home of pirate's treasure still waiting to be found.

July 23, 2014 was our last day in Nova Scotia. We visited the small fishing village of Mahoney Bay before stopping at Amos Pewter and learned the intricate artistry that goes into each piece. We next traveled along the beautiful Lighthouse Route towards Lunenburg. We explored this fishing village and discovered how early settlers turned to the sea for survival during the prohibition days. We returned to the days of the Rum Runners and "bottle fishing" during prohibition. This experience was completed with a visit to the Iron Works Distillery, which had its first huge iron pot used to make rum, but it is no longer in use today.

We started the evening along the waterfront sampling local mussels, oysters, and their world famous scallops prior to a spectacular farewell dinner with all of our fellow travelers. Before retiring for the night we exchanged email addresses with friends we made on the trip from Illinois and Edmund, Okla. Our friends from Oklahoma would be with us until we got back to Gainesville again.

The next morning after breakfast, we boarded our bus back to Halifax to meet our plane to Toronto, Canada. Then came the process of finding our luggage from the bus, and thanking the bus driver for his good driving and giving him an envelope containing the prescribed remuneration. Then we pulled our luggage into the airport to the ticket counter. With the help of our tour guide we got our boarding passes and got rid of our luggage. We had a little fatter envelope for the tour guide; we hugged her and thanked her for the very pleasant tour of the northeastern part of Canada.

Our luggage was checked through to Dallas, but in Toronto we would have to claim it and go through customs. That meant putting the bags back on a conveyor belt, going through security. We did not have to go through customs in Dallas.

It was a very enjoyable trip. The tour guide and bus driver where very good, and the people in Nova Scotia are very friendly. As I was writing this it was 34 degrees here in Muenster. I checked the temperature in Halifax, Canada—it was also 34 degrees. You recall that shortly after we arrived in Nova Scotia I checked the temperatures in both places, and they were both 66 degrees. That was when the rare cold front came through North Texas the first part of July.

Here are tombstones marking the resting places of victims of the Titanic. We visited the cemetary during this trip. My great-grandfather's oldest son tried to book a reservation on the ship, but it was full, so he was spared from the disaster.

CHAPTER 56

Our Mediterranean Cruise

Joey Anderson dropped us off at DFW Airport, and we started our journey. We boarded what looked like a late model 747. It had four engines and an upstairs passenger compartment. It was a British Airways flight to London. Our Business Class seats were different than anything we had seen before. I was flying in the window seat and was boxed in, and to get in/out I had to crawl over the feet of the passenger who was facing me along the aisle (I was flying backwards). Gracie was flying forward in her boxed seat next to mine, and we had a window between us so we could talk. The person in the seats ahead of her would crawl over her feet to get in and out to their window seat. The flight to London was uneventful until we got to London's Heathrow airport. Our plane sat on the tarmac about an hour while our flight to Venice was preparing to take off, and that was the last one from Heathrow that day.

An attendant helped us get seats on the next flight to Venice at Gatwick Airport. He also gave us express bus tickets to get there. We went down where the express busses were loading and waited. The bus we needed was one stop away from us, but something was holding it up. We did not have any time to spare, so I hailed a taxi, and we were on the way. I watched the meter pass—E25, then E50 . . . it kept on climbing. It passed E75 and kept going. I had to add 10 percent to the meter to compare it to the dollar. Finally at over E88 we reached Gatwick airport—I handed the cab driver a $100 bill, and he was happy. We rushed through security and made our way to the gate, which was the last one in that wing. They were loading, so we never stopped and walked right on the airplane.

(Later the ship reimbursed us for the taxi fare.)

At Venice we retrieved our luggage, went through customs and were met by a Viking agent as we came out. They took care of our luggage—the last time we had to handle our luggage, but Viking gave us super service. He put us in a holding group of people nearby until he had gathered up all who were on the flight. People were coming in from all over the States and from Canada. The ship had 900 cabins.

After everyone was there we walked a short distance to get to a medium-size bus that took us to the ship. The ship was not located in the best area of Venice. You could not walk to the business district or do sightseeing by foot.

We received a packet with our cabin keys, and we boarded the ship. We found our third-floor suite at the end of a long hall that ended up right at our cabin door at the very back of the ship. The door opened to a sitting room that led to a bedroom and bathroom with a walk-in closet.

The shower and large bathtub were in their own room and had a picture window over them—there were blinds that you could drop down. We had a balcony that started in our sitting room—it had another door from the bedroom and stretched around the corner of the ship to the starboard side. From this balcony you could look right into the picture window of our bathtub and shower. We were late making our reservations, so these suites were all that were left. Each of the seven levels of the ship had these suites at the back of the ship. We could have chosen any level.

One level down from our cabin was the sit-down dining room. We usually ate dinner here. We ate breakfast in the buffet on the seventh floor directly above. There was an elevator to take us to the seventh floor. We roamed around looking the ship over. The ship had a large sitting area in the middle on the bottom floor that usually had a piano or a combo playing.

Forward on the ship was a large theater that featured live entertainment each night and two small movie theaters on both side entrances that could be added to the large theater if needed.

There was a large gymnastic room full of every machine you could think of. The ship had 900 passenger cabins to sail in.

CHAPTER 57

Memories from The Grand European River Cruise

I thought you might be interested in what we saw on the Grand European River Cruise. It would get a little monotonous if I told you city by city what we saw. All cities had their cobblestone streets, old churches that were built in the 13th century or earlier, beautiful old buildings, and quaint sidewalk restaurants with plenty of cool beer. There were Opera Houses, half-timber houses and monuments to passed heroes. I do want to tell you about those cities that had something unique about them.

The first day we arrived in Amsterdam and boarded our ship, and we spent most of that day getting familiar with the boat. On the second day we were given a cruise of the city in glass-topped canal boats that ended up at the Van Gogh Museum. The museum contains the world's largest collection of Van Gogh paintings.

A 70-mile, tree-lined canal took us to the Rhine River. In Germany we did sightseeing in the towns of Cologne, Koblenz and Mainz. In Cologne we visited the magnificent Gothic Cathedral. It took 400 years to build the cathedral. The cathedral is a UNESCO World Heritage Site, and it largely escaped World War II damage that ravaged the city and Germany. Even though it stands close to an important bridge over the Rhine River that was destroyed, it had very little war damage. Today there is a large parking lot under the cathedral.

In Rudesheim we took a mini-train ride into town and visited the fascinating antique mechanical musical instruments museum. The player piano was taken to a new level—there were whole bands playing from a roll of paper with a bunch of holes in it.

As we passed through the most scenic part of the Rhine our program director pointed out the little towns, castles, ruins and other sights along the river. Sites ranged from the Katz and Maus Castles to Pfalzgrafenstein Fortress, which sits on a rock in the middle of the Rhine River.

The ship played the German song "Die Lorelei" when we entered a part of the river that narrows and becomes very dangerous to maneuver. The song tells about the legendary rock formation rising 440 feet above the river. It also tells about the maiden who would stand on the rock in past years and comb her golden hair in the nude and cause many shipwrecks.

Mainz Germany, was our next stop on the Rhine. While I was in service more than six decades before, I spent two years at an army base at Finthen, suburb of Mainz. Mainz lay in ruins except for the 11th century Romanesque cathedral. It had only minor damage. When I was there in 1951 the stone floor had been worn from foot wear through the centuries. What caught my attention as we toured it recently was that the stone floor of the cathedral had been replaced and showed no signs of wear.

In Mainz we also toured the Gutenberg Museum, home of the Gutenberg printing press and the originally printed Bible.

After leaving Mainz we entered the Main River. Our first stop on the 82-mile Main River was Werthelm. We sailed past the vineyards of Franconia on the way to our next stop at Wurzburg, and motor coaches took us to Rothenburg.

We entered the 106-mile Main-Danube Canal at Bamberg that took us to the Danube River at Kelheim. The canal was Charlemagne's dream in 793; it was completed in 1992 with locks that raise the water to 1,332 feet. Connecting the Main and Danube Rivers, today it enables continuous river travel from the North Sea to the Black Sea.

The canal took us to the ancient city of Nuremberg were I served six months in 1951 as a prison guard in the notorious "Palace of Justice" prison. At that time the prison held mostly American soldiers who got in trouble with the law—and Alger Hess, the only Nazi prisoner left in the prison. Only one wing remains today of the old prison, and it is fenced in and not occupied.

We sailed into Austria and stopped at Passau and Linz. Passau is at the confluence of three rivers: the Danube, the Ilz and the Inn. The Inn River, which flows off of the Alps, has a very milky color from melting glazers that, as the rivers converge, also gives the Danube its milky/gray color.

We were treated to an organ concert from Europe's largest pipe organ. We saw Linz as we sailed along the Danube.

At Melk we visited a 900-year-old, baroque Melk Abbey perched on sheer cliffs high above the Danube.

In Vienna we attended a concert in one of the city's palaces. The concert featured compositions of Mozart and Strauss performed by a Viennese orchestra.

In Bratislava, Slovakia, we took a mini-train ride to the city center and toured the beautiful St. Martin Cathedral, among many other sights.

We arrived in Budapest, Hungary, on the 15th day of the cruise. The Danube cuts through the heart of the city. The Buda Hills and old city are on one side, and elegant boulevards of modern Pest are on the other. We toured the city and visited a diamond factory. Some from the ship instead took an optional tour to discover the legendary Hungarian "cowboys," drank some Palinka Hungarian brandy and are their Pogacsa biscuits. The Captain's dinner was scheduled for that night, because it would be the last night we would spend on the boat.

During our 16-day cruise on the boat "Viking Pride," we stopped once or twice every day in the middle of the towns for some sightseeing. The boat had about 140 passengers who had come from all over the world, including Australia, England and Japan, as well as from many places in the U.S. We made friends with Jim and Felicia Jones from Round Rock, Texas. We shared a table with them when we ate and hung out together on tours. This made the cruise a lot more enjoyable.

We departed from our ship at Budapest and spent an extra night in the Budapest Hilton before catching a flight back to Frankfurt. It was a Sunday, so we attended Mass at St. Pious Church, next door to our hotel. The services were the same as ours—except it was all in Hungarian and Latin. The Latin was familiar, but the sermon got a little dull.

CHAPTER 58

On the Way to Peru

The strangest phenomenon happened as our airplane landed in Cusco, Peru. On every airplane flight I have ever been on, my ears would hurt and make strange noises as we descended to land—but not when we landed in Cusco. The altitude for that city is over 13,000 feet above sea level.

(More about Cusco later on.)

It was the start of a long day when we got up at 2 a.m. on Jan.17 to be in Gainesville at 4 a.m. to catch our ride to DFW airport for our trip to Peru. There was just Gracie and I and one other lady going from Gainesville. When we got to the First State Bank parking lot there was a large 40-passenger bus waiting to take us to Denton. In Denton the bus picked up people from Dallas and Colleyville and about 10 persons from Denton before taking all of us to the airport. When Gail, our tour guide, came aboard the bus in Denton she handed each of us a brown bag of snack food that I put on the top of my carry-on bag for easy access.

This trip marked the first time we had ever been to South America. Our first flight was to Miami, where we would meet people from different parts of the U.S. going to Peru with us. In Miami, our plane was due to leave for Lima, Peru, at 2 p.m. from Gate 42. After about an hour the word came that our flight would leave from Gate 44. Well, that was not much of a deal; we were just two gates away. We gathered our luggage and moved to Gate 44.

Then word came that our plane was going to leave from Gate 1. That is a long way from Gate 44 in the Miami airport. A man close by that worked for the airport suggested that we take the Skytrain, which would drop us off a short distance from Gate 1. An elevator took us to the Skytrain level, and we boarded a waiting car. It took a while before the car came to the designated exit, but, after taking an elevator down, we walked to Gate 1 at almost precisely the time we were supposed to board.

There was no effort to board us.

First came the announcement that there was a 30-minute delay to repair a problem with the airplane. Then came the announcement that there was another 30 minute delay to work on the plane. Finally, we heard the announcement that the plane was being taken out of service—and that our new plane would leave from Gate 16.

Everybody made a dash to get to Gate 16—that's 15 gates from where we were. I hoped that our luggage made it to the right airplane. American Airlines did not have a good reputation in Miami at the time.

As I was hoping, I was also wondering why we had to go to Miami, then to Peru, when there were direct flights from DFW to Peru. We try to go Business Class on long flights to get more legroom. The plane on which we finally ended up was an older plane, and the attendants gave each of us a small TV that sat on our food tray. With the TV came a very good headset that cut out all of the wind noise when I put it on. Because of a shoulder injury I struggled to put Gracie's and my carry-on luggage in the overhead. We have always found that other passengers are very helpful in stowing luggage or exchanging seats so that Gracie and I can sit together. This became especially true after I started wearing suspenders.

After a light lunch we settled down for the five-hour flight to Lima. Gracie started filling out the various customs forms (one for each of us) for me to sign, which we would need when we get to Peru.

The overnight flight landed in Lima at 9 a.m. It was a long and hurried walk to claim our luggage. It seems like we had to walk all around the terminal, twice. We kept our fingers crossed that our luggage got on the right plane after the problems in Miami. While I was waiting on our luggage, Gracie came up with a luggage cart. Eventually our luggage showed up, and we stacked it on the luggage cart and made our way through the door that took us to the customs agent. He looked the forms over that we had filled out on the airplane, tore one of the forms in two—stamped both copies, placed one copy back in our passport and told us to keep our copy ready as long as we were in the country. He did this for each of us. The next door took us to the hundreds of people waiting for someone from the flight.

We made our way to the gentleman holding up a Collette sign and were placed in a holding area where he was gathering up other members of our tour group from other parts of the U.S.

There were several busses waiting to take us to our hotel, and the Denton group was directed to a smaller bus for the short ride.

In the hotel we waited for our name to be called to get our key. After a day that started at 2:30 a.m. the day before, we were glad to get some rest. Peru is in the Eastern Time zone, so we lost one hour also in the process.

(Before I forget . . .)

I want to congratulate Chris, Joey and their team for completing the E7 10-gigabit ring in the heart of Gainesville. This is not just high-speed Internet service; these are rings. It means if a component fails or the fiber cable gets cut, service is not interrupted. Because we are seeing a decline in our wire-line telephone service even though the population in this area is increasing, it is so important that we find new sources of revenue, and there is a great demand for high-speed, reliable internet service. This is a great area to expand in. Again, Congratulations.

Now, back to Peru . . .

Machu Picchu

Because of the 4 a.m. rise to catch our bus to the airport, the delayed departure from Miami, and the long flight to Peru we had spent over 40 hours without a good night's rest. So we welcomed a late breakfast the next morning. We enjoyed a fascinating city tour through the center of Lima, a UNESCO historical site. We also enjoyed visiting the church on the site of The Cathedral de Armas, which was first built in 1538 and was designated a Cathedral in 1541. It was destroyed by earthquakes and rebuilt many times. The present Cathedral was completed in 1940 and is the third renovation following an earthquake. That evening we joined our fellow travelers for a dinner showcasing Peru's delicious cuisine and festive entertainment.

The next day, after a delicious breakfast, we were taken by bus to the airport, where we boarded our plane for the three-hour flight to Cusco, which is located high in the Andes Mountains in the southern part of Peru. It is nestled in a valley between mountains. During our flight to Cusco my ears gave the usual discomfort as our plane climbed toward Cusco, but I experienced no discomfort when we landed, for Cusco's elevation is close to 13,000 feet, higher than many airplane flights. At Cusco we boarded buses that took us to the Majestic Sacred Valley of the Incas, the agricultural center of their Grand Empire. We learned of the century-old methods of spinning, dyeing and weaving Andean traditional textiles when we made a visit to Asana Kacha, a living museum of Peruvian Andes.

After a short lesson in the local language we shopped in Pisac Village to browse the colorful handcraft market. Next we visited Pablo Seminarie's Ceramic Studio that teaches you about this internationally renowned artist's techniques and designs, inspired by ancient Peruvian culture. We spent the night in the Sacred Valley of the Incas.

On Wednesday, Jan. 21, 2015, we boarded the Machu Picchu train for a breathtaking view through the train's domed windows as we rode through the Andes Mountains on the way to the "Lost City of the Incas." Our train followed a winding mountain valley that had vegetation right up to the train windows. On the train I purchased a multi-pocket vest, a hat that drooped down over my head and neck to protect me—especially my neck—from the sun, for it was in the middle of summer and we were in the high altitude of Peru. We also purchased walking sticks to help our balance as we walked the narrow ledges. Hidden deep in the mountains covered with tropical jungle, Machu Picchu is the most spectacular sight in South America. The city and the surrounding mountains were hidden, but it was a flourishing region long before the Spaniards came and finally discovered it. Not even the Christian missionaries could find Machu Picchu.

We had a very nice room in our hotel in Machu Picchu. A roaring whitewater mountain stream passed close to our window. Below our balcony was the road up the mountains to the Incan ruins 1,000 feet above us in the mountains.

Incan Ruins of Peru

About 1,000 feet above us at an altitude of about 8 000 feet laid the ruins of the Incas people who lived and thrived about the time Egypt was building their pyramids. After lunch we walked a short distance to the Manchu Picchu staging area to catch a minibus that went up into the mountains. They divided us into two groups—one group would be the more aggressive group. The second group would take it easier. We chose the second group, for the air was thin and we did not want to go very high in the ruins with the many large stone steps.

After lunch we took a minibus to get to the Incan ruins high in the mountains. First we had to cross the raging whitewater stream that was flowing under our balcony at the hotel and through the valley. The mountain rose almost vertical, and the road was a series of sharp switchback turns that took us into the mountains to the Incan ruins. I believe there were 10 switchback turns that took us high into the mountains. Manchu Picchu became smaller and smaller as our bus climbed the mountains until the town was about 1,000 feet below us.

Once we reached the ruins a terraced walkway path led us into the area where the Incas lived and flourished. Here they built their walkways. They built their farmland on the side of mountains that were too steep for conventional farming. Terraces were built into the mountainside with a rock outer wall to hold the dirt—making about an acre or less of good farmland. These terraces were built one above the other. In this way water from the mountaintops would provide irrigation, starting with the highest terrace. The water would flow down to the next terrace below, and so forth, all the way down the mountains, feeding water to all the terraced land below.

We learned how the Incas people lived and worked. They lived on ledges on the mountain's sides. They made use of stones to build their home's stairway and footpaths. They built the terraces on the mountainsides to do their farming. One wonders how they were able to move the big boulders and cut the stone with no modern tools. It certainly is one of the wonders of the world. Spanish missionaries never found the Incas people, so there were no churches up in the ruins.

Because the ruins are over 8,000 feet above sea level, while we enjoyed what we were seeing, we found it difficult to get our breath to sustain any climbing and walking. It takes time to get used to the high altitude, so we took it easy up there. We used our walking sticks and walking canes to keep our balance, for the walkway had no banisters.

It was all very interesting, but we were all glad when we got back to the buses with no broken bones or bruises after our trek up and down the mountains. We saw people hiking back down the mountains. While our bus went back and forth on the switchback road, the hikers would go straight down. At places they had stairways for them to walk down on.

That evening we enjoyed an exclusive culinary demonstration before dinner. The next morning we had some free time to browse around Machu Picchu before returning by train to the Sacred Valley and on to Cusco.

En route we changed from the train to buses to visit a Peruvian children's orphanage supported by the Collette Foundation. This was summertime in Peru, and the children in the orphanage were all visiting family or friends— except for three young girls who had no place to go. The orphanage is run by three Catholic nuns. I am sure their annual budget got a boost when we left.

The next day, back in Cusco, we explored the former capital of the Incas Empire during a colonial city tour and experienced the architectural legacy visible in the Cathedral, Santo Domingo and the Plaza de Armas. We explored the important sacred Incan ruins of Sacayhuaman Fortress. Remember, we were back in the city of Cusco, whose elevation is over 13,000 feet. We had trouble moving around and had to stop often to catch our breath.

The next morning we told newfound friends goodbye and were bused to the airport for our flight home. At the airport we did something typical of Collette tours: we all lined up to get our plane tickets in one group, and we were in groups going to different parts of the country. We were going to Dallas, and they had us routed through Miami; another group was going to Minneapolis and they were routed through Dallas. Again, I got to wondering:

Why did we not get routed straight to Dall as?

CHAPTER 59

Portugal—Douro River

We left DFW at 4:10 p.m. and arrived at Frankfurt, Germany, after a 9-hour-and-55-minute flight, so it was the next day at 9 a.m. when we arrived in Frankfurt. The seats would lay back but were not very comfortable. I tried to get some sleep on the plane, but I got very little. After a three-hour layover at Frankfurt another Lufthansa flight took us to Lisbon, Portugal, arriving about 3:30 in the afternoon. That is a long time to be without sleep, and we were dead tired. Viking River Cruises had a van waiting on us when we arrived in Lisbon, and soon we were on our way to the Trivial Hotel.

After checking in, getting our room and cleaning up we sacked out. We were dead to the world. We are not as young as we used to be, and 24 hours without sleeping had us tired.

Following some sleep we moved around to learn more about the hotel we were in. We were on the second floor, and the rooms were very nice and roomy. Later in the evening they had us assemble on the top floor of the hotel for a briefing session. After the briefing we had dinner and returned to our room for some more sleep.

We had a buffet breakfast the next day, then we gathered our vox receivers and embarked on a half-day tour of Lisbon. The first place we visited was the Belem with a breathtaking view of the Jeronimos Monastery—a Hieronymite monastery that is arguably the city's most beautiful building. It is a UNESCO World Heritage Site, along with the Tower of Belem. Next they took us up a steep hill and drove through the maze-like (Bairro Alto) old city of Lisbon. We learned about Lisbon's long, multi-cultural history, exploring the narrow streets of the Alfama as we walked back down toward the water's edge.

After a good breakfast the next day we checked out of the hotel and took a scenic bus ride on the coast to the Portuguese town of Proto. A highway sign along the route indicated that we were close to the famous town of Fatima. I would liked to have visited Fatima, but it was not on our agenda. On the way to Proto we stopped at Colmbra, the birthplace of six Portuguese kings and home to one of Europe's oldest universities. We ate lunch before continuing to Proto.

Upon arrival in Porto, we proceeded to the dock at Vila Neva de Gaia in the middle of Proto. Our Viking ship was named after the river it sails on, "Douro," which empties into the Atlantic Ocean at Proto. The Douro has its starting point 556 miles away, back in Spain. For 77 miles it is the border between Portugal and Spain. In Portugal it plunges 1,250 feet within 30 miles in a series of gorges and rapids and flows generally westward across Portugal to the Atlantic Ocean. A series of six locks make ship traffic possible.

The locks raise or lower the ships as much as 140 feet at each lock. This is higher than any other locks that I am aware of. Our cruise did not go into Spain; it stopped short of the border. Most of the banks of the Douro have terraces clinging to their sides, growing grapes. This makes for beautiful scenery. Most of the grapes are made into Port wine.

After boarding the ship we were assigned our cabins, and we had a chance to see what our room would be like for the next five days. The Douro ship is only about two years old and especially built for the Douro river with its six locks and narrow riverbanks at times and high cliffs of fertile soil covering with terraces on the sloping banks of the Douro River.

Our stateroom was the smallest we ever have had. There was just enough space to walk around the bed. The French balcony was basically a sliding door that led a few feet to a rail. It was explained to us that they could not make the cabins with more room because the locks we would be going through would not allow ships to be any wider. The bathroom was nicer than what we experienced on our previous cruises, and it even had a shower with a door you could close while you showered.

Our room was close to the stairway we would use to go down two flights to eat. There was an elevator that went from the third floor (where our cabin was) to the first floor (where the dining room was). We never did use it other than to try it out to see how it worked. We were on the same level as the lounge area, where we could go for leisure time. There were about 120 guests on the ship.

Whenever we left to visit places away from the ship there were three buses labeled A, B and C. We were on the A bus. In our cabin on chargers were vox units. Whenever we left the ship or went on the buses we would need the vox units to be able to hear our guide. Each bus had its own local guide, and his/her vox units were on different frequency, so even if you were adjacent to another group you always heard your own guide. We did not have to stay within hearing distance of the guide, for this device allowed us to hear as long as we were in the general area of our guide.

There was a lot of walking, and most of it was up or down hill and in narrow alleys or cobblestone streets. It seemed like it was always uphill no matter which way you went, especially to get back to the ship. Portugal is an old country, and its irregular streets were all paved with cobblestones, each about four inches square with sand between them. They are difficult to walk on. Also, there is no such thing as going around the block and coming back to where you were in that locale. Our three-times-a-week exercising back home made us in shape to do the walking and step climbing that was necessary. We were in better shape than a number of other persons on this cruise.

We soon made good friends with several retired couples from England. They spoke English but were very difficult to understand. We were on different buses during the day, but we spent our evening meals together. We have been exchanging emails since we returned home.

After a good breakfast we took a city tour of Porto—a charming riverside community whose historical center is a UNESCO World Heritage Site. There are six bridges over the Dour River in Porto. Our guide took us through baroque Cathedrals and romantic 16th through the 19th century building set among narrow, cobbled streets. We saw Foz, an old fishing village where wealthy Porto families keep their summer homes.

We then visited a typical port winemaking facility, then returned for lunch. After lunch we took an optional excursion to Guimaraes. This is another UNESCO World Heritage Site. Guimaraes has a medieval quarter with narrow streets, a main square and palaces and monasteries dating back as far as the 10th century. This city was Portugal's first capital in the 12th century and home to its first king, Don Afonso Henriques. We returned to our ship, which had sailed to Bitetos.

For dinner the second night we disembarked and proceeded to the 11th century Alpendurada Monastery—now a small inn and museum with a sweeping view of the river Douro—for a leisurely dinner and Fado concert. Fado is a type of music that can be traced to the 1820s in Portugal but probably has much earlier origins. There are many Fado clubs in Portugal.

The next day we sailed along the Douro River, going through an amazing lock, arriving in late morning in Regua. Gracie and I have sailed on many rivers—the Voga River in Russia· the Rhein River in Holland and Main in Germany; the Danube through Austria, Czech Republic, Slovakia, to Budapest Hungary. We sailed the Yanze River in China and the Seine in France, but we have never gone through locks like these on the Douro River. The water on rivers is dammed up every so often to keep it deep enough for a ship to sail. Locks are built into the dams to raise or lower the ships to get by the dams. Most locks raise or lower a ship about 10 to 15 feet, but the locks on the Douro River in Portugal raise or lower a ship 140 feet. Ships sail into a lock, and a heavy watertight gate is closed behind it. The concrete sides of the locks are as high as the need to raise the ship to the level of the water above it. Then water is pumped into the lock until the ship is the level of the water above the dam. A heavy gate is opened in front of the ship, and the ship can sail on until the next lock. Most locks have a lake to hold the water until it is needed to raise the ship, then the water is pumped back into the lake when lowering a ship.

The Douro River locks are like a large square concrete silo with walls over 140 feet high—just big enough for the ship to fit in. There is a heavy gate just high enough at the down riverside for the ship to sail into the lock. When the gate closes behind the ship a concrete wall completes the rest of the 140 feet to complete the lock. There are rollers on each side to keep the vessel from rubbing on the sides.

To make the ship as low as possible to enter and exit the locks the captains bridge is telescoped down so that only the captain's head sticks above the deck as he guides the ship through low places. The radar mast lays down flat along with a covered area to flatten the ship out. When you enter the lock you can see the exit gate 140 feet high above in the front of the boat. This makes for an interesting sight. Water from the river Douro is let in to raise the ship to the river above. When we reached the top in about 10 minutes a gate opened in front, and the ship continued on its way.

The Viking ships are especially designed for river sailing and for easy maneuvering for docking. A motor in front and one in the back propel the boat as much as 10 miles an hour. There is no rudder. The propellers are mounted in such a way that they can be turned in any direction for guiding the boat. Front and back propellers work independently of each other.

Upon arriving at Regua we disembarked for a visit to Lamego, a small town famous for its baroque Sanctuary of Our Lady of Remedies, dating back to the 14th century and still used by pilgrims today. We visited the shrine, decorated with exquisite tile work in the Moorish manner, and descended to the grand baroque staircase. We also saw the town's Gothic cathedral and the ruins of 12th century Lamego Castle with its unusual vaulted cistern. We visited Quinta do Selxo, one of the area's iconic port wine-making institutions. We also saw the vineyard and toured the facility to learn how these unique Portuguese products are crafted, then sampled the wares in their tasting room. We returned to our ship for dinner.

We enjoyed the scenery as we sailed east along the Douro River. We saw dramatic, sheer rock formations, picturesque terraced vineyards and graceful bridges and trestles along the way; we passed through two more of the river's locks at Valeira and Pocinho dams, each raising our ship over 100 feet. We arrived at Barca d'Alva, not far from the Spanish border, during lunch.

Salamanca, Spain

Barca d'Alva was as far as we sailed east on the Douro River. This took us not far from the Spanish border. Because we were so close to Spain we took a fullday excursion to Salamanca, Spain. This ancient city, a UNESCO World Heritage Site, is a living museum that takes visitors back to the Middle Ages, yet it is a cosmopolitan, multicultural city with a large population of international students. We took a bus ride through the Iberian countryside to Salamanca, and then spent some time exploring the shops and the cafes of the Plaza Mayor (Main Square) on our own.

On the bus ride to Salamanca I watched almost as soon as our bus climbed out of the Douro River basin what appeared to be a lone aerial cable line that followed the highway the 30 miles to Salamanca. I believe it was the telephone communications for the towns we passed through on the way to Salamanca.

Lunch was served at a local restaurant and featured an unforgettable flamenco show. Then we had a guided city tour that took us to the Gothic House of Shells, the 13th-century Salamanca University and the New Cathedral, built from 1513 through 1733. The Old Cathedral is still there and can be visited during free time. Our ship had moved, and we joined it in Vega de Terron.

The next day they took us up a scenic road to the little village of Facaios. Our bus followed the winding road up and out of the Douro Valley. The top of the valley made for a beautiful scene with the vineyards hanging onto the side of mountains on the terraces and the Douro River flowing quietly at the bottom of the valley with our ship that looked like a toy.

We made our way to one of the last traditional bakeries in the Douro Valley. We discovered how bread was made in the old days and enjoyed a fresh sample. We had an English-speaking guide, but we had a problem communicating with the local people. They were taking a batch of dough and pulling off pieces of dough and putting it on a tray. I assumed this would then go into an oven for baking. We visited the local museum for wine and bread. We sampled all the different wines, and I purchased a bottle of Moscatel wine, along with several small bottles of port wine. Facaios is a typical village not yet discovered by mass tourism. That evening we dined at the Dou o Vine District (a UNESCO site). Our tables were set up outside in a grassy area in a vineyard with grape vines growing on three sides. I was really impressed by the well-dressed young people who waited on us and served the food. The boys had suits and ties on, and the girls had on nice dresses. I complimented one girl for the nice way that the young people worked and looked, but she stared at me and went on with her work, I assumed she did not understand what I said.

I sampled some local varieties of Port wine such as Moscatel. It was all good and well-suited as an after-dinner wine. I purchased a bottle of the Muscatel wine to take back on the ship. We had to do a lot of walking; it seemed like they never could park the buses close to the ship.

When we got back to our cabin on the ship we realized that we did not have our wine. We had left the Muscatel wine on the bus. I had given up ever seeing my bottle of wine again. We spent the last night on the ship.

That evening after dinner we were all called to the ship lounge and given our departure times from the ship. We had a 6 a.m. flight out of Lisbon, so it meant we were in the first group to leave in the morning. Our luggage had to be out at 3 a.m., and our bus to the airport was leaving at 5 a.m. We ate breakfast and waited for our name to be called.

When we were finally called we took our carry-on luggage and boarded the bus to the airport. I mentioned to the guide from the ship that I had left my bottle of port wine on the bus the previous day. He asked me to describe it. He said a bottle of wine was found and made a dash back on the ship and came back with my bottle of wine and the sampler bottles. I never expected to see them again.

We got to the airport and claimed our luggage from the bus and entered the airport to get our ticket. Here I was, going into the airport with my luggage in one hand and the sack with the wine in the other. In the middle of the airport line I opened my luggage and placed the package of wine in the middle of my clothes and zipped it shut again. Then I checked in my luggage with the wine. From Lisbon we were on a Lufthansa flight to Frankfurt—and then a United flight to Chicago—and then a Lufthansa flight to Dallas.

The United flight was on the new Boeing 777 plane. That is the first time we flew backwards. Our seats were in the last row of that compartment. By reversing our seats they were able to get two more business-class seats in the compartment. We probably were the only ones flying backwards on the whole airplane. When I looked out my window I had a full view of the left engine of the plane. When we arrived in Dallas our luggage did not and was delivered days later to the telephone office. The bottle of wine made it in good shape without breaking.

Portugal is an old country with many historical sites. Many cities date to before Christ and the Roman Empire. It has many Cathedrals built in the 14th and 15th centuries. The scenic Douro River Valley with its vineyards clinging to the sides, the friendly people, and the locks that raised our ship as much as 140 feet made for a memorable trip and an unforgettable journey.

CHAPTER 60

Our Russian Visit

For many years we had wanted to visit Russia and learn about the living conditions in the communist country. Our first opportunity came in 1965 when we learned about a "People to People Ambassador Program" started by President Eisenhower and sponsored by the U.S. State Department. We did not go because our children were too young to leave for so long a period.

The second opportunity came in February 1986 when the National Telephone Cooperative Association sponsored a tour to Russia. This was what we were looking for, so we signed up. Our boys were bigger by then and could take care of themselves. When the time came we flew to New York to meet the rest of our group and catch a plane to Finland, as there were no direct flights to Russia at that time. From Finland we were to take a bus into Russia to Moscow. We met the rest of our group, composed of telephone people that we knew, and looked forward to a trip into Russia.

We were in the JFK International Airport waiting room scheduled to leave in about an hour. Our airplane broke down about 20 feet from the boarding gate. Because of the delay in boarding, we were all given vouchers to a nearby bar to get a drink while we waited for our airplane. While we were in the bar, news of the Chernobyl nuclear disaster appeared on a news crawler display. A short time later we learned that a hydraulic steering hose broke on the plane and the hose would have to be flown in from Dallas.

A bus took us to a hotel in New York to spend the night. So we had the night to decide what to do. We watched the news reports on television that evening, and I was afraid we were not being told the truth about the disaster and how bad it really was. Gracie and I decided not go on to Russia. Our luggage was already on the plane, so we could not change clothes. All we had wasin our carry-on luggage.

We called home to Gene, and the first thing he asked was, "Where are you?' He was greatly relieved when we told him we were still in New York and had decided not to go to Russia. We had to wait for our luggage to come back from Finland so we spent three days sightseeing in New York waiting for our luggage to return. Less than half the group went on with the tour to Russia. They reported that no one there appeared to know anything about the disaster. Not long ago we learned of a Viking River Cruise that started in Saint Petersburg and ended in Moscow. It sounded like a great cruise, so we decided to try again to see Russia.

We landed in Frankfurt after an overnight flight from DFW. In Frankfurt we had to transfer to a Lufthansa plane to take us to St. Petersburg. We moved briskly through the airport up and down escalators to find the right gate. When the time came to board the plane we had to take a bus to the airplane that was sitting out on the tarmac in a row of planes. This was a special bus with a wide opening in the middle of the main bus and the trailer-like second part of the bus that was flexible in the center to make corners. The large center doors were designed to make it easier to get on and off the bus in a hurry.

The bus was crowded with passengers and their carry-on luggage. By the time we reached our plane a rainstorm was going through the area, and we crawled up an outside stairs to get in the plane during the storm. The stairs were covered, but the run from the bus to the airplane was not.

After about a four-hour flight we landed in St. Petersburg, Russia. We exited the plane on outside stairs the same as we entered the plane in Frankfurt. We stepped back in time when we entered the airport. There apparently was only one terminal to the airport, and it appeared to have been around for quite some time. There was only one baggage claim conveyor that clanked along on one side of the main waiting room of the airport. We claimed our luggage and went outside to catch a cab.

There was a cab outside that we took to our hotel. The cab driver helped us with our luggage, and I gave him a note with the name and address of the hotel we were staying at. It was a relatively new cab, and the driver drove like there was no tomorrow. There were a lot more cars than there are roads. Cars would park on sidewalks, and on the corners.

Apparently auto sales got way ahead of the roads to drive on. It was quite a ways to our hotel. When we got close to our hotel it was obvious thatthe driver did not know exactly where our hotel was. He finally stopped at a literal hole in the wall. On the side of the hole a small sign had the name of our hotel. He gave us our luggage and left.

Across the street from our hotel was a canal. On the other side of the canal and about a block away was a beautiful church, the Church of Our Savior on the Spilled Blood.

Apparently a well-liked Emperor Alexandra II was assassinated in 1881 on the place, and a church was built in his honor. They started to build the church in 1883, and it was completed in 1907. When we were there it was closed, but I understand that it now has been opened to the public again.

Gracie had made our hotel reservations on the Internet, and the hotel looked great there. We wondered what hotel she had picked out. The building looked like a multistory warehouse with few windows. We picked up our luggage and went through the opening in the wall that was wide enough for a car to drive through. The front of the hotel was on the inside of a courtyard and opened to a large area surrounded by buildings. It looked great and was a nice hotel. It looked like the hotel we picked on the Internet. We went in and registered.

They gave us room 201. We had to carry our luggage up the stairs to the first floor where we could take the elevator to the 2nd floor to our room. The room turned out to be really nice with a large bed and television. We rested a while, then we decided to walk around to see the neighborhood. Because it was close to noon we looked for a place to eat. We went into a small restaurant, and a young waitress came to wait on us. We had no trouble with selecting a sausage plate, but we were concerned about whether the water would be safe for us to drink, so we ordered a Coke. When we got our Coke it was a fountain drink and was still made with their water. The food was good, but we did not know about the water, so we had to drink their beer.

The taxi ride from the airport took the biggest part of the Russian money (rubles) that I had changed at the airport in Frankfurt, and we were told there was a bank not far away, where we could get our money changed. We had no concerns being on their streets wanting to change money, so we walked to the place. The Russian language signs made no sense with some of the letters appearing backwards to us. It turned out to be the wrong place, but they did tell us the right place to go to get money changed. We had to take a short five steps down to a place that would change our dollars to rubles. It did not look like a place to change money, but it had a sign on the side of the door thatsuggested it was a place to make a money exchange.

On the way back to our hotel I wanted to take a picture of where we were staying, so Gracie stood next to the entrance and I prepared to take a picture. Two well-dressed young men approached us and asked if they could take the picture so we both could be on it. We readily agreed, and it turned out that the men were Seventh Day Adventists doing missionary work in Russia. They were from the USA and enjoyed speaking English with us.

We came a day early to get over the jet lag. We would meet the ship and the others tomorrow.

After breakfast the second day we again took a bus—this time to "The Hermitage.' The experts say that if you were to spend a minute looking at each exhibit on display in the Hermitage, you would need 11 years before you could see them all. We went through room after room of pictures, frescos and statues. There were many groups of people following their guides. The guides would hold up a sign with the group designation. You needed the headset tuned to your guide to hear what your guide was saying as you went from room to room. The rooms were hot and stuffy. I always stood by an open window if there was one around. What I remember most about the museum was the carriages used by Catherine the Great, wife of Peter the Great. They were huge vehicles that needed four to six horses to pull them. Of course, the roads at that time were not very good.

The Hermitage Museum is Russias best gallery of world art, one of the most prominent art museums in the world and definitely the main tourist attraction of St. Petersburg. The museum was founded in 1764 when Catherine the Great purchased a collection of 255 paintings from the German city of Berlin. Today, the Hermitage boasts over 2.7 million exhibits and displays a diverse range of art and artifacts from all over the world and from throughout history (from Ancient Egypt to the early 20th century Europe). The Hermitage's collections include works by Leonardo da Vinci, Michelangelo, Raphael and Titian, a unique collection of Rembrandts and Rubens, many French Impressionist works by Renoir Cezanne, Manet, Monet and Pissarro, numerous canvases by Van Gogh, Matisse, Gaugin and several sculptures by Rodin. The collection is both enormous and diverse and is an essential stop for all those interested in art and history. (I got this off of the Internet. I could not describe it better).

The main building of the Hermitage Museum is the Winter Palace, which was once the main residence of the Russian Tsars. Magnificently located on the bank of the Neva River, this green-and-white three-story palace is a marvel of Baroque architecture and boasts 1,786 doors, 1,945 windows and 1,057 elegantly and lavishly decorated halls and rooms, many of which are open to the public. The Baroque Winter Palace was built between 1754 and 1762, and its first resident was none other than the celebrated Catherine the Great. Many of the palace's impressive interiors were remodeled after the huge fire that partly destroyed the building in 1837. Some of the best Russian and most famous foreign architects worked exhaustively to ensure that this Imperial residence was one of the finest and most luxurious palaces in the world.

The Hermitage's collections are displayed in adjoining buildings along the Neva embankment, which together form an enormous museum complex: the Winter Palace, the Small Hermitage, the Old Hermitage and lastly the New Hermitage. The Hermitage Theater, the private theater of the Tsars, is a beautifully decorated amphitheater, and still hosts regular lectures, concerts, opera and ballet performances. You can learn more and view pictures of the beautiful rooms and buildings of the Hermitage on the Internet. Go to Google and type in "The Hermitage Russia" to learn more.

It seemed like everyone in Russia owns a car—with not enough roads to drive on and no place to park. Cars were parked everywhere. They park on the sidewalks and on the street corners. Our bus crawled along in the traffic, especially on a Friday. At one time we were stuck in traffic and were only about a block from our ship, so we got out and walked back to the ship. We saw no road construction going on to improve the congestion.

We always came back to the ship for lunch before we would embark on an afternoon tour. We saw noted sights and toured St. Isaac's Cathedral, Peter & Paul Fortress and the Nevsky Prospekt. This is the main thoroughfare in St. Petersburg with the majority of the city's shopping and nightlife, as well the most expensive apartments, which are located on or right off of the Nevsky Prospekt.

They also gave us leisure time to relax on ship or go out and shop in the local stores. That evening we attended a performance of traditional Russian folkloric music and dance group.

The food was always great, and the waitresses were always friendly. We found the local people always friendly and wanting to help. When going on shore we always had to go through an area with booths, custom jewelry, trinkets, rings, charms, necklaces and ornaments. If you did not have rubles they would take American dollars; in fact it seemed they would rather have the dollars than the rubles.

As we went to breakfast on the third day and looked out the window we realized that we had left St. Petersburg and were now on the Neva River on our way to Moscow. Again I was amazed with the fact that there were no housing developments. There were large apartment buildings but no individual homes. People were fishing along the banks as we passed by. I set my portable GPS in the window of our cabin to see how fast the boat was traveling. Going upstream we were making only five or six miles an hour. I had my laptop computer with me, but I was not able to get my Internet messages. We had registered with AT&T for service in Russia, and my cell phone worked in Russia. The technology used in Russia and all of Europe is the same as what AT&T uses in the USA. Verizon USA phones will not work in Europe.

We then crossed Lake Ladoga, Europe's largest lake. We cruised the Svir River to Mandrogy, where we had some time to explore this museum village, visit the vodka museum or shop for handmade Russian craft items. There was an optional visit to a banya (traditional Russian bath house). This place looked to me like it was built special so that river boats had a place to stop when passing by. We continued along the Svir's 139-mile "Blue Route" toward Lake Onega.

Cruising through the night we arrived at Lake Onega, Europe's second-largest lake. We arrived during breakfast at the island village of Kizhi. There were three other Viking ships together, and there is only room for one boat to dock at a time. So the boats docked side by side, and we were the outside vessel. We had to walk through two other Viking ships to get to shore.

After breakfast we set out on a walking tour through the Open Air Museum of Architecture, a UNESCO World Heritage Site. There we saw a collection of wooden houses, windmills and churches representing ancient Russian architecture, highlighted by the famous three-tiered Preobranzhenskaya (Transfiguration) Church—a fairytale-like structure built in 1714, all out of wood without a single nail. I noticed that time was taking its toll on the wooden church, for it started to lean. Heavy wooden poles were set on each side to keep it from leaning further.

There was a Dutch-type wooden windmill that they would turn when the wind changed direction. There was a cabin where a middle-age couple told about early life on the island. The winters were severe, so the livestock were on the ground floor, and the owners lived in one room on the second floor above the livestock. Heat from the livestock would rise to the second floor and help to keep them warm. Everything was built from wood, but there was not a tree on the island. In wintertime the lake freezes over, and locals can bring the wood from shore.

Departing late in the morning and cruising through the afternoon gave us time to see the countryside. We continued through dinner and cruised along the Volga-Baltic Waterway. This system of rivers and canals, spanning 229 miles and seven locks, links the Volga River with the Baltic Sea.

Kirillo-Belozersky Monastery

We arrived in Kuzino, a typical Russian village, and took buses to the historic Kirillo-Belozersky Monastery, founded by Saint Cyril in 1397. Apparently phone service to the area was buried, for the poles that once carried open-wire lines still stood, but the wire was removed. Upon arriving at the monastery we had a long walk and went through heavy iron gates in 22-feet-thick walls to gain entrance to the main monastery.

A local guide took us on a walk through several small wooden chapels, the Assumption Cathedral and a museum, and we visited a children's art school and restoration workshop. A stand sold a variety of gifts in the entrance gates. The vast walled area of the monastery comprises two separate priories with 11 churches, most of them dating to the 16th century. Of these, nine belong to the Uspensky (Assumption) priory by the lake. The Assumption Cathedral, erected by Rostov masters in 1497, was the largest monastery church built in Russia up to that date. Its 17th-century iconostasis many ancient icons arranged in five tiers above a silver heaven gate endowed by Tsar Alexis in 1645. A lot of valuable objects kept in the sacristy are personal gifts of the tsars who visited the monastery.

Statue honoring Leannine

Painting in Moscow

CHAPTER 61

Communist Cuba

Arriving in Havana:

Our 59th wedding anniversary was coming up, and we wondered what we should do to celebrate. Collette Travel Service had a Person to Person Tour scheduled to Cuba around our wedding anniversary, so I thought this would be a good way to celebrate. We have been on a number of Collette tours, and we always have enjoyed them.

Our passports were still valid, but we had to get a visa to go into Cuba. The tour schedule was for us to fly to Miami, spend the night, then take a charter plane to Cuba. We struggled to keep our luggage and carry-on at less than 44 pounds.

On Oct. 7 we rose early, and Julian Hernandez took us to Gainesville First State Bank Conference Center, where we met the others from Gainesville that were also going. The only other person from Gainesville was dropped off by her husband. Our ride to the airport took us to Denton, where we met four more persons going on the tour. We continued on to DFW International Airport and were dropped off at the American Airlines check-in point at Terminal B. After going through security and some delays we finally boarded a 737 airplane that was fully packed with over 200 passengers. The reasons I know that it would hold over 200 persons is because we were in row 33 with six persons to a row, and there were more seats behinds us. The good thing about that seat was we were close to the restrooms in the back of the plane.

In Miami after we retrieved our luggage we were met by a young man who was to be our guide on his first trip with Collette. He was to stay with us while we were in Cuba. That night we got acquainted with our fellow travelers at a welcome dinner at a popular Cuban restaurant. There were two persons from Wisconsin and two more from New York, making a total of 12 persons making the tour.

In Miami we were given instructions on traveling in Cuba. Collette Travel Service had been issued a license to legally travel to Cuba, to participate and engage in a full-time schedule of authorized educational exchange activities in Cuba. This included meaningful interaction between us and people in Cuba. Prior to departure, Collette provided us with a letter of authorization to confirm our legal travel status, of the authorized travel agenda and activities, and our record-keeping responsibilities. We had to keep this letter on us at all times. No one checked us while we were in Cuba, and we moved around freely in Havana.

The next morning after a breakfast buffet we boarded the bus to go back to the airport. We were to take a King Air charter flight 90 miles to Cuba. At the ticket counter they weighed our luggage carefully, and we had to tell them our weight, which Gracie reluctantly did while I was close enough to hear. They examined our visas and passports carefully. Then we went through regular security and waited at the gate for our plane to leave. Because of the weight restrictions I was expecting the charter plane to be a small plane, but it was a 200-passenger 737. There were less than 40 people on the plane so I wondered why the weight restrictions.

It was about an hour flight over water from Miami to Havana, and after we landed, the plane pulled up to the terminal which was not much larger than the airport at Denton. We deplaned on an outside staircase that was pulled up to the plane, and we went into the terminal. The waiting room was also the baggage claim room, and there was only one belt for luggage. The luggage came out sporadically, mixed with saran wrapped, package after package. Apparently some people go to Miami and buy goods and bring them back to Havana. Maybe that explains why we came over on a big plane and were restricted on weight. We went through customs with no particular problems. I understand there are two more terminals in Havana—one for domestic flights and one for international flight. The one we came in on was for U.S. traffic only.

Here we met the local guide that would be with us through the duration of our visit to Cuba. She was around 40 and a heavy smoker. I never could understand her name, and it was never written out. She seemed to be well versed in Havana and spoke fluent English. We walked a short distance to a parking lot that was not much larger than the parking lot at the Muenster Community Center and boarded a 12-passenger Chinese bus for our 45-minute ride to the hotel. The well-covered engine of the bus was behind the driver, and the shotgun seat that the guide used. The driver had a door he could get in and out of, but the guide had to crawl over the engine and get out the same door on the side of the bus that we used.

Gracie and I got the back seats in the bus, and there were very few springs under that bus—we got bounced around on the way to the hotel. The ride to the hotel was a real eye opener. Half of the buildings were vacant, and weeds and tall grass were growing everywhere. The vacant buildings had doors and windows missing. Nobody seemed to worry about the tall grass, much less mowing a lawn.

We checked into the Hotel Quinta Avenida Habana, a very nice modern hotel—as nice as any in the U.S.. It had modern elevators that apparently had been added in the open area around the staircase since the hotel was built. We could not buy a newspaper that was in English.

Our room was also very nice and was on the second floor. About the only thing missing from the room was Internet service. We were told there would be no service, so I did not even bring my computer along. However, a number of people would go to a certain area in the lobby and use their computers. I do not know if they had an Internet connection. A window in our room opened to the front of the hotel, and we could see an open area between us and the road that had been mowed but not trimmed. The hotel had no vacuum cleaners; the staff would use a broom and sweep the carpets and raise a dust storm. We were supposed to hear a lecture on life in Cuba when we arrived that would tell us about the educational system, but we did not hear or see anything. While walking around the hotel I noticed that the flowerbeds were being neglected.

We were taken to the Divina Pastora Restaurant overlooking Havana and its harbor for dinner the first night we were in Cuba. It was a nice restaurant. There was always plenty of fish on the menu, and Gracie does not like fish (or the fish does not like her). She always had trouble finding something to eat. They had chicken on the menu. Gracie tried this one time, but obviously they never had to fix chicken before.

After dinner our bus took us to the Cabana Castle, and we took in the Canonazo Havana's cannon-firing ceremony. Apparently they went through this ceremony each evening, firing this huge cannon at 6 p.m. A large crowd gathered on an elevated open area of an old fort to witness the pageantry associated with the firing. This open area had about a 25-foot drop-off with no guardrail. We made sure we stayed away from the edge. When they finally fired the cannon it rattled the windows of all Havana. Later in the week, no matter where we were in Havana we could hear the cannon when it was fired. The cannon is fired to commemorate Cuba's independence from Spain with the help of U.S. troops.

In 1898, the United States assisted in a war to protect Cuban citizens and businesses. This war was known as the Spanish-American War. The United States declared war on Spain after the U.S. warship, the Maine, exploded and sank on Feb. 15, 1898 while visiting Havana, Cuba. No one really knows what caused the warship to explode, but the United States blamed Spain. Thousands of United States troops fought in Cuba.

On the next day, Tuesday Oct. 9, 2012, we enjoyed a very good breakfast—a very well stocked buffet that even featured smoked salmon. Then we boarded our Chinese bus for a tour of Old Havana. It was a step back in time. We then took a walking tour of the four main plazas. We learned about the city's architecture and restoration efforts as we visited the Maquet a Vieja Habana Museum, which houses a model of the city.

We parked our bus and walked past the Catedral De la Habana to a pedestrian-only plaza, where we met the students of a primary school in the city's center. According to our schedule the school administrator would give us an interesting talk about the school. We toured the area and looked into classrooms but no one told us about the school. The kindergarten class was taking a nap on blankets on the floor when we walked through their area.

Coming back to our bus we walked past the Cathedral again. Our itinerary said we would visit this Cathedral, but our guide continued to walk past it. I wanted to see what it looked like inside, so I went past a man at the entrance and went inside. It looked like any other church with the long row of pews in the center. Before I could see very much the man came and asked me to leave, which I readily did. By this time I was way behind the rest of the group. I don't believe our guide liked churches, for the group was supposed to visit this church and we did not visit any of the many churches in Havana. Our guidebook said that we would visit this Cathedral. Catholicism is very prevalent in Cuba even though it is a communist country.

Next we visited Santovenia, a Catholic non-governmental charity focusing on caring for the elderly. It was run by nuns and was built around a Catholic church. It was a very nice and clean place to live in. They were eating when we visited the care center. One area had husband and wife still living together. In other areas the men and women were separated. There were more than 400 persons living the facility. They had something you would never see in the United States: an outdoor laundry. They washed the clothes and hung them on racks out in the sunshine to dry. There were no clotheslines, just racks. The overworked nun running the place gave us a talk on some of the interesting facts about the place.

That night, we enjoyed a Cuban favorite as we dined at the El Aljibe in the modern part of the city.

Cuba—Day 3

After another good breakfast, we boarded our Chinese bus and drove west out of Havana. I thought it was strange that we had to drive through the front entrance of a nearby hotel to get to the street.

We were going to the lush region of Pinar del Rio to the town of Vinales. This is the most picturesque area of Cuba. It was a good four-lane highway. For some reason our bus would stop running, and we would all get out of the bus and walk around. It was bad diesel or the bus was overheating. The driver did not seem to be concerned and did not seem to do anything, and we would all get back in and drive another 25 miles or so when it would stop again. After about a three-hour ride we left the main highway and followed a country road. There was a power line and a telephone cable along the road. Electric power and telephone service seemed to be prevalent throughout the area. I do not know how good the service was, but some kind of service was available. After an additional hour drive we came to the town of Vinales.

It was noon when we arrived and we ate lunch in a unique local restaurant. Lunch included the famed Cuban sandwich. We took a tour of the town and talked to various persons and learned about life in this small town. Very few spoke English.

In the afternoon we visited a colorful tobacco farmer, who explained his crop while showing us the tobacco-drying process. He gave a cigar-rolling lesson, and we met his family at their home. The rural houses in this area were two-room, flat-roofed homes. The kitchen consisted of a two-burner electric cooktop sitting on a table. They had no cabinets. The farmer was building a new home of stone and cement, but it was no larger than the home he was living in. Parked halfway in his single-car garage was a 1956 Chevrolet automobile. Lying next to his home was a wooden plow. It consisted of two five-foot pieces of tree limbs. One piece was the plow from handle down to the plow shear. The lower end was turned slightly to make the plow shear. The other limb was attached to the handle section about two feet above the plow shear and provided the hitch to the oxen. It struck me the way the plow angle attacking the soil was controlled by a metal turnbuckle about 16 inches above the plow sheer and the hitch section.

This farmer spoke good English and told us about his farm being in the family for generations but now taken over by the government. He still lives on it and farmed it, but 90 percent of what he made each year went to the government. On our day in the country we saw only one small tractor working in the fields.

While we were visiting the tobacco farmer, his neighbor, standing on a harrow, was leavening a field with a pair of oxen pulling the harrow.

We next visited an organic vegetable farmer. Again, the house was a flat-roofed, two-room home. They served us lemonade and showed us their large vegetable garden. I guess they can raise vegetables all year long, for it never freezes. It would seem strange to me that there were no seasons all year long—just summertime.

While we were visiting this farmer, two of the neighbor boys were standing around so I gave each a Cuban coin worth about 50 cents. They were so excited that they ran all the way home, and when they got home the sister must have heard the excitement—she came out and examined the coins and hugged the boys.

Our bus had no problem going back to Havana. That evening we ate dinner in a local restaurant. Every time we ate we were serenaded by a threepiece Mariachi band—some were quite good.

Day 4—Province of Guanabacoa

That day we visited a daycare center for underprivileged children run by nuns who dedicate their lives to helping these children and their families.

Only about four or five children were at the daycare center while we visited. They seemed to be well kept, and the place was clean. There seemed to be a high school nearby, for there were many uniformed high school age children in the area. I do not believe they were taught by the nuns; at least, that was never mentioned. Attached was a small Catholic church that would hold about 100 persons. This was the only church that we visited officially in Cuba. There are many large churches in Cuba, but we did not get a chance to visit inside of any officially.

Next we were taken to visit an Afro-Cuban museum. We saw how they lived. Our discussions were limited because we had a language problem. A small band was playing, and they took several of us to dance to their wild music. I tried to stay up with one girl but she soon gave up. I recorded some of their music on my cell phone, and I can play it to anyone interested in their music.

We visited Ernest Hemingway's home in Havana. He gave it the name of "Lookout Farm." He was living there when he wrote his final masterpiece, "The Old Man and the Sea." His home remains much like it was when Ernest left in 1960. His large (12 meter) fishing boat named Pilar was propped up in a dry dock close to his home. The whole area was not well preserved and was full of weeds. The house was in need of a paint job, and the premise was run over with cats and dogs. Each dog even had its own dish when they were fed. We were not allowed in the house, and we could not see much looking in the windows to get an idea of how they lived.

Next we visited the Arte de Cufa Gallery of Fine Arts. Since its inception in 1995 the objective of Arte de Cuba Gallery has been to foster an environment of goodwill through the sharing of cultural ideas and the celebration of diversity. Half of the buildings there were vacant. I do not know if the owners abandoned them or what happened to them. Occasionally a door or window would be missing. The weather never changes in Cuba, and the grass is always green all year long. While it did not rain while we were in Cuba the grass was growing out of control.

In walking down a street we would always have to be careful—there would be a manhole covers missing or just big holes in the sidewalk with no warning around them.

Not all staircases had handrails. You had to balance yourself when you went up or down a stairway. Beggars were everywhere you went. They had nothing to sell or give in exchange for a handout. In China, at least they tried to sell you something. One day I was without any small bills, and a woman about 40 years old came to me pleading for some money. I did not want to give her a big bill. The only word she knew was "please," and she pleaded with me all the way to my bus. It troubled me greatly that I was not able to give her some kind of money, for she seemed desperate.

The food was always good, and restaurants looked clean. The main dish was almost always some kind of fish, and, as I noted earlier, fish do not like Gracie.

They showed us a number of schools; they looked clean, and the students all had a clean and pressed uniform.

Sunday evening we went to a church that was close to our hotel for Mass. It was a large church that would kneel about a 1,000 persons, but there were fewer than 40 people in church. Of course, we would not find many people in Sacred Heart Church on Sunday evening, either. An elderly priest said Mass. He was assisted by a lady. There were no altar boys, no ushers to take up a collection. This one lady read the gospels, including the proper of the Mass, she passed the basket to take up a collection and helped to give out communion. One lady from our group also went with us to church.

About the time we went to Cuba the National Geographic magazine had an article on the country. They pretty well had the same impression of Cuba that we had. In it they quoted a local telling a reporter, "We pretend to work and they pretend to pay us." I am sure that the embargo the U.S. has on Cuba is the cause of many of their problems.

Cuba—Day 5

We were supposed to do a lot of things. First we were to discover the secret of Cuban cigars at a cigar factory and learn why they are treasured around the world. Other than the tobacco farmer we visited earlier we saw none of this. Then we were to learn about the healthcare system in Cuba when we were to stop by a local healthcare facility and meet with the staff. None of this took place.

We did arrive at the National Aquarium, where experienced divers would swim with graceful dolphins in an oversized aquarium. We also saw all kinds of fish in large tanks. The dolphin was swimming wildly around and around in his own tank. I do not know what was upsetting him; maybe he was just exercising. However, there was no one in the tank with him (her? it?). The aquarium covered about a city block but was not very well maintained. The grass was not mowed and the flowerbeds in the aquarium area were neglected.

After lunch we were to attend a workshop on marine conservation efforts and Cubas diverse marine ecology. Of course, none of this took place.

We did stop at a very interesting ceramic shop that had everything around this place built out of ceramics. There was a lot of beautiful ceramics. There was even a love seat built out of ceramics. There were stairs to the second floor on which you had to be very careful, for there were no banisters on it.

We thought this would be a good place to get us a souvenir. We found out the ceramic pieces were very expensive. For visitors everything was very high in Cuba. They had a lower price for the natives—even different money. They sure did like to get some American money—however, this is true throughout the world, especially among the Russians and the Chinese.

The agenda said we would meet local artists to discuss modern day art in Cuba, and the importance of art in their society. None of this took place. On Saturday, after a good breakfast, we traveled east along the shoreline to the easternmost part of the island of Cuba. Havana is located near the east end of Cuba. There we enjoyed the view of the brilliant Caribbean Sea from the second floor of the Famous DuPont House in Front of the Sea. It was there that we viewed the only golf course we saw in Cuba. I am sure this was a major tourist attraction before the days of Castro. The DuPont House was in need of repair and had an elevator that would not always work. We never saw large groups of people, but everywhere we ate lunch or dinner the restaurants were set up to handle many large groups.

On the way back we rode through the narrow streets of Varadero, where we joined a group of young people in a pottery-making demonstration in a well-equipped pottery workshop, Taller de Ceramica Artisticas. One person demonstrated pottery making out on the side of the street. There could have been a well-equipped factory in the back off of the street, but we did not see any.

After winding our way through the narrow streets we ended the trip with classical music concert in a former church and interacted with the musicians and historians of this special place. This former church was located on a high hill overlooking the city. A large cemetery was close by. It must have been a Catholic church for many generations—why it no longer was a church was never explained. The very talented musicians were all of one family. I was able to buy a CD of their music.

On our final day in Havana we were picked up at our hotel by vintage cars and taken to the famous Plaza de la Revolution, the location of many well-known addresses given by Fidel Castro before we visited the nearby Museum of the Revolution, one of Havana's foremost institutions. The area was decorated by old tanks, artillery pieces and vintage fighter planes that were used by Fidel when he defeated the Bastista Administration to take over Cuba. Each couple rode in a different car. Gracie and I rode in a 1959 Buick convertible. If you remember, large tail fins were the fashion in 1959. We experienced lunch at the La Ferminia, a popular restaurant at the end of legendary 5th Avenue.

All of the cars in Cuba are no later than 1959 models. They cannibalize cars for spare parts. It was not unusual to see a car broken down at intersections or on the side of the road. They cannot get new cars from the U.S. because of the embargo. Why they did not have Japanese or European cars I do not know, unless they could not afford them.

Later, we learned about policies between the U.S. and Cuba in an informative discussion session hosted by a local Cuban scholar. The scholar seemed genuinely interested in getting ideas as to what Cuba could do to improve the life of the Cubans. I told him that if the people had access to the Internet that it would greatly improve their lives. He explained that the embargo by the U.S. does not provide them with high-speed broadband Internet service. Only slow service is available, even though high-speed lines are on all sides of them going to other countries in the Caribbean. It would be very difficult to provide Havana with high-speed Internet service over their phone system. Their phone system consists of a mixture of cables and wires attached to whatever is available. They did not seem to have a uniform way of doing anything. The same was true of electric lines.

I suspect the Cuban government is not too interested in letting the Cuban people know how the rest of the world lives. High-speed Internet service would be readily available by satellites, and would go directly to their homes. It is possible that the people are too poor to pay for Internet service. We never saw a satellite dish in Havana. I would have liked to talk further with him about Cuba, but it was Sunday afternoon, and we still had not been to Mass, and there was church service about a block away to which we could walk, so we left early.

Finally, we savored dinner the Café del Oriente as we celebrated completing an amazing journey to Cuba.

Wrap-up of Cuba

The next day we checked out of our hotel, and our bus took us back to the airport. We went through customs; they looked over our papers and waved us on. In other countries, Gracie and I could go up to customs together, but here it was one at a time. We had no problem leaving Cuba. This time there was a twin-engine, turboprop plane waiting to take us back to Miami. Apparently there is very little freight going back to Miami from Havana. In Miami we changed to an American flight and we were home that evening.

Cuban trip summary

Cuba is a very poor country. It appeared to us that there is only one class of people: poor. No one lives in big fancy houses. They all live in apartment buildings. Everything seemed like it needed repair and paint. Grass grew tall everywhere. No one seemed to mind the weeds.

I do not know, if Cuba was given to me today, that I would want it. It looked to me that you would have to take a bulldozer and push everything into the sea and start over. Over 50 years the country has done nothing to keep it up. Nobody owns anything, and the government does not have the money, nor does it not bother to keep things up. From what was shown to us, the schools and retirement homes were well taken care of. The retirement homes seemed to be well run—thanks to the nuns. From what we saw of the schools they were clean and well managed. I am sure we were shown the best of the retirement homes and schools. They did not show us any institutions run by the government. If they mirrored everything else run by the government it would be in shambles.

There was very little business activity on the streets—no display windows. They did not even have signs telling what kind of store they were. Gas stations did not post the price of gas or even that they were a gas station. Grocery stores had painted on one side of their flat roof that they were a grocery store. Inside, half the shelves were empty. Each row had an inconspicuous person watching what you picked up. Once you checked out, but before you could leave, another person at the door compared every item in your sack with the cash register receipt.

There was one place in Havana that was crowded with people and with a lot of activity going on. It was a large building covering about a block or more (we never got to the far end). The building was divided into row after row of small booths with people selling goods. It was like a farmers market, but there was everything under the sun for sale. This was a sharp contrast with the rest of Havana. As you walked by they tried to entice you to buy what they had to sell. On one aisle, this very energetic girl was selling little wooden boxes. She spoke good English and offered me a prize if I could get it open. The box had no top or bottom. It looked like it was made out of a number of different wooden pieces glued together. I worked with it, but there was no visible way to open it. I gave it back and she readily opened by pressing on the certain corners and it slid open. I tried it and I could also open it as well. It was a good conversation piece, so I purchased it. I put a Cuban 3 Peso (about 3 dollars) bill in it and closed it. To this day I cannot get the box open again. The Cuban money is still in the little wooden box.

The people living in Cuba today know only Communism. Very few people in Cuba remember being under anything but communism.

The restaurants we were in had good food and seemed to be prepared for large groups of people, but we were the only group eating. A Mariachi band always played when we ate. Seafood was always the main item on the menu, but beef and chicken was available. Gracie found out not to order chicken. Apparently they do not have to prepare chicken very often.

It appeared to me that they did not have a standard way to build phone and Power lines—esPecially from the Power transformer to the homes.

Why is Cuba communist?

Throughout our trip I was wondering why we had communism only 90 miles from our shores. I remember some about how Cuba got like it is today, about why Castro was able to gain power and why it is communistic. But that was way back in 1959 when Castro gained power. The Internet is good way to refreshing one's memory, and here's what I learned by doing a simple online search:

Castro was a young lawyer in Havana who petitioned the courts for the overthrow of the Batista government, which he accused of corruption and tyranny. Castro's arguments were rejected by the courts. Castro then gathered a force of armed rebels and attacked the Moncada Barracks in Santiago on July 26, 1953. They were defeated and sentenced to 20 years in jail. Castro was pardoned, along with a group of political prisoners, and Castro immediately formed a new army in the mountains to west Cuba.

The Cuban Revolution was an armed revolt conducted by Fidel Castro's 26th of July Movement and its allies against the regime of Cuban dictator Fulgencio Batista. The revolution began in July 1953, and Batista was finally ousted in January 1959. His regime was replaced by Castro's.

This was in the heyday of Communist Russia, and the U.S. did not help Castro to overthrow Batista, but Castro got help from Russia. Castro's government was then formed along Communist lines, becoming the present.

CHAPTER 62

Oklahoma City

For years Gracie and I talked about taking the Heartland Flyer to Oklahoma City with John and Mary Lou Leftwich of Gainesville—spending a couple of nights and coming back again on the train a few days later. We finally made it on Tuesday, Nov. 15, 2011.

At the time our train was due a three-locomotive freight train rolled in and stopped on the tracks. Then it slowly started backing up again. Apparently it was parking on a side track to allow our passenger train to arrive. Most of the freight cars rolled silently by, but a car that was two cars behind the locomotives made a noise like it was going to tear itself up as it rolled by. After about a 25-minute wait our train finally rolled in. You could hear it from miles away, for the engineer sat on the whistle as it came into Gainesville. With the sound of escaping air it came to a complete stop. The conductor came out and took us to an open door a bit down the train and put down a stool that we stepped on to get into the train. It would be a three-hour ride to Oklahoma City.

A church group of about 35 members filled the car with forward-facing seats, so we had to ride facing backwards—looking at where we had been. It was pitch dark outside, so you could not see anything that was going by. We asked the conductor if we had come to the Red River Bridge yet, and he said yes—in fact, we had passed it some time ago.

We were hungry and had planned to eat on the train. One car forward and down the stairs was a snack bar, so we paid it a visit. For Gracie and I the lady heated up a ham and cheese sandwich. The cinnamon roll looked good, so I got one, too. Diet Pepsi was our drink.

Before the train got to Oklahoma City it stopped at Ardmore, slowed down at Paul's Valley, stopped at Purcell and again at Norman, Okla., where the church group got off.

At Oklahoma City we came down the circular staircase and looked for our missing luggage. It so happened that the conductor had already set our luggage off of the train. We grabbed our bags and took off for an elevator to street level. It was cold—45 degrees. Our hotel, the Marriott, was only a block away. We got a nice room with a king-size bed in a handicapped room on the eighth floor.

The next morning after a good breakfast we walked to where we could pick up the Trolley that went to the Oklahoma Museum. This Museum was all about Timothy McVeigh's bombing of the Arthur Murray building in Oklahoma City.

After we got off of the trolley we walked past the Empty Chair Memorial; looking down we could see the chairs that symbolize each person killed by the blast. Farther on we passed several wire fences that served as the parameter for paraphernalia memorials left by visitors to the museum.

CHAPTER 63

Our Trip to Alaska and The Cruise (from Gracie's Perspective)

On June 29, 1992, we started our day at 4:30 a.m. We were going to Anchorage, Alaska, for the OPASTCO summer meeting. We left home at 5:30 a.m. to stop in Denton to pick up Gene to head for the airport. Alvin and I left DFW Airport on Delta Flight 1845 at 8:25 a.m. headed for Anchorage. Gene left on an American Airlines flight at 10:55 a.m. for Anchorage, also. The reason we did not go on the same flight is because we booked ours with our cruise.

We landed in Salt Lake City for a brief stop. We did not leave the airport. We arrived in Anchorage at 1:55 p.m. We rented a care while we waited for Gene's flight to arrive. We stayed at the Sheraton Anchorage Hotel. It is a really nice hotel. On one side is a cemetery, and on the other side there used to be the famous 5th Street, with all the call girls and a soup kitchen. The girls have gone, and the soup kitchen is a gift shop now. We were in room 732, and Gene was in room 722. On the evening we arrived at Josephine's in the hotel. It was a very nice and elegant restaurant. At 11:30 p.m. in June, it is like daytime in Anchorage; sunset comes at about 2 a.m. It never really got dark.

On Sunday, June 30th, we went to the 10 a.m. Mass at the Holy Family Cathedral. At 1:30 p.m. we boarded a bus for the Palmer golf course. Tee time was 4 p.m. All three of us played in the OPASTCO golf tournament, which was run rather loosely. They did not have any golf carts assigned, and some had to pull carts. It worked out okay, and everyone finally got started playing via a shotgun start. My team won second place and received a trophy. Alvin won an umbrella that was given away at the party after the tournament. While we were playing golf we had some of the most beautiful views anyone has ever seen.

On Monday, July 1st, we took the Anchorage City tour. In the afternoon we rested for a little while before we went to the OPASTCO reception in the evening.

On Tuesday we went to the General Sessions. We had lunch with John and Carolyn Rauh. In the afternoon the men went to the meetings, and Carolyn and I went shopping. I won a $100 travel certificate from Co-Bank. I signed up for the gift in their hospitality suite. That evening we all went to the Fred Follies banquet and show. It was a lot of fun.

On Wednesday we had the OPASTCO breakfast with John and Thelma Calendar. They are always so much fun. That afternoon we all attended different seminars. We had lunch with OPASTCO.

The trip lasted through July 13th, and we had a lot of wonderful moments during our stay, particularly during our cruise. On July 8th I entered the fashion show. While I was getting ready for the show, Alvin went to see the communications room on the ship. The Captain arranged for Alvin and some of the men on the cruise to do this. They missed my turn as a model. I modeled a hot pink jogging suit. I purchased a blue jogging suit. Later, we were on deck looking at many beautiful glaciers, as we were in Glacier National Park. We played ping pong and spent a lot of time on deck that day. After dinner we went to see "Cabaret Showtime" and "The Music Man." After the show we went to the casino but the machines did not pay off for us. Later we went to the midnight buffet—one thing about a cruise is that you get to eat a lot.

On Tuesday, July 9th, when we woke up the ship was rocking back and forth a little. I was looking in the mirror and could see that I was holding myself so as not to fall into the mirror, then, suddenly, holding myself because I was falling away from the mirror. My cosmetics never knew where they were; they kept shifting around.

Eventually, we docked at Skagway, left the ship and were told to return promptly at 6 p.m. We were told that if we were late, they would leave us. Skagway was a unique little town. We took the White Pass Railway tour, then, after the train ride, we walked all over town and ate in a little restaurant. Without tourists this town would close down.

Later, we walked down to the telephone office. There were two employees in the office, and they were very friendly, showing us all around the place. They seemed to be a little more relaxed with their work than we were with ours. We returned to the shop on time, and after our evening meal we went to see the show "In the Mood." Before the show started we danced a little. It was kind of funny when we were dancing—sometimes when you lifted your foot it did not come down right because the ship was leaning one way or the other. After the show we visited the casino again, but, alas, our luck hadn't changed.

On Wednesday, July 10th, we docked at Juneau, the capital of Alaska. It appeared that the only way to get into the town was by boat. That morning, while Alvin was washing his hair, he wanted to use some hair conditioner. He reached for it, but instead picked up the bottle of Woolite instead. That gave us something to laugh about. Once we made it to shore we took a gold panning tour and found some gold. Later, we took the Taku Glacier Tour and then went up in a float plane that took us to the Taku Lodge for a salmon dinner. It was delicious. The scenery on the way back was very beautiful. The airplane flew very low over several glaciers, and I felt like I was in heaven—it was just gorgeous.

We returned to the ship at 5 p.m. After dinner we went to the show "Cabaret Showtime." The entertainment throughout the cruise was great, as good as any Las Vegas show. After dinner Alvin and I entered the "Twist Contest" before trying our hands at the casino once more. Our luck still hadn't changed.

After breakfast the next day we went to the horse races and won a little money. Then we went to the newlywed game. We entered but were not chosen to participate. We had an early lunch because we were going ashore at Ketchikan. We had to dock offshore and take a "tender" to shore and back. They really packed many people in these small people movers. It was kind of scary—I guess I will follow Alvin anywhere. It rained and rained—we got all wet. We took a tour but could not see much because of the rain. We returned to the ship at 6:30 p.m. for the formal dinner, after which we attended the show "Tin Pan Alley." Then we went to the Lip Sync show and paid another visit to the casino. Of course, our luck was the same. We attended the midnight buffet.

On Friday, our next to last day on the trip, we stayed on the ship all day. We were heading for Vancouver. It rained some more that day; in fact, it rained pretty much all day, making for a cool, yucky time on deck. We bet on the horse racing again and won a little. We played bingo and didn't win at all. We walked on the walking and jogging area on deck. Alvin purchased a gold watch. Another visit to the casino produced the usual results.

Because we were soon to leave the ship we packed that evening. It was hard to get everything back in the luggage. I think luggage grows when we travel. As our last dinner concluded we tipped all of our waiters, who were marvelous the whole time we were on the ship. So, too, was the dining experience—seven-course meals were the norm. After dinner we attended "Cabaret Showtime and the "Talent Show." Finally, we attended the midnight buffet. You know how in the movies when there's a scene on a cruise ship, you always see the couple out on the deck late at night and the moon is shining so brightly and everything is so romantic? Our late strolls weren't like that—it was almost always rainy, windy and cold. The setting wasn't so romantic for us.

So . . .

We made it romantic. We ran outside real quickly, kissed and hugged each other, and then ran back inside. The ship was really rocking that night after we got to bed.

Our cabin attendants could not speak English, so we did a lot of sign language. That last day we found out one could speak German. That might have come in handy, knowing that earlier.

On Saturday, July 13th, we got up at 5 a.m. so we could see the ship come into Vancouver. Breakfast was at 6:30. After breakfast we cleared out our room and waited to be called for check-out. We were checked out with the yellow #1 tag. We left the ship at about 10:30, and, of course, it was raining. We watched our luggage come off the ship. How it survives is a wonder. We said goodbye to our friends and departed. Each of us went our ways. Alvin and I took a but to the Vancouver airport to catch our Delta flight to Los Angeles. We changed planes there and headed to DFW International. Gene and Mark Johnson picked us up at 11 p.m.

Our tour cost us $1,589 each. This included airfare to Anchorage, our cruise and airfare to Dallas. This was the first cruise that I had ever been on. Alvin and I really enjoyed it.

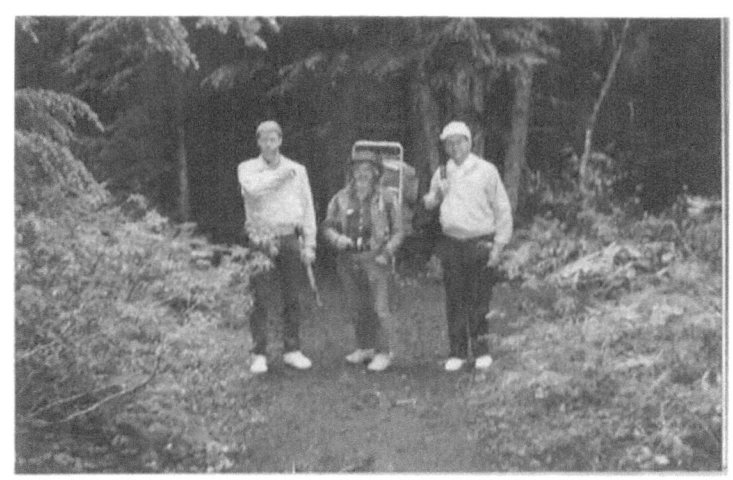

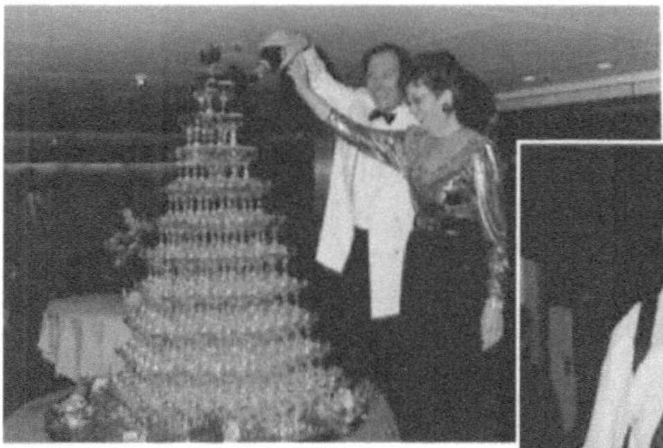

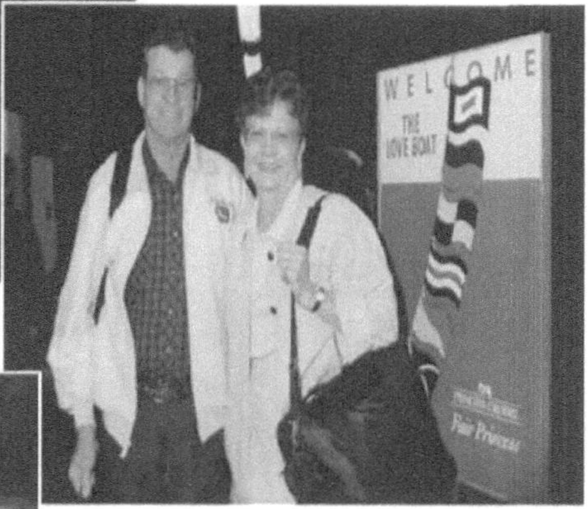
WELCOME
THE LOVE BOAT
Fair Princess

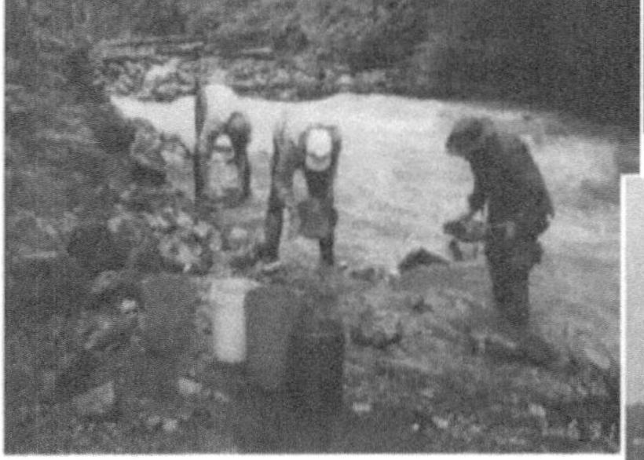

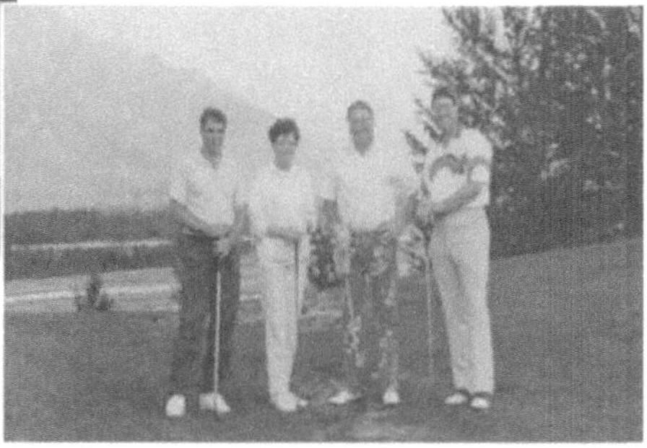

STORIES ABOUT MUENSTER, ABOUT GOD, ABOUT OUR FRIENDS AND ABOUT HIS FRIENDS

From the beginning when Muenster was founded
in 1889, it was a town of celebrations.

CHAPTER 64

The Muenster Men's Choir (Historically Speaking)

From the very beginning in 1889, Muenster had a men's choir. The founders had been members of the choirs in their Midwestern congregations and were endowed with fine, clear voices. Their musical talent was a great asset to the new foundation.

That is how Brother Thomas R. Moster tells about the beginning of Muenster Men's Choir in his book "The Diamond Jubilee History of the Sacred Heart Parish 1889-1964':

The founders of Muenster certainly possessed a great love and zeal for God's honor and glory. He had the uppermost part of their heart, and He must be served first. So it happened that on December 8, 1889, on the occasion of the first Holy Mass celebrated in the new colony by the Reverend Henry Brickley of Saint Mary's church in Gainesville, the men sang the third Plain Chant without organ accompaniment. Frank Hesse, Bernard Wiesmann, Theodore Wiesmann, Emil Flusche, Doctor Carl Flusche and John Koester were, among others, members of the first choir of Muenster.

Brother Thomas continues:

During the early days of the parish, the various teachers like Mr. Kaupe, Mr. Tharp, Mr. Boerger and the Reverend Barnabas Held, O.S.B., had charge of the choir.

In 1902 the much esteemed John Luke, Sr., took charge as organist and choir director, and his harmonious music still rings in our ears.

In 1915 the choir members were: Henry Henscheid, Jos Markowitz, John Luke, Franz Hoenig, John Herr, Al Hoenig, Father Joseph, Theo

Wiesman, John Henscheid, Albert Bauer, Henry Henscheid, Ben Luke, Bill Henscheid, Charlie Markowitz and John Rohmer.

In 1928 John Luke Sr. had the pleasure to celebrate his golden jubilee as organist. Then sickness forced him to retire from active work. Mrs. Bertha Trachta took up the position as organist under the direction of Leo Henscheid and fulfilled her duties well until her tragic death in 1935. Since 1936, Mr. Anthony (Tony) Luke, grandson of the late John Luke, Sr., has discharged the organist's duty.

The untiring zeal of the choir members deserves not only our praise, but our admiration. In sunshine or rain, in heat or cold, the faithful men are at their posts to sing God's praises, not only in the morning, but also afternoons or evenings for vespers and benediction. Indeed, the good Lord must look upon them with pleasure.

Choir members in 1939 were:

First tenors—Leo Henscheic, Jos. Hesse, Werner Becker, Walter Becker, John Wimmer, Lawrence Wimmer.

Second Tenors—Joseph Weinzapfel, Alois Kleiss, Andrew Hofbauer. First Bass—Wm Henscheid, Clement Hofbauer, Frank Walterscheid, George Koelzer.

Second Bass—Meinrad Endres, Bernard Luke, Henry Luke, Wilmer Luke.

The Director was Leo Henscheid, and the Organist was Anthony Luke.

Members who deserve special mention for long and faithful service, and who have now joined the choirs of Heaven are: John Luke Sr., Frank Hesse, Henry Hensheid Sr., Franz Hoenig, Jos. Markowitz, Sr., Alois Hoenig, Theodore Wiesmann, John Koester and the Flusche Brothers.

Without the zeal and sacrifice of these earlier members the choir would never have achieved what it did.

Brother Thomas concluded by saying, "Singing is twice Praying."

Tony Luke playing the organ - 1990

1964]   MUENSTER, TEXAS   139

This program conveys an idea of the type of music rendered by the
Men's Choir of Muenster.

JOINT CONCERT

Given by

"MUENSTER MAENNERCHOR"
"GESANGVEREIN FROHSINN" of Dallas
"LIEDERHEIM" of Dallas

Muenster Parish Hall, Sunday, April 18, 1937 at 3:00 p.m.

REFRESHMENTS AFTER CONCERT

★ PROGRAM ★

Saengergruss
Begruessung
Der Jaeger Abschied .... Felix Mendelssohn-Bartholdy
Wohin mit der Freud .... Friedrich Silcher
Still ruht der See .... Heinrich Pfeil
Muenster Muennerchor-Frohsinn

Monologue .... Franz Koegl
Guter Rat .... Rudolf Wagner
In der Waldschenke .... M. Osten
Frohsinn

Nacht Lied der Krieger ....
Saengerbund ....
Muenster Maennerchor

Selected ....
Oscarovitch Pulowinchsky, Violin Virtuoso

An der Weser .... Pressel
Margareta .... R. Meyer Helmund
Frohsinn

O Schutzgeist alles Schoenen .... Mozart
Muenster Maennerchor-Frohsinn

Nusshaum .... Schumann
Lena .... Hildach
Liederheim

●   E V E R Y B O D Y   W E L C O M E   ●

CHAPTER 65

The Choir As I Have Known It

The unsung heroes of the Men's choir are the wives who made it possible for the men to be at practice each week and at church on Sundays. Without them going to church by themselves with their children as the men sang, without their encouragement, the choir could not exist.

I joined the Men's Choir around 1946. We had to audition behind a curtain to see if they thought we had talent. We had to follow Tony on the piano playing the scales. We were behind a curtain so the old choir members did not know who was singing, and if we got thumbs down we did not know who had rejected us. I must have gotten thumbs up, for they placed me in the Bass II section with Ben Luke, Henry Luke, and Wilmer (Bill) Luke. We had to just listen at first before we could join in and sing. Finally, they allowed us to sing along with our section.

Alfons Koesler, First Tenor; Gerald Bayer, First Bass; Rufus Henscheid and Dennis Hofbauer, Second Bass, auditioned with me.

I don't remember who all was in the choir at that time, but I remember Smoky Koelzer was in Tenor II along with Bill Henscheid and Martin Becker. Werner Becker was a Tenor I, Clem Hofbauer was a Bass I, Leo Becker and Lawrence Wimmer sang Tenor II.

We were still in the choir loft in the old church; Tony played the organ with his back to the altar. There was a big mirror over the organ located so that he could see the altar while playing the organ. An electric pump provided air for the big pipe organ. You could hear the motor running when you entered or left the church. During power failures, there was a large wooden lever sticking out of the organ on the east side that we had to pump up and down to provide air to the organ.

After I joined the choir in 1946 we sang in the old church about three years before the church service was moved to the old parish hall in preparation of tearing down the old church and building a new one. The pipe organ and bells in the old church were sold to a church in Dallas. The parish hall had a choir loft in the back, and an organ was moved in, and we sang from there. We used music stands to hold our music as we sang. In 1951 the new church was completed, and a new organ was purchased. An outdoor Mass was held on the north side of new church before the organ was moved into the new church. The Lady of Fatima statue was moving across Texas at the time and came to Muenster. The Men s Choir sang for the Mass with Tony at the new organ. After the outdoor Mass the organ was moved upstairs into the new church choir loft. A high-reach forklift from the Shamburger Lumber Company was carefully moved into the church through the west doors and used to lift the organ to the choir loft.

By this time Gracie and I were married, but I was not allowed to bring her upstairs with me in 1953. The only time the old members would consider for her to come upstairs would be at Christmas Midnight Mass because the church was so crowded. Old timers like Ben Luke and Bill Henscheid did not like to have women in the choir loft. They were afraid that if women continued to stay in the choir loft, they would soon be singing with the choir.

The Men's choir was singing for all church services—High Mass on Sunday, all weddings, funerals, Masses for the dead, novena services. Of course, we had to practice. Weddings and funerals were held in the mornings so Tony would have to leave his variety store to go play the organ. Leona, his wife, would keep the store open while Tony was gone.

Requiem Masses for the dead were usually sung at 6 a.m. Most of the time Tony had help from Bill and Leo Henscheid. Many times Tony played the organ and sang the Requiem Mass by himself. Ben Luke was a mail carrier and could not be in church always to sing.

"Missa Tertia," a two-voice Latin Mass, was almost always sung for weddings unless another Mass was requested. Lawrence Wimmer worked for the milk plant and could get off regularly. I remember him, along with Bill Henscheid, singing for weddings. I was there some but not nearly as often as some of the others.

None of the members, except Tony and Frank Luke, could read music very well, but we had a file cabinet of music that we could sing.

When the church changed to English we still sang mostly in Latin. We gradually changed to English. But the choir continued to sing one Mass each month in Latin until it was disbanded in 2000.

Leo continued to direct the choir as he got older. He selected the songs we sang, and it got to where we were singing more and more the same songs and he was following the choir more than he was directing it.

He died suddenly in 1982. Fr. Placidus Eckart never was very fond of the choir and asked what the choir was going to do. I told him we could go on with Tony at the organ and directing. The choir continued 17 more years after Leo died.

In 1971 we were using the Saint Joseph Club for choir practice. At one of the practices we recorded a Christmas program.

Members of the choir in 1971 were:

Second Bass: Dennis Hofbauer, Val Fuhrman, Ben Luke, Alvin Fuhrman, Gene Gieb and Melvin Luke.

First Bass: Clem Hofbauer, Clyde Fisher and Doug Yosten.

Second Tenors: Martin Becker, Lawerence Wimmer and Thomas Knabe.

First Tenors: Werner Becker, Henry Yosten, Alfons Koesler, Fred Knabe and Tommy Felderhoff Jr.

Organist was Tony Luke, and Leo Henscheid was our director. Muenster Men's choir always had good relations with the Dallas Frohsinn Singing Society. Brother Thomas writes in his Diamond Jubilee History of Muenster having a joint concert presented by "Muenster Maennerchor" and "Gesangverein Frosinn" of Dallas in the Muenster Parish Hall, Sunday, April 18, 1937 at 3 p.m. Some of the songs they sang were "Der Jaeger Abschied," "Wohin mit der Freud" and "Still ruht der See." The Dallas Frohsinn also sang "Monologue," "Guter Rat" and "In der Waldschendke."

CHAPTER 66

Prelude to Germanfest

Our relationship with the Dallas Frohsinn started up again 20 years later in 1957 and continued for over 20 years. They would charter a bus and come to Muenster each year for a concert and dance. Mrs Lehnertz would always cook a very delicious meal. We would eat in the basement of the old parish hall, and the concert and dance would be upstairs.

On the Frohsinn's first visit to Muenster in 1957 at the dinner, Herman Meiners, president of the Dallas Frohsinn, gave a long speech in German; he did not realize that not a one of us could understand what he said. He still laughed about this, years later.

The Polka Peppermints band always played for the event. Teddy Trept, Hermann Meiners, Willie Gotlieb, Charlie Heck, Gary Nelson and their wives and others were some of the Dallas members coming to Muenster.

It was usually cold, as they came in February. We would always set them up on the downwind side of the old Parish hall. There was no insulation in the walls, and the side of the Hall would always be cold from the wind.

The Dallas Frohsinn would sing three numbers, then Sacred Heart Choir would sing three numbers, then we combined the choirs and sang three numbers together. All would be in German.

At intermission Gary Nelson would get out his accordion, and German beer songs would fill the hall. A good time was had by all.

The Hall had one commode in each of its men's and women's restrooms, so lines would develop.

We would return their visits by chartering a bus and going to Dallas to join them for a concert and dance in the "Sons of Hermann Hall" on east Elm Street and in the Ceck Hall on Greenville Avenue.

One year Dr. Martin Kralicke, a local physician, took a new doctor along that was planning to relocate to Muenster. We had our usual chartered bus and had our usual party on the way to Dallas and back. Beer cans began to roll back and forth in the bus as it slowed down and sped up. When we got back to Muenster, the doctor left town, and no one ever saw him again.

When the old Parish Hall was torn down and a new Community Center was completed in the 1970s, we continued with our joint concerts and dance. It was the most popular event of the year in Muenster. Our success with German music, song and dance contributed to the establishment of Germanfest in Muenster.

When the Germanfest was founded in 1976, we continued the joint concert with the Dallas Frohsinn. The first two years we continued in Sacred Heart Community Center, but when Germanfest moved to the Muenster City Park the crowd was split, cutting down on attendance of the dance.

We continued to exchange visits with the Frohsinn with performances in the Pavilion at the Park. Their 20th straight visit to Muenster was celebrated with a concert in the Pavilion and the dance in the Community Center. Rain poured down that night.

The visits discontinued, and the older members in both choirs died. That was the last time they came to Muenster for many years.

For the 2003 Germanfest, Teddy Trept, who was 93, was able to arrange for the Dallas Frohsinn to come back to Muenster and sing for us again. By then they were a mixed choir, with very few men still singing. It was Teddy's dream that the Muenster choir would again join the Frohsinn one more time to sing together.

There were only about four of us still singing. We planned to sing, "Das ist Der Tag Des Herrn" (This is the day of the Lord), which Muenster could still sing. The Dallas Frohsinn did not have music for their mixed choir, so we did not try to sing with them.

Muenster has many good men's voices, and it is my hope that the men's choir tradition in Muenster will become a reality again someday.

CHAPTER 67

God Got His Money's Worth

Tony Luke became the organist for Sacred Heart Church in 1936 when Bertha Trachta, who was the church organist, was killed in an automobile accident.

Tony was drafted into the service during WWII and fought the Germans in Europe. He fought at the Battle of the Bulge. He promised God that if he would let him survive the war, he would return to Sacred Heart and play the organ as long as God would let him. He returned to raise a family and became the church organist again.

In those days there was one high Mass on Sunday. There was one choir and one church organist. You had to be good to satisfy the choir members of those days. Tony played for all church functions: High Mass on Sunday, weddings and funerals during the week, novena services several times a week. When he played for a funeral or wedding during the day, Leona would take care of the variety store that he owned so he could play the organ.

There were church holidays, like Ascension, Forty Hours Devotion, and New Years Day. Then he had to play for choir practice at least once a week. Masses for the Dead were usually read at 6 a.m. Sometimes no choir members would be present, and Tony would sing the Requiem Mass by himself.

Music for a men's choir is hard to find, and that was especially so in later years. Many times new music would have to be rewritten to fit the Men's Choir. At times Tony would take songs and add harmony for the choir. As members got older they no longer could reach the high tenor notes. Tony would rewrite the music in a lower key. At times he would transpose a hymn as he played it.

After Leo Henscheid died, Tony also directed the choir for about 18 years. About five years ago Tony's health started to fail him. Doctors would not let him climb the stairs to the choir loft. The full choir disbanded, but soon Tony was at the organ again playing for several of the choir members singing at least one Mass a month until his death in July at the turn of the century. He played for Novena services the week he died.

Yes, "God got his money's worth"

The last Mass sung by the choir members still active was for Easter in the year 2000. At the Mass Werner Becker sang tenor and I sang bass. We sang the two-voiced Easter hymn "Paschum Nostrum" with Tony on the organ.

Tony died the next day, and that song was sung by members of the Sacred Heart Men's Choir. Werner Becker died a few months later.

THE MUENSTER MEN'S CHOIR: FOUNDED ON THE FEAST OF THE IMMACULATE CONCEPTION 1889. DIED EASTER 2000

CHAPTER 68

The Medders Hoax

The town was all excited in 1960 when a couple of millionaires from Tennessee purchased the Alois Hess farm a few miles north of town. Ernest and Margaret Medders had spread the word that they were heirs to the Ruben Medders Phelen estate of Beaumont, Texas. They would soon be receiving a large sum of money. An arrangement with the Poor Sisters of Saint Francis gave them money to spend until they received their fortune. The Sisters would get the fortune for giving them money now.

I came in contact with the couple when they applied for telephone service at their ranch. They had purchased 152.4 acres of land and a 30-acre tract of land from Alois Hess for $57,000. The deal called for $14,000 cash and a note to Hess for the balance payable, $14,000 annually, all due on or before June 1, 1963. The Medders home was then constructed on the 30-acres of land.

The home they built had many bedrooms, each with a bathroom. It had a large living area and a large kitchen. They wanted so many telephones that I decided to install a Norelco Private Automatic Switchboard. About 1,000 feet north of their house they built a large party barn. The party barn office was also connected to this phone system with the house. They drove Cadillacs, and they wanted a mobile phone in each car. I had just changed our mobile system to an Improved Mobile Telephone System, "IMTS."

They sponsored large parties in their party barn in which the men had to have tuxedos and the ladies wore evening gowns. They invited celebrities and even got to ride in President Lyndon Johnson's Air Force One plane. They attended White House dinners with congressmen of the Democratic Party.

The Sacred Heart Men's choir held their annual Concert and Dance in their party barn. Mrs. Lehnertz cooked the meal. It was the largest crowd we ever had at our annual event, which normally took place in the Community Center.

The couple eventually fell behind on paying for their telephone service. I contacted them for payment, and they told me not to worry because they were wealthy and they would pay as soon as they got their money. They tried to give me one of their Cadillacs, but they did not have a title for it. Ernest also had a set of cufflinks that he said was quite expensive, but I had no use for them. Their security man came in one day and opened his pouch on my desk and poured out a bunch of coins; it looked like they robbed everyone's piggy banks. We all got in the business of counting coins. I turned their service on again until they got behind again. I told them we have many wealthy patrons and that they all paid their telephone bill on time, and I disconnected their phone service. Their cars were out of town, but as soon as one came to Muenster I removed the mobile phone. I was featured on Channel 8 removing a mobile phone from one of their vehicles.

Remember: The word we had heard was that they were heirs to the Ruben Medders Phelen estate of Beaumont, Texas. However, efforts to locate such estates there had not been successful. The estate was also reported to have been under the jurisdiction and supervision of a bank in Memphis, Tenn. However, authorities consulted there reported no knowledge of the estates described. The Medders would give no information concerning the estates. They were supposed to be getting their money from the Poor Sisters of Saint Francis who would then fall heirs to their wealth when they died.

Ernest Medders died while they lived here in Muenster and is buried in Sacred Heart Cemetery. Margaret Medders was tried and convicted for embezzlement, and the last I heard she was serving a term in a penitentiary.

CHAPTER 69

It Was a Great Party

The celebration of my 90th birthday started on a Thursday, when a high school choir from Sacred Heart came to the telephone office and gave me a vase with beautiful flowers and sang "Happy Birthday"—and in beautiful harmony they sang the National Anthem. Then they presented me with a "Happy Birthday" banner with the signature of every student in school. After that, the phone company's "NORTEX CHOIR" sang me "Happy Birthday"—at least, I think that is what they did! It was great, but I would suggest they don't do it again. Actually, it was not in harmony for the fun of it. They sing it that way to each employee when they have a birthday (never in tune).

To help make it a wonderful party my friends Bob and Joy Burns came all the way from California in their mobile home. It worked out well, for they could park their mobile home close to Fuhrman Hall and get power from one of the vender power hookups in the park. The water was off in that area for the winter, but they had an internal supply. They spent their weekend with us and left Monday afternoon. Bob is a real handyman to have around. Someone had used a grease pencil and wrote graffiti in one of the stalls in the men's toilet in Heritage Hall, and he took acetone and removed it without harming the paint.

Then when I showed our rent house next door he noticed that the toilet lid was broken, and I bought a new lid and he replaced it. I would like to keep him as a neighbor. Bob will have to come back, for I found graffiti in another toilet behind the stage.

Pat and Vikki Cathey, a niece and nephew also from California, flew in Friday, stayed with her sister in Dallas and came up Saturday for my birthday party. They returned for a visit Sunday. They had to drive many times from Dallas through all of the road construction to get to Muenster and to the DFW airport. Then from Lubbock, Kaylynn, our daughter-in-law, and our 13-year-old grandson Conner, drove over 300 miles to be here for the occasion. They made a special trip, staying only one night before going back again Sunday for him to be in school again on Monday. These three (Vikki, Pat, Kaylynn and their families) truly helped make it a splendid occasion.

I really appreciated that most of our employees took the time to be there. I enjoyed their presence, and we were able to get a group picture with all employees present—we even had a number of our retired employees with us, as well. I want to thank all of them for making my 90th birthday a memorable occasion. I know that the few that were not there were sick, or circumstances made it impossible for them to make it. It was a big surprise to me when Chris McNamara, Nortex Network Operation Manager, presented me with a plaque from Drew Springer and the Texas House of Representatives honoring me on my 90th birthday. Not able to make my party was Nortex General Manager Joey Anderson and Nortex Chief Financial officer, Alan Rohmer, who were attending a telephone conference in San Diego, Calif.

Then there were the friends of our late son Gene—Troy Wolf, Jamie Moster, Sam Hess and others—who spent many a pleasant summer day with us on Lake Texoma skiing and boat riding and who attended the party. When they were young I launched and drove the boat while they learned how to ski. As they grew older and more mature they were able to launch the boat and go out and ski without me. We got to the point on Saturdays where we would go out to Texoma. The boys would take the boat and go skiing; Gracie and I stayed at our cabin mowing the grass and grilling chicken. I put the chicken on the grill until they turned brown and then I put them into a large roaster with water on the bottom and poured barbecue sauce on the chicken and let it simmer until the meat would just fall off of the bones.

In the meantime, Gracie would make a big skillet of fried potatoes. She would cook them with onions until they were brown and then open a can of Pork and Beans. The boys would come back from skiing hungry as a bear, and soon all the food we prepared was gone. When they left I always told them to "come back when you cannot stay so long." At my birthday party on Saturday night they insisted I tell them again, "Come back when you cannot stay so long' when they left.

The caterer, Vine and Branches, had a table with a large assortment of snack food set up on it. The folks who worked there appeared to have gone out of their way to provide a great assortment of food. They sent a box of assorted food and a cake home with us, and I tell you it was all excellent. Everyone told me they enjoyed the food. Serving refreshments from the kitchen by way of a serving line worked out real well, and more drinks could be taken from the cooler as needed. I want to thank Josie for keeping our guests served with refreshments.

I was overwhelmed by the turnout of friends and neighbors. There was a benefit for Doyle Klement over at the VFW Hall, and friends John and Mary Lou Leftwich had their 80th birthday celebration in the First State Bank Conference Center in Gainesville. Many of the people from there came over as well. We had planned for a crowd of up to 200 persons, and the actual attendance was close to that. We set up about a couple dozen tables in front of the stage so attendees could sit down and watch a slideshow of events from our past.

I want to thank Tara Zielinski for adding the finishing touches to the slide show, and for managing to keep the program from becoming too long. I hope everyone had a chance to view the slides.

Finally, I want to thank Gracie for planning the party—and for putting it together. She had every detail covered. As always, she put together a great party. She is a "keeper."

Yes, it was a great party!

CHAPTER 70

My Army Buddy

Not long ago I walked into the barbershop in Lindsay, and there was Hugh Perry, my army buddy from way back in the early 1950s. We were both stationed in Kurmainz-Kaserne close to Mainz, Germany. I was in "B" Battery, and he was in the Headquarters Battery of the 2nd Armored Division. Even though we now live in the same area we had not seen each other for about 66 years. He looked great, and we had quite a conversation catching up on each other since our names were called to go home. When we left the barbershop we said we would get together a lot more in the future, but we never did.

Jason Beck, my barber, is normally quiet as he cuts your hair. One day after I had the chance to reunite with Hugh, Jason told me that Hugh had come for a haircut not long before. I asked him how he was doing, and he said that he did not believe very well. He told me his wife died and he was using a walker. Well, I felt I had put it off long enough and I would go out to see him that afternoon. From our earlier conversation I remembered him saying he lived on the old Curly Fuhrman place north of Lindsay.

After getting my haircut I drove east on Highway 82 to the Marysville/Moss Lake Road and headed north. Driving on Marysville Road I realized I was back in my old stomping grounds, and where I grew up brought back many memories. On the corner of Highway 82 and Marysville Road a little over 91 years ago a beautiful baby was born. Yes, that is where I began.

My Mom and Dad lived on the Robert Flusche farm that belonged to my mother's brother after they moved from Iowa because of Dad's poor health.

Further north on Marysville Road is a gravel road shortcut to Gainesville. I remember that, when I was about five years old, I was riding in an iron-wheeled wagon pulled by a team of horses going to Gainesville with my

Daddy on this road. I had to stay with the horses and wagon as Dad shopped.

Some kind of a tragedy happened, for there was a crowd of people around the wagon. I believe someone fell off of a power pole.

We lived farther north where the roads now split, one to Marysville and one to Moss Lake. When we lived there, the split did not exist. A series of corners took the road around our place.

I knew that the Curly Furhrmann place was on the Marysville Road where there was a road going east that had never been opened. I went up to the house, but no one was at home, so I asked a neighbor, and he told me I was on the wrong road.

I was on the Marysville Road, but Hugh Perry lived on the Moss Lake Road. I looked for a road that would take me from Marysville Road to the Moss Lake Road. I found none, so I went back to where the roads split and got on the correct road. The Moss Lake Road did not exist prior to WWII. Now it goes right through the middle of our place as it existed before the war. In fact, the road goes right through where Dad had his machine shed. As children we spent many an hour playing around the machinery.

That pasture is where I practiced driving Dad's 1929 four-door Chevrolet touring car. The back doors on the car opened from the front, and one time when Dad drove through the gate coming home, I opened the door while going through the gate and it tore off. That is the only time I can remember getting a spanking.

On the north side of the machine shed under the trees, Dad had an old steel-wheel Fordson tractor. I remember only one time he started it and tried to plow. It had no battery; ignition was by permanent magnets embedded in the flywheel. When the flywheel was spinning it provided battery to the four coils, providing spark to the four cylinders. To get it started one would have to connect a car battery and crank it. After we got it running he tried to plow, but it could not pull a two-disk plow, so Dad went back to his horses until he bought a new John Deere tractor in 1936.

Dad had sold this place to Leo Mosser when I was about nine years old and bought the larger Phillip Berendt farm when Phillip died. We now lived on a farm on the north end of what became the Gainesville airport.

Getting back to what I started, I got on the right road, and I was soon driving up to Hugh Perry's farm yard. I came to find out that the west side

Hugh Perry's farm was adjacent to the east side of the old Curly Fuhrmann farm. That is why he said he lived on the Curly Fuhrmann place. He just did not tell me he was on the other end—or I did not hear it.

One of Hugh's two daughters met me at the door. He was sitting in his lounge chair with his walker by his side. Hugh's health had deteriorated drastically since I had seen him. His wife had died some time ago, and because of low blood pressure he had passed out, breaking his hip in the process. He attributed the low-blood-pressure problem to a clogged filter he had in his veins that limited blood flow. His children that live close by are helping him. His son has been doing the farming. He had high praise for the Muenster hospital where he spent six weeks in rehabilitation after they replaced his hip in the Gainesville hospital. I was not aware that he was in Muenster hospital, or I would have visited him. He was impressed with the number of people exercising in the hospital every day.

When I left Hugh I went past our old Berend place on the north side of the Gainesville Airport. I thought about the time we had to leave it. It was a nice home over a full basement, with a double, two-story garage. It had a big red barn, many smaller buildings, and a 20-tree peach orchard. Cooke County Electric had just brought us electricity, and crops in the fields were ready to harvest. But bulldozers were pushing over our old giant oak trees, and we had to grab what we could during the two weeks they gave us to get out.

It was 1940 and the beginning of World War II.

CHAPTER 71

The Story of Heritage Park

The people we serve have been good to us, and we wanted give something back to the community. I have been active in Germanfest from the beginning. I was on the founding committee in 1976 and was Chairman or Co-Chairman of the fest in the earlier years for more than 10 years. Gracie and I feel it is only proper that we contribute a major part of Heritage Park.

While Gracie and I contributed the major part of Heritage Park, the park would not have been possible without over 50 contributors of money and/or services to complete the project. I need to give special recognition to Matt Sicking for the use of his grader and backhoe, and to the people who served on the board for their guidance—their wisdom has made Heritage Park what it is today. Also, it would not have been possible without the financial assistance given by Nortex.

Heritage Park

A permanent home for Germanfest has been a dream of mine and of most board members of the Chamber of Commerce for many years.

Land was offered to the Chamber sometime in the early 1980s by John H. Bayer to build a permanent Chamber/Germanfest office and land to hold the festival. A drawing of the office building was found in Chamber papers after Margie Starke became the Secretary of the Chamber of Commerce in late 1989. She asked about this drawing, and Charles (Chas) Bayer told her it was part of a dream for a Chamber/Germanfest office, but the Chamber had to provide the plans and funding for the office and festival grounds. The Chamber had hoped that they might someday bring this to reality, but after several years they just dropped it due to lack of raising any funding and to lack of interest from the community. Margie said she had already made a lengthy list of things she would like to accomplish while working at the Chamber. On the list was creating a permanent home for Germanfest, but she feared this would be something that would be a long time coming—or something never be. Nevertheless, she left it there on the "To Accomplish List."

It was in spring of 2006 when I visited Margie's office, located across Highway 82 from Rohmer's Restaurant. I wanted to discuss the possibility of a permanent home for Germanfest. So much of GermanFest in the park was on private land, and I didn't know how much longer the land would be available. The fest ties up the park for two weeks where no one else can use it. I told Margie that if there was enough local interest to buy the land that Gracie and I would be willing to donate $1.5 million toward starting the project.

Margie said she did not know if the interest was there, but promised she would call a meeting to find out what the interest would be. I told her that the people of Muenster were good to my family and that we wanted to give something back to the area.

I realized that an attempt to do a project of this sort had been made earlier but had died for a lack of funding, so I wasn't sure what would come of my proposal.

Margie called a special meeting of the Chambers members, and we met in the telephone company's meeting room. We explained the aforementioned facts—and concerns—about the private land situation. I also noted that it cost over $30,000 a year to sponsor Germanfest, money that isn't recovered without a sponsor. While we would have some 30,000 visitors each year, because the event was held on private property, the funds raised at the event would go to rent. Besides that, I said, parking is along Highway 82 and on streets of Muenster and in many private parking lots, and I was concerned that one of these years someone would be injured or killed crossing the highway. I noted that the park we used for was getting too small for the Germanfest. Each year vendors had to be turned away.

Thirty two members attended the meeting, and to my joy, a great deal of interest was shown among the attendees. An overwhelming number of persons present agreed to proceed with the project.

A few months later, a second meeting was held on July 8, 2007 in the K C Hall. Matt Sicking and others gave a barbecue dinner for the group that attended. I made my presentation explaining how important it was for Germanfest to have a permanent home. Bayer Brothers had given us an option to purchase 92.6 acres of land on the west city limits of Muenster for $5,000 an acre. The Muenster Industrial Board agreed to purchase 96 acres on the west side for $350,000, leaving another $113,000 to complete the purchase of the land. Gracie and I offered to donate $1.5 million to build the pavilion if there was enough local interest to purchase the land. The Fisher Family had agreed to donate $100,000 toward the construction of an amphitheater. There were just three or four people opposed to the idea; it was overwhelmingly approved.

How Heritage Park came to be

A fund drive was started to see if the $113,000 could be raised to buy the land. Some 30 local persons came forward to purchase the land, making the Heritage project a reality.

Germanfest Inc. was incorporated in May 2007. It received its non-profit status locally on May 23, 2008 and with the state of Texas in January 2009. Hess Drilling Company doing the dirt work.

A governing Board was established and consisted of me representing Nortex Communications; three Chamber Board members: Matt Sicking, Kirk Klement and Carolyn McPherson; Industrial Board Member Charles Bayer; City Manager Stan Endres and Chamber Secretary Margie Starke. I was elected President Matt was elected Vice President and Carolyn was elected Secretary. It was decided to call the project "Heritage Park." Our first order of business as a Board was to hire Terry Harden as our Architect. We also appointed the John Bezner civil engineering firm to prepare the site plan and appointed Dave Isabel to be our construction engineer. Dave agreed to provide his services at no charge.

The lowest bidder for site preparation was Hess Drilling Company. Alliance Building Systems designed and manufactured the 180-foot x 360-foot steel building, and Mages Construction Company of Gainesville was awarded the building contract. Matt Sicking agreed to act as the General Contractor for Heritage Park.

We held a groundbreaking ceremony in September of 2010 and we looked forward to a new home for Germanfest and other activities throughout the years when the park was completed.

Site work started in 2011, and the building arrived six months later.

The site area was an old field, and it had old iron junk lying around and a number of idle uncapped oil wells. A creek with heavy brush undergrowth runs through the middle of the proposed site. There were old oil tanks that had to be moved, and a powerhouse sat idle. We would liked to have kept the powerhouse for show, but the owner moved it to Nocona. The place that would become Heritage Park was a mess when we purchased the land.

Herman Grewing, owner of the oil lease, capped the three or four old oil wells on the site. The Industrial Foundation sold about 10 acres of their land to Giles Walterscheid for a machine shop, and the city laid a sewer line and a water line past our place to serve them. We agreed to share the cost of the water and sewer with Giles. Matt Sicking buried a 4-foot drainage pipe from the railroad bridge to Brushy Elm Creek to take the place of the creek that ran across the parking lot. All the down drains of the large building were also connected to this line when the building was complete.

We had an empty building when Mages completed its part of the contract. In fact, we had a beautiful 64,800-square-foot empty shell for a building, as it took all the money to build the building. The inside of the building was not in the contract, and we planned to fill it out as we had the money.

The Clyde Fisher Family donated $100,000 toward the purchase of the amphitheater, which was constructed by Giles Walterscheid. The Fisher Family named the amphitheater "Fisher Stage.'

Donations did not come in to help complete the project, so I made my first advancement of $100,000. In addition, four more $100,000 contributions were made to complete the building and lawn area. The contract to lay the concrete blocks to finish out the toilets on the east side went to a Mexican contractor. This was the only bricklaying contractor we were aware of. Along with the east toilets, an office and storage area were also completed.

The inside of the building was completed and in 2013 the Firemen Bar-B-Que was the first event held in the new park. Three Big Ass Fans

Company fans were added to make the pavilion comfortable during the event. Since then, in 2015, a kitchen was installed.

On August 3, 2007 Annette Walterscheid amd Kathryn Hicks joined the Germanfest Inc., and the board consisted of nine members; Matt Sicking, Kirk Klement, Charles Bayer, Carolyn McPherson, Stan Endres, Margie Starke, Annette Walterscheid, Kathryn Hicks and me. In 2010 Annette Walterscheid left the Board.

Jeff Walterscheid joined the board in 2013. Claude Walter joined the board in 2014. Kirk Klement left the board in 2015. Jeff Walterscheid left the board in September of 2015. Claude left the board in December of 2015. Pat Lutkenhaus joined the board in March of 2016. Bernard Hesse joined the board in June of 2016, and John Bartush joined the board in June of 2016.

In April 2018 the first Germanfest was held in Heritage Park. A second entrance to Heritage Park from Highway 82 is under construction. The parking lot west of Fuhrman Hall is being graveled to make room for an additional 1,000 cars to park along the highway.

It is planned to have the carnival and the Bar-B-Que Cook-off on the south side of Brushy Elm Creek with the cook-off east of the carnival. A bridge gives access to the Germanfest grounds for these areas.

A panel of stars will give credit to those who donated money or their services to complete Heritage Park. There will be 25 Plexiglas stars framed with a blue background for those who paid cash and 15 Stars framed on a red background for those who provided services. The more you gave, the larger the star. Stars will be mounted on both sides of the stage. The blue stars will be mounded on the east side of the stage, and the red stars on the west side of the stage. An LED light will outline each star and light up the donor's name.

The pavilion in Heritage Park is named Fuhrman Hall in honor of our son, Gene, who was killed by a drunk driver in 2003. Gene, our second son, was the manager of Nortex Communications Company at the time of his death. His wife Kaylynn was pregnant, and we now have a 13-year-old grandson, Conner.

The whole town benefits from Germanfest taking place in their town, but the following community organizations and their sponsors are benefiting directly from Germanfest: the Muenster Library, Sacred Heart Alumni,

Knights of Columbus, Muenster Jaycees, Muenster Kiwanis and Muenster Boy Scouts.

The 34th Germanfest took place this year (2018) in Heritage Park. We went all out to show off our new home. The Schroeder Group from Wichita Falls, Texas, was hired to direct publicity.

The new 64-acre Park features a 75,000-square-foot Fuhrman Hall, where the major activities took place.

We hope the community has many years of enjoyment from the Heritage Park Complex.

The start of the Heritage Park

Heritage Park Fisher Stage

CHAPTER 72

Germanfest

Heritage Park inside the tent—GERMANFEST

From the beginning when Muenster was founded in 1889, it was a town of celebrations. In the years before WW I it was a Schueitzenfest. The local gun club shoot-off was held on the north side of the church grounds. At that time that was an open field. The town artist would carve out an eagle out of knotty hardwood. This would be mounted on top of a pole so that all shots would go up in the air. Shooting at this eagle would start Wednesday and continue until the last piece of the eagle would fall to the ground about Thursday afternoon.

Beer made it more difficult to shoot chips away from the eagle. Everyone used the same gun, which was mounted some distance away. It was mounted on a pole in such a way the only thing you could shoot at was the eagle. The man who shot off the last piece of that eagle, felling it to the ground was declared "Schueitzen King." He would then select his Queen. His Queen would then select her "Ladies in waiting." These usually would be close friends of the Queen.

They would reign over the festivities ending with the grand ball on Saturday night. Celebrations would continue each day with parades through town led by the town band and the Men's Choir singing. This celebration would continue late each night.

In one of last Schueitzenfests, Joe Noggler was the Schueitzen King, and Jenule Sieger was his Queen. Ladies in waiting to the Queen were her close friends Mrs. Henry Roberg and Mrs. Frank Schaech.

When WW I came along all activity of this kind was stopped and no one even spoke German. Many of the local people were afraid that they would be put into detention camps until after the war.

The Sacred Heart Choir and the Dallas Frohsinn

The popularity of the 20 years of concerts and Dances held with the Dallas Frohsinn played a great part in the success of the expansion of Germanfest. The Choir joined the Texas State Singer Bund Society, and in 1935 the State Singer Bund convention was held in the Muenster Parish Hall. A relationship was started with Dallas Frohsinn Singers that continued off and on for 40 years.

As I noted previously, our relationship with the Dallas Frohsinn started up again in 1957 .They would charter a bus and come to Muenster each year for a concert and dance. Mrs. Lehnertz would always cook a very delicious meal. We would eat in the basement of the old parish hall, and the concert and dance would be upstairs.

On the Frohsinn first visit to Muenster in 1957, Herman Meiners, president of the Dallas Frohsinn, gave a long dinner speech in German; he did not realize that not one of us could understand what he said. He still laughed about that years later.

The Polka Peppermints band always played for the event. Teddy Trept, Hermann Meiners, Willie Gotlieb, Charlie Heck, Gary Nelson and their wives and others were some of the Dallas members coming to Muenster.

It was usually cold, because they came in February. We would always set them up on the down-wind side of the old Parish hall. There was no insulation in the walls, and the side of the hall where the wind blew in would always be cold.

The Dallas Frohsinn would sing three numbers, then Sacred Heart Choir would sing three numbers. Then we combined the choirs to sing three numbers together—all would be in German.

At intermission Gary Nelson would get out his accordion, and German beer songs would fill the hall. A good time was had by all.

The hall had one commode in each of its men and women restrooms—needless to say lines would develop.

We would return their visits by chartering a bus and going to Dallas to join them for a concert and dance in the "Sons of Hermann Hall" on east Elm Street and the Ceck Hall on Greenville Avenue.

One year Dr. Martin Kralicke, a local physician, took a new doctor along who was planning to relocate to Muenster. We had our usual chartered bus and had our usual party on the way to Dallas and back; beer cans began to roll back and forth in the bus as it slowed down and sped up.

When we got back to Muenster, the doctor left town and no one ever saw him again.

When the old Parish Hall was torn down and a new Community Center was completed in the 1970s, we continued with our joint concerts and dance. It was the most popular event of the year in Muenster. Our success with German music, song and dance contributed to the establishment of Germanfest in Muenster.

The First Germanfest

The bicentennial of the United States was approaching in 1975. Gerald Ford was president of the United States and had urged towns to have special celebrations to honor the occasion. Also, new signs had just been posted on Hwy. 82 proclaiming Muenster to be the "Home of German Hospitality."

The Chamber had just started up again after being inactive for a number of years, with Bertha Hamric as president. The membership agreed to a weeklong celebration with an event almost every evening. Bertha appointed a committee to plan the big bicentennial celebration.

The founding committee consisted of Leonard Endres, chairman; Bertha Hamric, Jane Monday, Alvin Fuhrman, David Bright, Al Wiesman and Lawrence Bruns.

The Bicentennial and German Week celebration was held at the new Community Center, which had just been completed. The parking lot was not paved, and everyone stumbled over the rocks and gravel to walk around. A large 60 x 120-foot tent was erected along the north side of the parking lot, running east and west. The tent was packed with local organizations sponsoring food, arts, services and entertainment booths. Electrical problems plagued the booths serving food. There were too many cookers and not enough power.

We had a weeklong celebration, with something taking place almost every night: Wednesday night featured Opening Ceremonies and a Bicentennial Pageant at the public school; Thursday night offered a Queen Pageant in the Community Center where Barbie Hess was chosen Queen.

Pia Woodall of Irving brought her folk dance group of young girls to dance on an improvised stage on the west entrance of the Community Center.

Alois Wiesman manned the information booth and supervised the guest book, a job he has continued for many years. Al Walter supervised security and continued to do so for the next 10 years. Almost everyone in Muenster had a job that week.

Dan Hamric and Ronny (Rumpy) Hess directed a 10-mile Fun Run, which started and stopped in front of the celebration on Main Street. We were amazed at the number of runners in the first fun run and the number of people who attended our first Germanfest.

There were also softball tournaments, horseshoe tournaments, tricycle races, skateboard contests, bicycle rodeos, a tug-of-war, a turkey shoot, a motorcycle rodeo, an arts and craft show, with plenty of German food, beer and soft drinks. Friday night the first of three dances took place in the Community Center and featured "Cherry Rhones."

On Saturday night, the "Polka Patriots" played. As a prelude to Germanfest, each year, for nearly two decades, a bus load of the Dallas Frohsinn Singing Society members would join the Muenster Men s Choir for a concert and dance in the Community Center. In the early years this would take place in February; starting that year, the dance was changed to

Saturday night to correspond with the Centennial celebration. The choirs held a joint concert singing German songs separately and together. The Dallas Frohsinn Schammelkapella Band played dinner music and led the sing-along at intermission. This event was very popular, and the place was packed with some people seated in the meeting rooms of the community Center. Tables were resold when someone would leave. The choirs also performed on the west entrance to the Community Center.

And on Sunday night, the festival closed with the Centennial Ball. Barbie Hess was Queen of the Ball, and we danced to the music of the "Art Tofte Band." Everyone dressed up in their finest, and the band played into the night. We were very tired by then, but we enjoyed every minute of it.

After paying all the bills the first year, the committee thought they had made $25. When the second year came around, Edgar Dyer and the FFA boys and girls were asked to clean up the grounds again. They said they would be glad to; however, they hadn't been paid the $25 to clean up the previous year. There went the $25 profit from the first year.

Germanfest has continued every year since.

The second Germanfest

On a summer day in 1976, I was working in the equipment room of the telephone office when Bertha Hamric, Chamber president, called and asked if I would be the general chairman for the 1977 Germanfest. I readily agreed, for I was anxious to keep Germanfest going. I felt it would be great for Muenster to celebrate our heritage with a festival each year.

Right away, I ran into a problem. It so happened that the Texas Telephone Association convention was held in Austin the same week as our Germanfest, and I was on the TTA Board. I would need to make the board meeting after the convention Wednesday before coming home.

In those days, the Chamber of Commerce had no office. The general chairman and his committee planned and carried out the event.

So there would be no confusion, I wrote a manual with a description of what each job consisted of—it covered all aspects of the festival. Each job had a volunteer overseeing that part. This manual served as a guide for many years. I still have this manual in my files today. Needless to say, Germanfest took place that year without any problems. When I got back to Muenster on Wednesday afternoon, the fest was well on its way.

The same size large tent was again used in the second Germanfest. This time it was turned north and south in the middle of the Sacred Heart Church parking lot. By this time, the parking lot had been paved.

I was determined not to have an electrical problem again during the second year, so I dug through the cheese plant junk box with their approval and came up with two used 200-amp fuse boxes that we could use for the main power panels. We mounted them on poles on each side of the tent. TP & L hooked up the power to these panels, and we ran the electric cables from the power panels throughout the tent. This redesigned electrical system replaced the troubled system from the previous year, and we had no problem with the electricity.

We still were not sure what the fest should be called, so we just called it "Germanfest.' More than a dozen persons took on the job of planning for the festival and called on an army of volunteers to help them with Germanfest. This was the same group of people who worked on the 1977 festival. This included me as general chairman, with Bertha Hamric as co-chairman. Other officers included Lawrence Bruns, publicity; Dan Hamric, Ronny (Rumpy) Hess, sponsoring the KC's Fun Run; Edgar Dyer and the FFA, clean up; me and the telephone company, electric power and sound system; Alois Wiesman, information booth; Al Walter, security; Al Hess, concessions; David Bright, finance; Jane Monday, decorations· Leonard Endres, tent; Frank Luke, entertainment; and John Monday, games.

The KC's sponsored the second 15k German Fun Run with 569 runners. The race started and finished on the street in front of the Germanfest on Main Street by Sacred Heart Church.

Roller skating skills were added to the contests, and Gene Fuhrman, my late son, won first prize.

Debbie Zimmerer was crowned Miss Muenster in a pageant held in the public school auditorium on Thursday night. She was honored at the Choir's concert and dance Saturday evening.

On Saturday night, Sacred Heart Men's Choir again held its popular concert and dance with a bus load of the Dallas Frohsinn Singing Society members joining us in the community center. Again the place was packed. The choirs sang German and English songs separately, and then the choirs were combined for a finale. Gary Nelson played the accordian and led the spontaneous German singing during the intermissions. The Honorary German Consulate from Dallas, Gershon Canaan, and his wife, the Honorary Consulate from Monaco, in Dallas, attended Germanfest.

Pia Woodall's ballet dance group was back again this year and performed on the entrance to the Community Center.

The estimated total of visitors the second year was 12,000. Finance chairman David Bright reported a gross income of $8,559.16 with total expenses of $4,610.55. Net income the second year was $3,599.16.

1978 Germanfest

"GERMANFEST WAS GREAT" was the Enterprise headline, after the third Germanfest, which was held in the City Park in 1978 for the first time. Johnny Pagel, general chairman, reported that remarks made about Germanfest were highly favorable and estimated that about 30,000 persons attended the weekend event. He was highly complementary of the several dozen persons who did a good job with organizing the event.

The principal attraction was the German Fun Run with 1,165 runners— this had developed into one of the leading distance races of the state. Obviously Germanfest and the Fun Run each are helpful to the success of the other. Over 100 volunteers in town and along the rural routes provided drinks and sprayed runners to keep them cool. Chairman Dan Hamric said 1,345 persons registered for the Fun Run, but only 1,165 finished.

Other headline events were the Miss Muenster Pageant the preceding Thursday. Cindy Sangster, daughter of Mr. and Mrs. Tom Sangster, was named Miss Muenster. This took place Thursday night and was the first event of the 1978 Germanfest.

On Saturday evening, the Sacred Heart's Men's Choir's combined concert and dinner dance with the Frohsinn Singing Society Men's choir from Dallas took place in the Community Center. This was the 18th year that the Dallas Frohsinn joined the S H Men's Choir for a concert and dance.

There was constant entertainment at the Jaycee pavilion and a free street dance. There were vocal concerts by two S H Parish singing groups, and instrumental presentations by the Muenster High School Band. Also a German Band from North Texas State University entertained for three hours on Saturday. There was a free street dance in the park Saturday evening.

Most of the festival's success can be credited to the hard working volunteers who did the "heavy lifting"—both figuratively and literally. Besides erecting and dismantling booths they spent long hours serving the crowds at the concessions. Others prepared baked goods at home for sale in the big tent.

Special credit was given to Edgar Dyer and boys of the F F A chapter who served the duration by keeping the tables cleaned during the fest, as well as cleaning the grounds the morning after.

The guest book was supervised by Mr. and Mrs. Al Wiesman and contained about 1,700 signatures and told a story about the Germanfest. Fortunately, the names were mostly from out of town and revealed that some came great distances to attend the Germanfest. The listing showed visitors from towns around Muenster and from 27 states and three foreign countries. Amazingly, Germany appeared on the list 27 times, along with Saudi Arabia and Guam.

Food, drinks and souvenirs were the main features. The National Guard Armory display included a first aid station and a heritage museum and a battle tank. Also this year for the first time was a Ferris wheel and a Merry Go Round. These were very popular with the children.

Organizations operating concessions included the VFW Auxiliary, the Garden Club, St Ann's Society, the Blue Bonnet Club, the HD Club, Fischer's Market, the Quarterback Club, Catholic Daughters, Young Homemakers, the Muenster Fire Department, the Band Parents, Gary Fisher's, Pagel Grocery, H and W, the Dairy Inn, the Center Restaurant, Sacred Heart Trust Fund, Nocona Leather Goods, Anderle and Hudspeth, and Muenster Public School Seniors. All agreed that the third annual Germanfest was highly successful—far exceeding the previous Germanfests that were held previous years. Germanfest has been a real boast for the town, bringing in new money that is circulated many times in our small community.

1979 Germanfest

"The fourth annual Germanfest was another delightful event." That is how the Muenster Enterprise described the fourth-annual Germanfest held for the second year in Muenster City Park. The total attendance for the three-day event was estimated to be 30,000 persons. I was chairman again, and I reported at the time that the event was highly successful and credited dozens of pleasant, hard-working people for making the event so successful. Monica Hess took over publicity for the first time. The brochures took on a new look. Frank Luke continued with entertainment.

The entertainment program for the Germanfest started Thursday evening with the Miss Muenster Pageant in the MPS auditorium. Miss Cathey Flusche was selected 1979 Germanfest Queen. She reigned over the Germanfest festivities and represented Muenster in various events throughout the year.

The Highway 82 overpass had been demolished and all Hwy. 82 traffic was routed past the Germanfest main gate on Maple Street. Dick Ferber was new in Muenster and helped direct traffic past the park. Courtesy vans provided by Wilde Chevrolet and Endres Ford helped move the crowd from town to the park. Parking was provided by private individuals.

For the first time there was continuous entertainment in the Jaycee pavilion for the three days. There was a variety of bands, vocal concerts and folk dances, as well as many other dances, including street dances, a polka dance, a country western dance and a disco dance. In addition, there were horse shoe contests, motorcycle riding, costume contests, folk dancing and a beard contest. Twenty-four booths were set up for business in the big tent on the tennis courts in the City Park.

Saturday night there were two dances. There was a country western dance in the VFW Hall and a polka dance in the community center. The Dallas Frohsinn Singing Society joined the Muenster Sacred Heart Choir in a concert and dance in the Community Center.

This was the first year the Jaycees used their specially equipped beer van with 16 beer spigots on both sides of the van. The beer van has become a featured attraction of Germanfest.

"Muenster's fabulous Fun Run was super" is the way Ramie Fette, editor of the local paper, described the Fun Run in the Muenster Enterprise that year. According to the sponsors, Dan Hamric and Ronnie Hess, 1,402 persons registered for the Fun Run and 1,068 completed the race. This year was the first time the race was held on Saturday; in previous years it was held on Sunday. The winner was Hector Ortiz, a 26 year old man from Fort Worth. He came in second in the 1988 race. He finished the 15-kilometer race in 48 minutes and 46 seconds. The first person to finish from Muenster was Dale Schilling with a time of 53 minutes and 4 seconds. Hamric said one of the gratifying features of the Fun Run is the praise received from the runners, commenting on how well it was organized and the pleasant atmosphere along with the way and drinks at stations along the way.

In regard to food, 3,400 pounds of sausage was consumed along with 500 pounds of sauerbraten, 475 pounds of barbeque, and 40● chickens. These dishes were served with all the trimmings and washed down with 250 kegs of beer served in 20 ounce souvenir cups. The beer was sold at a dollar a cup. An additional 38 kegs of beer were served at the Fun Run party and at the two dances held Saturday night.

Mr. and Mrs. Al Wiesman supervised the guest book again this year. More than 1,900 persons signed the guest book. This is some 300 more signatures than last year. Nearly all persons signing the guest book are from out of town—many of them coming from afar. They came from 31 states not counting Texas and Oklahoma. 13 came from foreign countries. Germany again led the list with 18, considerably less than last year with 23. Others came from England, Canada, Panama, West Indies, Mexico, Australia, the Philippians, Holland, Venezuela, Singapore, Scotland and Lebanon.

Germanfest has become a real boost for the city and surrounding area. Most local organizations use the opportunity to raise their operating budgets for the year. It is estimated that over one million dollars is spent in the Muenster area the weekend of Germanfest.

Germanfest grows and grows

As the fest began to become increasingly popular, we began to make changes to accommodate the big crowds. I found an abandoned country bridge, and county personnel helped get it across Bushy Elm Creek in the Muenster park and drove steel pipe into the ground on each end to support it. We laid corrugated metal roofing on the floor and covered it with 4 inches of concrete.

We also buried concrete holding tanks on each side of the tent to catch the waste water. Steve Moster, city manager, would not let us connect the run-off from these tanks to be connected to the city sewer system. We would have to have them pumped out when they got full. Water was piped to both sides of the tent. We gave them no hot water—they had to heat their own.

A telephone switchboard was installed on the south side of the tent. Phones were installed on all strategic locations. A paging system was installed through the park. It is necessary to have a way to communicate with the crowd in the event of severe weather or danger.

Thunder storms would come through usually at night and I would be called out to secure the tent. At times vendors would leave the merchandise on shelves when they left at night. One occasion during a violent storm I took all of the ceramic displays off of their shelves and laid them on the floor to keep them from being damaged by the storm. The lady came the next day and was most distressed because her display was on the floor. She was most grateful when she learned of the storm that passed during the night and none of her pretty vases were damaged.

Helga Beckman and her Polka Combo entertained along with Mike Ott Disco, talent show, square dancers and the Cooke County Chorale. By 1980, The German Fun Run had 2,010 runners. The Dallas Frohsinn Singing Sociality joined the Muenster Men's Choir and a joint concert and dance. The 1980 Germanfest was the last time that the Dallas Frohsinn and the Muenster Men's choir had a joint concert. I presented the Frohsinn with a plaque honoring their 20th year of coming to Muenster.

A new look in 1981 included three new flag poles, displaying the United States, Texas and West German Flags. An enormous banner, a gift from the city of Munster, Germany, was hung in the pavilion. New features for this year included hot air balloon rides, fireworks, a carnival attraction and a visit by an Air Force helicopter. Special vests sewn by Jr. Elite were worn by the Germanfest committee. Total expenses were $21,570.31 and revenue was $22,605.42. Admittance to the park brought in $16,182.01. German bucks were used for the first time.

The 1982 Germanfest was bigger than ever. Blessed with perfect weather there was a gain in attendance of almost 50 percent. Newly completed restroom facilities, financed by the Chamber, were used for the first time. The first bike rally drew 119 participants; the Fun Run had 3,250 runners, with a total attendance of the three day event estimated at 45,000 to 50,000 people. Months of intensive planning for new activities and improvements pointed toward maintaining the larger number of visitors to 1983 Germanfest. All popular features of the fest continued this year, including improved security and van service furnished by Wilde Chevrolet from town to help facilitate the parking problem.

A high, straight wind this year created problems with the big tent throughout Sunday afternoon and the Fun Run. The wooden stakes holding the tent kept coming out of the ground, and Larry Aldridge was kept busy driving them back down. We had to use two stakes, one behind the other to hold the tent. The main tent was vacated for a while because of the high wind. We had to keep people from leaning on the poles inside the tent, as they were going two-to-three feet off of the floor and coming back down hard.

Each year telephone company crews would go to Lindsay, and Sacred Heart church grounds to pick up tables and chairs and haul them to the fest. Monday after the fest they would have to haul them back. At times they would be damaged and have to take them to a repair shop for repairs before returning them. Our bucket truck has to be used each year to put the ropes in the flag poles.

David Fette was concessions chairman for the first year. VFW sponsored a country and western dance at their hall. Security was improved in the park under Dick Ferber's direction with the uniformed sheriff deputies. Because of the increased cost of sponsoring the fest, an admittance of $1 was charged to enter the park, collected by the Myra Fire Department.

The Texas stage was added in the west side of the park featuring western music. Edgar Dyer and the FFA continued with the park cleanup.

Germanfest 1984, 1985 and 1986 maintained the phenomenal popularity of the fest. Louis Stephenson headed the 1985 fest. Thunderstorms passed through almost every year, usually at night, causing concern for the big tent. The German Fun Run became the second largest in the state. The bike rally continued to grow. Visitors seem to level off at around 40,000/50,000 each year.

The barbecue cook-off started in 1986. The Myra Fire Department took over the cleanup of the park. The Gainesville Kiwanis Club took care of the gate. Ethnic heritage was stressed more strongly in later years, and booths were requested to decorate in this theme, with awards given to the most outstanding.

German costumes became popular to support this theme, and the food continued to be great.

Margie Starke started in 1986 to head the Chamber of Commerce and Germanfest and continued in that role for 23 years. The Chamber office was started in 1986 with the office in the building occupied by Weinhof today.

The gate fees were increased to $3 in 1987 and 1988 to help finance the ever-increasing cost of producing Germanfest. Volunteer help continued to decrease, while the entertainment and publicity budget continued to increase. The cost of security and emergency medical service also increased. Dumpsters were incorporated to help with the huge amount of trash that the three-day event generated. The visitors continued to enjoy the popular entertainment and booths of food, drinks and gifts. Planning began in 1988 for an extra special Germanfest for the Muenster Centennial year, 1989. That year the library started selling centennial books at the Germanfest.

About 1986 we opened the Chamber office at what is the Weinhof today. Margie Starke continued as Chamber of Commerce manager and managed Germanfest since the office was opened.

Proceeds from Germanfest finance the Muenster Chamber of Commerce in its yearly effort to promote Muenster and the surrounding area. This also gives the various organizations of the area an opportunity to earn money for their yearly activities. Germanfest has helped to publicize Muenster and make it known as the tourist attraction for Northern Texas.

It is estimated that the Germanfest since 1980 has brought an average of one million dollars into Muenster each year. It is also believed that this money spent in Muenster for Germanfest has re-circulated over seven to ten times in the community.

I was chairman or co-chairman during 10 of the first 12 years of Germanfest. Others chairing the festival since have been John Pagel, Dick Ferber and Wayne Klement. It took an army of volunteers to produce Germanfest. In the early years Germanfest was organized with about 25 persons heading various activities, who in turn had a group of people working with them to stage the festival. My original organizational manual was used until the Chamber hired Margie Starke.

Those who worked many years with Germanfest through the earlier years include Al Wiesman, who worked many years in his information booth. He gave out information and supervised the guest book signing visitors from around the world. Monica Hess arranged the entertainment in the pavilion for many years. John Pagel headed Germanfest the third year when it was moved to the city park when the church parking lot was too small. David Fette had the task for many years supervising the food venders in the main tent. Dick Ferber supervised the security during Germanfest until his untimely death. Bertha Hamric was Chamber president when Germanfest was started in 1976 and served as co-chairman at times. Al Walter and his volunteers provided security at night. Edgar Dyer and the FFA boys and girls were in charge of keeping the place clean. Dan Hamric and Ronnie Hess started the Fun Run. Gary Fisher was in charge of entertainment on the west stage. Ray Wilde Chevrolet has provided vans, with Gene Gieb driving them for transportation to and from up town. All of these people volunteered their help, so it was a town effort each year to stage Germanfest.

Lilly Palmer is now the head of the C of C Volunteers, who still provide drinks and encouragement to the fun runners and bicycle riders as they come by their farms in the rural areas.

Today Gracie and I wear our German costumes, and we have had young people from out of town come up to us and ask about Germanfest. Some come to learn about their German heritage.

Heritage Park hosts the 2018 annual Germanfest

For the 2018 Germanfest, the layout of Heritage Park was patterned after the popular Germanfest in the City Park. Fuhrman Hall, the main building, hosted many food venders along the north side and the Polka bands. It opens to a wide grassy area on the south to the Fisher Stage. There are extensive toilet facilities that open to the outside as well as the inside on the south side of Fuhrman Hall. Additional food vendors were located around the grassy area along with the many Arts and Crafts tents between the grassy area and the creek. They fill the area between Fuhrman Hall and Fisher Stage. The children play area was located along the west side of the grassy area.

Three large parking lots accommodated more than 2,000 cars. Three lighted bridges over Bushy Elm Creek connected the carnival and Bar-B-Que cook-off with the rest of the complex. One bridge gave access to the carnival on the south side of Bushy Elm Creek.

There are two entrances to the park: One off of Ash and a new entrance that was completed off of Highway 82. A well-lighted boulevard led visitors from Hwy. 82 past the carnival parking area over a newly constructed bridge over Brushy Elms Creek to the west parking lot and on to the west side of Fuhrman Hall. A buffer area at each entrance kept cars from piling up on the roads. A bridge for people to cross Brushy Elm Creek from the carnival parking area provides a short cut to the GermanFest. The Ash Street entrance lines up with 2nd Street coming from downtown. It is anticipated that 2nd Street will be opened some day to give access to downtown Muenster. 2nd Street will have to be routed around the spillway of the Weinzapfel Lake.

The present north entrance to Heritage Park from Ash St. has become a limited access for vendors only. They are able to go in and out without mixing with visitors coming to the park. This is controlled by a pole gate that requires a code to open, which they receive when they register.

CHAPTER 73

The Barn Swallows

Not long ago, I came home and noticed that a pair of Barn Swallows had built a nest on top of the motion detector in our garage. Our garage is open in the back, so they had access at all times. I will call the birds Cherio and Rodger—Cher and Rod, for short.

When I got closer, Cher hopped out of her nest and sat on the solar screen as though to say, "How do you like it, and can we stay"? We welcomed them to stay. We were fascinated as the young bird couple prepared for their family.

The nest was made out of mud and straw. It had a beautiful lacy design. You could not see Cher or Rod when they sat in the nest. Sometimes, you could see their heads if they stuck them up to look around.

A week or two went by and we noticed both Cher and Rod were spending a lot of time in the nest. We assumed they were keeping the eggs warm. We did not get close to the nest to see how many eggs were there.

Then I came home one day last week and saw four hungry heads with their mouths wide open and Cher and Rod flying in food for their hungry family.

In the meantime our cat that is renowned for getting a bird for a meal now and then was licking his chops over the possibility of getting himself a dinner of four young birds when they became ready to try to fly. Cher had built her nest too high for the cat to reach, and the pipe post was too slick for her to climb. At night the cat lay on the hood of Gracie's car dreaming about the meal he was going to get.

This went on for weeks, and the family grew. Cher and Rod kept flying in the food. As the young ones got bigger the nest got more crowded. Soon some of the little ones, fully featured by now, would have to sit on the edge of the nest, for there was no room inside.

We knew that they would have to fly off soon, so we left the garage door open so the little ones would have a straight shot to take off. I came home last week and the little ones had successfully left the nest and were all sitting on our solar screen. As I drove up, Cher flew back and forth several times then landed on a nearby perch. She chirped as if to say, " This is my family—how do you like them"?

When I got out of my car, Cher flew back and forth, wildly screeching as if to say, "Now go—get going." One by one they took off flying through the open garage door. All took off except for the little one. He looked like he was not paying attention to his mother. Cher and Rod landed nearby, and it looked like they were deciding what to do with the little one. Meanwhile, I walked closer to the young bird, and all at once she took off, right through the open garage door and was gone. Cher and Rod, then a few behind her—then they were gone.

The cat was nowhere in sight. Cheo had picked a time when the cat was not home for the birds to make their maiden flight. Gracie then cleaned up the mess they made on the floor and sprayed some water on the mud nest, and it came tumbling down.

Every day Cher and Rod would come by to see us, coming into the garage, making a few circles and flying away.

The other day when I opened the garage door and drove in they came in as usual, circled a few times and stopped on the solar screen. They seemed confused, and they had something in their mouths. They apparently did not expect to see me right away. Finally they dropped what they had in their mouths and flew away. I picked up what they had dropped—it was mud with some straw. They were rebuilding the nest that had come tumbling down. I looked up, and they had a half-built nest back where the old nest was.

Here we go again.

THE END

EPILOGUE

A TRIBUTE TO GENE,
FROM HIS MOTHER

As this book has been dedicated to my wife Gracie—and to the memory of our son, Gene—I thought a fitting ending would be to share some of Gracie's favorite memories of him. I hope you'll see why we considered him to be so special.

Gene H. Fuhrman was born March 27, 1964. He was born at 1 p.m. in the old Gainesville Hospital (formerly M&S Hospital). Gene arrived two months pre-maturely and weighed only 4 pounds, 4 ounces. (Alvin and I said that he was a little bag of bones, because he was all arms and legs.)

He was so tiny when we brought him home that you could not hear him cry. So, at night, we kept him next to our bed in a bassinet so we would hear him. It was not too long before Kent brought his neighborhood friends in to see if Gene had any teeth yet.

Unfortunately, Gene was very sick his first five years of his life. He caught everything under the sun. He had the flu, and Kent caught it. I also got the flu. Alvin escaped it. Then, Gene had a second round of the flu. He cried and said it was Daddy's turn.

When Gene was four Alvin noticed that Gene was not feeling well. I took him over to our next-door neighbor, (our illness consultant) Mrs. Odessa Morrison, and she thought he had scarlet fever. The next day Alvin took him to the baby doctor in Sherman, and when he entered the doctor's office, Alvin told the receptionist that this baby probably has something very catching. Her reply was, "Just take your seat and wait your turn." When Gene's turn came, and the doctor diagnosed the illness, they ushered him out the back door. When Alvin and Gene arrived home and Alvin told me what it was, I called the doctor back and said Gene was going to a day nursery and he had exposed all of the children to scarlet fever. The doctor said, "All of the children have been exposed, and there is nothing to be done at this time." He told us not to say a word, and, maybe, nothing would happen. Fortunately, none of the other children caught scarlet fever.

Gene suffered with tonsillitis for several years before he was old enough to remove them. The year Gene was five years old we had taken him to the doctor 17 times in three months. Finally, one day the doctor said, "This is the best I have seen his throat. Let's take his tonsils out tomorrow," which was a Saturday. After this, Gene felt so good that we threatened to put them back a few times.

He also had chicken pox—right around the time he was supposed to be in Darlene Lueb's wedding as ring bearer. Luckily he was over them by the time of the wedding.

Eventually, he became a healthy boy who lived a wonderful life. And, now, I would like to share some of my favorite memories of Gene. I'll start with the early years . .

- Gene attended kindergarten at Muenster Public School. The morning he started kindergarten he was eating breakfast and started to cry. We asked him why he was crying, and he said, "I do not know how to learn." We told him that is why he was going to school: to learn.
- We always told our children that if they got in trouble in school they would also get in trouble at home for it. In kindergarten one day another boy squeezed Gene's hand hard, and Gene hollered, so the teacher sat him in a corner. He did not tell us about it until the third grade because he didn't want to get in trouble at home, also.
- When Gene was small, he attended day care at Sylvia Hofbauer's. He really liked it. In fact, after he started school, he would always stop on his way to the telephone office and play with the children. I called Sylvia to tell her to send him on his way so he wouldn't be in her way. She said, "Oh, I like him there. He plays with the children, and they really like him."
- When he was in the first grade at Sacred Heart school the time changed in October. Gene, still not knowing how to tell time, was

crying at the breakfast table again. This time he said he was late for school. We asked why he thought he was late for school. Gene said, "The sun is way up, and the birds are singing." That was how he knew when to be at school.

- We had taught Gene his prayers before he went to school. One day he came home from school and was disgusted. They were learning the Apostles Creed, and we had not taught him this prayer, and Sharon Voth knew all of her prayers before anyone else. He could not stand that he could not out-do her in prayers.
- He loved to read his MAD books. When his brother Kent got in trouble, Gene would run and get his MAD magazine and find the right saying for the infraction. He had a great sense of humor.
- We used large, brown paper bags for our garbage, and every time Gene wanted to open one his Kitty was always snooping in it. Gene would then take the cat and put her in the bag and shake her around so the bag would open up. Gene loved kitties.
- One time I told Gene not to do something, and he came back with, "You don't have a reason." I said, "Mothers do not need a reason."
- One summer when Gene was 9 and his good friend Bob Hamric was 10 we took the boys to Denver, Colo., to an OPASTCO meeting. There was a gas shortage that year, so the boys had to entertain themselves at the hotel. We thought they would go swimming all day at the indoor pool. Well, the pool had sprung a leak, so they couldn't swim. Every time Gene went to play with Bob, he would come and tell me he was going. In reply, I would always caution him to watch for cars when he crossed the street. One day he walked out the door and then returned to ask why I always reminded him to watch for cars. I told him so that one day he would not forget to look.
- Gene taught himself to play both keyboards on the organ.
- When he was small, he had a guitar, and he would always sing with it.
- Gene was a Cub Scout. I was his Den Mother for several years. He was very conscientious about working for all his merits.
- Years ago Alka Seltzer had a commercial that had this line in it: "Plop, plop, fizz, fizz—oh, what a relief it is." One day, Gene was

sitting on the commode singing, "Plop, plop, fizz, fizz—oh, what a relief it is." I had to laugh at that.

- One day when Gene was young he came to me and asked if I had noticed anything about Dad. I could not imagine what he was noticing about Alvin. I asked what is wrong with him. Gene said, "He can fix anything."

- I was using a canister vacuum cleaner and had laid the nozzle down to do something. Gene picked up the nozzle and made swirls on the television screen wit it. We had to get the repairman out to fix the TV. Needless to say, Gene did not do that again.

- Gene had blond hair when he was little. One day Alvin took him for a haircut, and he asked the barber to make his hair dark. He thought he was the only little kid that had blond hair until he went to school.

- Gene always came down to the telephone office after school. One evening, Gene was doing his homework. He needed some help, so I helped him with his homework. After he left my office, all at once a paper airplane came flying in. Gene had made a paper airplane, and inside it he had written a thank you note to me for helping him.

- Chris Moster, one of Gene's classmates, found out that Gene came down to the telephone office after school. Chris began coming down to play with Gene, and he was constantly getting Gene in trouble. So when Chris would show up, Gene would hide.

- One Saturday Gene, Kent, Greg Gieb and Chris Stoffels dug a hole in the backyard deep enough and wide enough for the four of them to sit in. They also found something to make a cover over the top. They pooled their money and went downtown to buy some French fries. When they came back, they laid their French fries in the hole and came into the house to get a drink. When they returned to the dugout, they met with great disappointment—Queenie, our dog, had crawled into the dugout and had eaten all of the fries. Talk about some mad kids.

- One evening after Gene came down to the telephone office after school he was crying. He was in the first or second grade then. It seems the Hartman boys that lived behind the telephone office were shooting sparrows with their BB guns. Gene could not stand to see a bird killed.

- The morning Gene was to start kindergarten he was eating breakfast and began to cry. I asked what was wrong, and he said he did not know how to learn. We told him that is why we were sending him to school.
- Gene played little league baseball. One season, he was the right fielder, and very few balls came that way. Gene got bored and started to watch the birds, etc., not paying attention to the game. Alvin went out and told him to pay attention to the game. When we got home, Gene said, "Dad, don't do that again." Alvin told him that if he watched the birds again he would. One evening Gene had a little league game in Muenster, and when I came to the game he came running up to me, and he had the back of his uniform torn. I always carried a needle and thread with me, so I took him to the school bus and sewed him up.
- Gene liked baseball, but he liked fishing better. He quit the team so he could go fishing with his daddy. His coach said he could still play, even though he missed practice. Gene told the coach that would not be fair to the other boys who all came to practice each time.
- Bob Hamric and Gene were very good friends for many years. They lived across the street from each other. On Saturdays they would go to see what each Mother was cooking and then would decide at which house they were going to eat lunch. They would spend the night at each other's homes. Bob had two little sisters, Dana and Lisa. When Gene and Bob were sleeping on the floor in the den, the girls would sneak downstairs and pull the pillows out from under the boys' heads, and their heads would go plunk on the hard floor. Gene always said he did not want any sisters because Bob's were always in his things, like his models and so forth. However, after these two little girls grew up, Gene saw them and said, "Boy, did they grow up cute."
- Gene and Kent shared a bedroom. Kent was always aggravating Gene. One Sunday morning when we returned from church, there was a big commotion in their bedroom. Alvin called in there and

said, "Boys, nothing better be torn up." Gene's answer was, "Only Kent." Evidently, Gene had enough of his brother, because Gene was not typically a fighter. Except two other times . . .

- One day, when Gene was really small, Greg Gieb was here playing, and Gene did not like what was going on, so he grabbed Greg around the waist and bit him. I gave Gene a lecture and then he went to the Giebs to apologize.

- When Gene was in the fourth or fifth grade in school he beat up Alfred Hennigan. Gene was not a fighter, so this came as a complete surprise to us. Alfred always bugged Gene during class, so Gene could not concentrate on his lessons. Gene asked the teacher if he could move, but the teacher refused to let him do that. So, one day, Alfred was especially annoying during class, and Gene decided he'd had enough and beat Alfred up after school. Alfred's mother came to school, and Gene got into trouble. That evening, I made him tell his daddy what he did, and Gene did not want to do that. We talked to Gene and told him we thought Alfred only wanted to be his friend but did not know how. If you knew his mother and father, you would understand Alfred's problem. Years later, Gene and Alfred were good friends. Alfred just didn't know how to be a friend in the early years.

- When Gene was very small he loved stuffed animals. He would stack them all around him when he went to bed at night. Sometimes, he had so many that they were pushing him out of bed.

- In those days I would sing to him. One day, he made a turn with his hand on my chest and said he was turning off the radio.

- When Gene started school he started calling me, "Mother," instead of "Mama." I loved this. He was quite old before he went to "Mom."

- When he started school he always gave Alvin a hug and a kiss before he left in the morning. He always called Alvin, "Dad."

- Gene loved skateboarding with Bob Hamric. Bertha Hamric would take the boys to skateboard parks on a routine basis. He and Bob won some contest at Germanfest with the skateboards.

- One time we went fishing at Eisenhower Park at Lake Texoma. Gene caught a great big fish, when not one else caught one.

- Once while Gene and Alvin went camping the dog was missing all night. Gene did not go to sleep until the dog returned early the next morning. He was five years old.
- Gene always liked to build a campfire when we went camping.
- Gene put many models of cars, airplanes and ships together.
- Even when he was young Gene loved to cook. We bought some easy cookbooks, so he could cook. He always baked his French fries. We had an elderly couple that lived next door. Every Sunday morning Gene would bake sweet rolls and take them to this elderly couple, Pa and Dessie. Dessie always made one of Gene's favorite dishes. It was applesauce with red hots.
- Gene also liked bologna sandwiches.
- Gene loved to look at my jewelry. I always knew he was in it. He always locked it when he got finished looking.
- When we had company he would crawl under our headboard on our bed with his flashlight and read. He did not like company when he was little.
- We went to Iowa to visit relatives when Gene was six. Dorthy Berte had a basement in her home. It was where her four boys played. Gene loved the basement, and when we had to leave he started to cry and asked, "Why don't we have a dirty room under the floor?"
- When Gene was in the fourth or fifth grade the mothers were asked to come to the school and observe the math class. I went to school and was sitting in the classroom for Gene to show what he could do in math. I noticed that he did not participate and was reading a comic book hidden in his math book. When he came home that evening, I asked him why he did not participate. He said, "I did all those problems last week and had all of them right."
- Alvin sang in the church choir when the boys were small. We would all go to church and then, when we entered church, Alvin would go up to the choir loft and the boys and I would got up in church. Evidently, Gene was wondering what happened to Daddy, because he turned around in church one Sunday and saw Alvin in the choir loft and said, loudly, "There is Daddy!"
- Gene loved Christmas. He had a printed place card. Every year he would set out this name card for Christmas, so Santa would know

where to put his presents. After the boys knew who Santa Claus was, we started wrapping their gifts. Gene was always very inquisitive. One year he unwrapped all of his presents and then re-wrapped them before Christmas. Another year he would look at the size of the boxes under the tree and then go down to the Ben Franklin store and check out all of the sizes of the things he wished for. The next year I wrapped all of his gifts in larger boxes.

- Gene always loved to help decorate the tree at Christmas. One year, when we still had hardwood floors in the living room, he dropped an ornament, and it splattered all over. He was sad when that happened. The next year we had carpeting, and he dropped an ornament that didn't break, and he said, "Thanks for carpeting."

- Alvin always liked to take the boys with him on Saturdays when he went somewhere. One Saturday he asked Gene to go along, and Gene asked, "Do I have to meet people?" In later years he learned to meet people very well.

- We did not have room for a garden. Our neighbor, Annie Flietman, had some garden space she was not using, and she said we could use it. Gene wanted to plant a garden. He and Alvin planted potatoes, and, as they grew, they got potato bugs on the plants. Gene had to go out and pick them off. One day he said he felt like the Orkin man.

- When Gene was small, and he did not want to go with Kent and Greg Gieb, he would just lie on the ground, and they could not make him go.

- Our boys did not know the Friske grandparents. They did not pay attention to our boys.

- Years ago, when you purchased a Coke, it was in bottles, and they were returnable for five cents each. The rule at our home was that you do not take these bottles and cash them in. I would take them to the grocery when I bought more Coke. Well, the Saturday before Mother's Day, I missed all of my empty Coke bottles. In questioning both boys, I realized they had taken them. Of course, I fussed at them for doing this. Neither one confessed what they did with the money. Come Mother's Day, here they came with a present for me that they had purchased with the Coke bottle money. Boy, did I feel bad.

Gene's junior high and high school years . . .

- When Gene was about 13 or 14 he always wanted his back rubbed before he went to sleep. I would rub his back for him.
- When Gene graduated from the eighth grade some of his fellow students told me Gene was the smartest student in the class. They did not give any awards for this in the eighth grade. Gene would never brag on himself. He never said anything about this to us.
- When Gene and Britt Smith were in the eighth grade and playing basketball they had a game one Saturday afternoon. Britt's father and I were the only parents there. Both boys would not shoot because they were afraid they would miss. Britt's Father and I started yelling, "we will give you a quarter for each time you shoot, hit or miss." Both boys began shooting, and their team won the game.
- When Gene was in the seventh grade he wanted to play basketball, but not football. The kids in school told him if he did not play football he could not play basketball. Alvin went to talk to the coach, and the coach said he wanted Gene to play basketball. In the seventh and eighth grades Gene had Coach Stock. He was not very good. In Gene's freshman year Coach John was the coach, and even in the first game Gene came on the court, you could see the difference in Gene as a player.
- When Gene was practicing for track they ran on gravel roads. He fell one day and really skinned himself up. That evening at the supper table, Kent was teasing him about being clumsy. Gene said, "I can't help that I do not know where my legs are going."
- Gene's friend Bob Hamric loved motorcycles, and Gene did not. One day, Bob was going to the river to ride and asked Gene to go along. Gene did not want to go, but he did not want to tell Bob no. I told Gene to go to Bob's and say his mother would not let him go. This satisfied Gene.
- While in high school he played on the basketball team. Gene got 90 consecutive tipoffs for his team. When they got ready for the tipoff the other team would all be on the other side.

- Gene received many honors in basketball. He was All Tournament in 1981 at Krum and Forestburg, to list a couple. He also played in the state tournament in San Antonio. One evening, when his team was playing at Callisburg, they started the game without a tipoff. When Gene came home that evening, I asked him why there was not a tipoff. He smiled mischievously and said they were not allowed to do any slam dunks during practice. If the refs saw a slam dunk there would be a penalty. The other players dared Gene to do a slam dunk, and he got caught.

- In his academic work Gene received several honors. He was Salutatorian of his class of 17. Some of the other honors he received included Science, English, History, Math and Biology. He was on the Honor Roll all four years of high school.

- When Gene was in Sacred Heart High School there were no computers. He and his father solicited donations from Sacred Heart parents until they had enough money to buy computers. Gene would teach his fellow students about the computer after school and in the evenings. The principal, Steve Bayer, would not let Gene and the other students in the school after hours to learn the computer. A nun would come over and let Gene in.

- One winter evening with snow on the ground we came home and Gene heard a little kitten crying in the alley. He went to see the kitty and brought it in our shop to keep it warm. The kitty was sneezing; Gene said it needed to go to the vet because it was sick. The next day, Gene took the kitten to the vet and paid for it himself. He brought the kitten home, but that was the last he saw of the little kitty.

- Gene loved kittens. One time our kitty was lost for some time, and we put a notice on Channel 2. One night at about 11 o'clock, Imelda called and said she found a kitty at the car wash. This was way over in the east part of town. She brought it over, and it was our kitty.

- Gene was always handy and able to fix things. He fixed his stereo to turn off automatically. Somehow he would set his alarm, which, in turn, did several things—including turning off the stereo. We had purchased a stereo for Kent, but when Gene got old enough to have one, he wanted a much nicer one for himself. We told that we would pay what we did for Kent's, and he would have to pay the rest. He had us purchase the stereo, and he made monthly payments until his part was paid. He was never late with a payment.

- During Gene's senior year in high school he decided to grow a mustache. Now remember: he was very blond-headed. One Sunday we had Grandma Fuhrman over for dinner. Grandma's eyesight was not very good. During dinner she looked at Gene and asked, "Are you growing a mustache?" Gene's reply was, "Oh, you finally noticed." Some Sundays when we were going to be out of town, Gene would take Grandma out to lunch. He always thought Grandma was cute. One day, after he took her out to lunch, he said he knew why she and Coralee, her daughter, didn't get along on politics—Grandma had given Gene her view of politics.

Gene's college years . . .

- When Gene went to college he came home one weekend and said he did not know toothpaste cost so much.
- When he was growing up he never used anything of Alvin's, like clothes, shoes, etc. But when he went to college he took Alvin's vitamins without asking. Alvin could not believe this.
- Gene attended North Texas State University the last year before the name was changed to the University of North Texas. He had a grade point average of 4.0. He graduated "Cum Laude" with a Bachelor of Business Administration degree and belonged to the Beta Gama Sigma fraternity. Gene loved astronomy and studied it on his own.
- Gene and Troy Wolf lived in an apartment in Sanger but were planning to move to Denton to go to school there. Prior to moving they cleaned the apartment, so well that they apartment manager commented on how clean they were leaving it. The boys said, "Our mothers taught us how to clean."
- On the first report card he received from college Gene did not get an "A" in English. He was very disappointed. He called home very unhappy. I told him it was very hard to get an "A" in college. His answer was, "I am not used to getting 'Bs.'" The next semester he had a different teacher, and she worked with him, and he received his "A."

Gene at the telephone company . . .

- Gene started with the company mowing the lawns when he was about nine or ten. When he was in high school he was our custodian for a while. He used a lot of pine oil, and it always smelled so clean. One day, I remarked that the office always smelled so clean. He said that was why he used so much pine oil—that it just smelled clean.

- When Gene went to work for the telephone company he said, "Dad, I am not going to keep the many hours you and Mom kept." As he started work he did keep many hours—and late hours. I would tell him to come in later in the morning, and he said that most of the employees did not know he worked late, and they would think he was coming in late because he was the bosses' son. He never wanted any employee to think that he was getting some extra perks because he was the bosses' son. So, at 5 p.m., off would come the tie, and he would lay his head back a few minutes and rest, and then he would continue to work late. When I was ready to go home I would go into his office if he was not resting and hug his neck and tell him to tell Kaylynn hi. One evening he asked me not to hug his neck so hard, so I lightened up a little. He would always push his chair back and get ready for the hug.

- Gene was also my computer desk help. I would peek around the door and wait until he noticed me, and he would make a face and come help me. One day he told me his office was too close to mine. He always did say that, for my age, I was doing fine with the computer. I think he was just being kind.

- After Gene graduated from college and had just started working for us there was an equipment show at Texas A&M. He was not supposed to go. The show was starting many things with the computer, and many of our employees were not versed in it yet. They came to Alvin and asked if Gene could go, so Alvin let him. When Gene returned home, he said, "Dad, I didn't know so many people knew you." This helped him overcome some of his shyness in meeting people.

- We were fortunate to be able to have lunch with him most days. We kind of had this routine set up. On Mondays we each paid for our own lunch. Tuesday was his day to buy. Wednesday he had lunch at the Kiwanis meeting. Thursday and Friday Alvin paid for our lunches. We would tease Gene on Tuesdays when he went with a salesman or something and we had to pay for our own lunch. When he went to lunch with Alvin they always talked electronics or something technical. When he and I went to lunch he would visit with me more about his life and what he and Kaylnn were doing.

- Sometimes, on company trips, we all three did not fly together. For one OPASTCO meeting in Orlando, Fla., we flew American, and Gene flew Delta. We told him that, by the time we got our luggage and rented a car, he should arrive and that we would pick him up. I went into the Delta terminal and could not find him anywhere. We thought that maybe he ran into a friend and got a ride to the hotel. We got into the car and left for the hotel. When we arrived, there was Gene in the room across the hall from us. He said he was waiting outside the terminal for us and saw us drive by. Because we didn't stop, he hailed a cap and got to the hotel before we did.

- Gene was quite a prankster. One of the last pranks he pulled on the front office personnel happened a few days before his accident. At 5 p.m. everyone rushed out of the building on their way home, so this one evening Gene laid a fake $100 bill on the floor at the back door where everyone could see it and check it out. Then he hid in a dark office nearby and waited for the reaction. They all stopped and picked it up and were excited—before quickly realizing it was fake. Gene enjoyed spying on them and watching their reactions.

- This last one everyone should enjoy: Ray Wilde, a customer who everyone likes here in the company, called Gene one day. Ray was running Alvin down right and left. Gene finally got tired of listening to Ray. He told him that he owed him an apology for talking about his father like that, and they hung up. A few minutes later, Ray called back and apologized to Gene.

Other special memories . . .

- Gene always had a quiet sense of humor. He would say something, and then after it soaked in, you would laugh.

- After he married the employees would ask him almost daily if Kaylynn was pregnant yet. After about two years they quit asking. When Kaylynn was pregnant, Gene wanted to see how long it would be before someone in the office would know. They found out on our 50th anniversary.
- We were at an OPASTCO meeting in Minnesota. We all went to a ball game on a bus, and it was quite a distance. Some friends of Gene and Kaylynn had four little boys. On the way home the children became tired and cranky. Gene started making funny faces, and soon the boys were laughing and nearly rolling on the floor of the bus. He also did this in church one Sunday when he was about 10 years old. Gene was kneeling very still, and I thought he was behaving. I noticed the little boy in front of me turning around and beginning to laugh. Well, Gene was making awful faces at him.
- One Christmas when we had Alvin's mother over for dinner we served wine. When Grandma took a drink of the wine, she choked a little. Gene's comment was, "Grandma cannot hold her booze."
- He always liked the way Alvin and I teased each other. He would use some of these same tactics on Kaylynn.
- One of his and Alvin's sayings came when I would fix a new dish to eat: "Mom, it is good, but you don't have to make it again."
- When Gene became engaged to Kaylynn his little niece said that Gene was going to change his name. They told her that Kaylynn was going to change her name, not Gene. She still insisted that Gene was going to change his name. They finally asked what he was going to change his name to, and she said, "Uncle Gene.'
- When Gene ate out he would always look for something exotic to try. When we were in Hawaii he talked Rick Rauh into eating alligator with him.
- Gene was a stargazer. While we were in Seattle I called home and asked him if he saw a certain star in the sky. He said yes. I said, "But it first appeared at 5 in the morning." He said he went to bed and got up at 5 and looked at it and then went to bed until time for school. We purchased warming gloves and socks so he could stargaze at night when it was cold. He also built himself a rotating reclining chair so he could be more comfortable stargazing.

- Alvin and Gene did a lot of night fishing under the Willis bridge. One night, Gene wound the boat up backwards on the trailer. He thought he had it secure, but when they started to drive away, the boat fell off. They had a lot of problems with the boat when they went out. One time they were fishing, and Alvin looked at Gene's hair, and it was standing straight up. Alvin told Gene they better hurry to shore because a storm was coming.
- One day Alvin, Gene, Grandma and I were going to Fort Worth to visit Bill and Kay. Grandma loved to talk, which she did very well. When we got to Denton, Gene said, "Well, she finally took a breath."
- Gene received his first communion at Sacred Heart Church. He received his scapular medal that day and wore it every day. He had it on the evening he was killed.
- He served as a Mass Server (altar boy) at Sacred Heart Church. He was always on time for serving. By living only two blocks from church he served 6 a.m. Mass many times. He had to set his alarm and get himself up and ride his bicycle the two blocks to church. The only time I would take him to serve was if it was raining. He also served if a guest priest was in town and said Mass. The last time he served was Christmas Eve Mass the year he graduated from high school.
- Gene never went around shirtless. In fact, he was very meticulous about clothes, in general. When I went to school for any of his activities, Gene would go to my closet and pick out the dress he wanted me to wear to school. I had a pretty dress with many colors, and this was the one he always picked. One day when I came home for lunch, Gene had a shirt on that I had thrown in the trash because it was so threadbare it would not hold buttons any more. Well, he had it on nicely ironed with a crease in the sleeves and buttons on it. He pulled the cloth together and sewed his buttons on. I told him I had thrown that shirt in the trash. He said, "This is my favorite shirt."
- Gene also never came to the table without his hair being combed.

- There was one area where he didn't care to be so meticulous. I always told him his handwriting was awful. He said, "I can't help it if my mind goes faster than my hand."
- When Gene and Troy Wolf were living in the Sanger apartment, Gene acquired a little kitty. He would feed it every morning when he came home from work. One day the apartment manager said he was going to get rid of all animals around the apartment. Gene brought his kitty home to us and asked if we would keep it. So, we did. The kitty stayed at our house until three days after Gene died, and we never saw it again.
- After Gene died Sacred Heart hosted a tribute to him, Virgil Henscheid and Shelly Hoedebeck at the State Theater.

AUTHOR'S BIOGRAPHY

Alvin Fuhrman began his telephone career with Muenster Telephone Company during the ice storms in 1949. The company's only repairman left town when the ice storm left all the telephone lines on the ground. Alphonse Hoenig of Muenster Telephone came to Alvin and his brother, Bill, for help. They were doing electrical work at the time. The company had only 12 telephones still working because of the ice storm. With no prior telephone experience they rebuilt the system, which has grown to over 10,000 telephone, Internet and cable television accounts today.

In December 1950, Alvin was drafted into military service and served two years with the 2nd Armored Division in Germany. At this time Bill left the company to further his education.

Alvin returned from service in December 1952 and became the sole repairman of Muenster Telephone Company. He married the girl of his dreams—who was still in high school when he was drafted into service, but who waited two years for him to return—and they raised a family.

During the next 10 years, Alvin was instrumental in bringing modern telephone service to areas around Muenster. This included the first dial telephone service in Montague County to Forestburg in 1955, the same year the town celebrated its 100-year Centennial, and dial service to Myra in 1956, replacing Don Hoskins' one-wire line telephone system.

Using first electronic equipment, service was extended to Rosston in 1957 and on to Leo community the following year. Muenster's system was completely rebuilt starting in 1960 and cut to dial service in 1963. Ten years later, all open-wire lines were replaced with buried cables, and party lines were replaced with one-party service. Then in 1983 the electro-mechanical dial switching system was replaced with a digital switching system, adding touch-tone and custom-calling features.

Today, fiber optics have replaced the copper and coaxial cables in all areas except the remote rural areas, bringing phone, high-speed Internet and television service to the homes and businesses. With the large companies neglecting the small towns, we have extended full service to small towns and schools around us.

The company has grown from its original five employees in 1952 (one repairman and four telephone operators), to just under 50 employees serving close to 10,000 accounts with state-of-the art telephone, cable television and Internet subscribers with over 200 miles of fiber optic cables.

Today, the company is extending its "Fiber to the Home" fiber optic network to a fiber ring in downtown Gainesville and surrounding towns and schools. Nortex serves a number of new subdivisions in Gainesville, Collinsville and Tioga. The reluctance of the larger communication companies to provide the demand for faster Internet speeds in these small towns is opening up markets to Nortex.

The Nortex staff consists of talented persons led by a capable young leader, Joey Anderson, who was recently promoted to General Manager. This title, along with the company presidency, was held by Alvin more than 50 years.

Alvin is a recognized leader within the telecommunications industry. His involvement in the telephone industry and the Texas Telephone Association is noteworthy. He was elected to the TTA Board of Directors in 1972 and served continually for 17 years. He went back on the TTA board again in 1993 and served until his retirement from the Board in 1999, at which time he received the Neville Haynes Award, Texas Telephone Association's highest award.

He has served in various other leadership roles within the Industry. In 1990, he chaired the TTA Historical Committee, which compiled and published the history of the Texas telephone industry, "Hello Texas," for which he received the "Distinguished Achievement Award.' His other leadership roles have included chairman of the TTA Convention and Member Services Committee, the United States Telephone Association's Small Company Committee, and Texas Statewide Cooperative's Legislative Committee. He was President of the Texas Telephone Pioneer Association Board, serving two terms. His family was honored in 1998 with the "Distinguished Family Award' by the Texas Telephone Pioneer Association.

He not only helped build a successful communication company, he also helped build and continues to actively participate in growing and serving his community. He was president of the Sacred Heart Men's Choir, singing Bass II with the choir for 65 years. When the parochial Sacred Heart School needed computers, Alvin and his late son, Gene, were instrumental in getting computers started in the school. He was on the founding committee of Germanfest in 1976 and served as general chairman for over 12 years. He received numerous awards through the years for his support of Germanfest. Recently, he put the finishing touches on a $5 million new home for Germanfest, which is on 64 acres called Heritage Park. The park is used all year for benefit events such as the Firemen Bar-B-Que, the Sacred Heart Church Thanksgiving Picnic, benefits to help individuals in need, etc. Surplus revenue from the events go toward scholarships and other worthy causes.

Alvin grew up on a farm north of Lindsay, Texas. In 1940, the government took his father's farm during WW II for an Air Force training facility—now the Gainesville Municipal Airport. The Fuhrman family later lived on a farm east of Muenster. He attended Lindsay school until his junior year and finished high school in Muenster, graduating in 1944.

His dedication to his communication company and the support of his community is surpassed only by his dedication to his family. Gracie, his wife of 63 years, has been by his side as each vision became reality. His son, Gene, was following in his father's footsteps until he was killed by a drunk driver in 2003. Alvin continues to be dedicated to service to the community. Alvin and Gracie have a daughter in law, Kaylynn Fuhrman, and one grandchild, Conner Gene Fuhrman.